BIGGER THAN GALLIPOLI

BIGGER THAN GALLIPOLI

WAR, HISTORY AND MEMORY IN AUSTRALIA

Liz Reed

University of Western Australia Press

First published in 2004 by
University of Western Australia Press
Crawley, Western Australia 6009
www.uwapress.uwa.edu.au

Publication of this book was made possible with funding assistance from
the Monash University Publications Committee and the Centre for Australian
Indigenous Studies.

National Library of Australia Cataloguing-in-Publication entry:

Reed, Elizabeth Marion.
    Bigger than Gallipoli: war, history and memory in Australia.

    Bibliography.
    Includes index.
    ISBN 1 920694 19 6.

    1. Nationalism—Australia.   2. World War, 1939–1945—
    Australia—Anniversaries, etc.   3. Australia—Civilization—20th
    century.   4. Australia—Social conditions—20th century.   I. Title.

320.540994

Cover images: Australian War Memorial: (front) Abbott, Harold, VP Day,
Canberra 1945, Oil on canvas on board, 45·4 cm × 60·8 cm (ART22923);
(back) crowd gathered in Bourke Street (Neg. No. 112839).

Permission to reproduce commemorative logos is gratefully acknowledged
from the Director National and International Memorials, Canada Remembers
Division, Veterans' Affairs, Canada; the Manager, Heritage Operations,
Ministry for Culture and Heritage, New Zealand; the Head of the
Commemorations Branch, Commonwealth Department of Veterans' Affairs
and the Australian War Memorial.

Produced by Benchmark Publications Pty Ltd, Melbourne
Consultant editor: Fleur Goding, Purr Communications
Series design by Robyn Mundy Design
Cover design by Ron Hampton, Pages in Action, Melbourne
Typeset in 9½pt Garamond Light by Lasertype, Perth
Printed by BPA Print Group

*Dedicated to all those around the world
who strive to prevent wars.*

FOREWORD

In the 'history wars' that erupted in Australia in the final decades of the twentieth century, one of the more intriguing skirmishes has taken place between those seeing World War I as the true focus of Australian national identity, and those who would give that honour to World War II. It has been a battle between generations, between imperial and national loyalties, between the two prime ministers, Paul Keating and John Howard, who have been the most successful in the stage management of national mythology. Gallipoli's role in social memory has long attracted academic attention. This is the first sustained analysis of how a social memory of the Second World War entered the process of imagining the nation.

Liz Reed provides much more than a comprehensive narrative of *Australia Remembers, 1945–1995*, the Keating Government's commemorative program celebrating the fiftieth anniversary of the end of the war. She sets it in an illuminating international context—the difference from the UK and the USA, the similarities with Canada and New Zealand. She draws another instructive comparison with other recent forays into formal national myth-making—the Bicentenary, the Sydney Olympics, the Centenary of Federation. She reveals the ways in which the commemoration exploited nostalgia, turned memory into spectacle, marginalised women and Indigenous Australians in the very act of recognising them, and brilliantly appropriated the memories of 'ordinary people'. This is dispassionate analysis, a major new contribution to our increasingly sophisticated understanding of social memory.

And yet it is written with passion. On the one hand, a heartfelt conviction about the waste of war; on the other, a frank admiration for how, comparatively, this national celebration worked. What is most intriguing is the intricate and surprising relationship between social memory and individual agency. CEW Bean's role in shaping and selling the Anzac myth has long been recognised. For *Australia Remembers*, the dominant figure was an equally unlikely candidate, the Minister for Veterans' Affairs, child of Sicilian migrants, Con Sciacca. It is a tribute to Reed's scholarship that the dispassionate analysis can sit side by side with a deeply troubled reading of the national commemoration of war and a deep admiration for the humanity of the individual at the centre of that commemoration.

Richard White
Department of History
University of Sydney

CONTENTS

Foreword   *vii*

List of Illustrations   *xi*

Preface   *xiii*

Chapter 1   Introduction—Memory and World War II   *1*

Chapter 2   Small nations remember—Canada, Australia
             and New Zealand remember   *11*

Chapter 3   History and memory—*Australia Remembers
             1945–1995* and uses of the past   *52*

Chapter 4   Nostalgia unbounded—VP Day as spectacle   *99*

Chapter 5   *Australia Remembers* and national identity   *119*

Chapter 6   The legacy of *Australia Remembers 1945–1995*   *152*

Notes   *177*

Bibliography   *195*

Index   *201*

LIST OF ILLUSTRATIONS

Figure 1   *Australia Remembers 1945–1995* logo   *19*

Figure 2   *Canada Remembers* logo   *34*

Figure 3   *New Zealand Remembers* logo   *41*

Figure 4   *Australia Remembers* commemorative
            poster—women   *73*

Figure 5   *Australia Remembers* commemorative
            poster—POWs   *85*

Figure 6   George Silk's photograph, Christmas Day 1942   *139*

Figure 7   Australia Remembers commemorative
            poster—Indigenous Australians   *149*

Figure 8   Brisbane's 'Freedom Wall'—detail of plaques   *158*

PREFACE

In the more than half-century since the Second World War ended, its legacy has loomed large in innumerable ways. The greatest and forever inescapable legacy, of course, has been 'the bomb' and the increasing proliferation of nuclear weapons throughout the world, both acknowledged and denied. Another significant legacy has been the ways in which the war interacted with existing movements for decolonisation within the British, French, and Dutch empires, and the overthrowing of colonial rule.

The Cold War has been and gone, leaving the United States with the task of learning the lessons of being the sole remaining superpower. Although this may be a status to which it has aspired since the end of the Second World War, the US Government, in its attempts to 'liberate' Afghanistan and Iraq for example, is learning that absolute power does not diminish the strength of those who oppose war.

Since the Second World War, nations and peoples have sought to find meanings from their experiences, and as the time has become more distant, the relationship between memory and history, commemoration and forgetting, has become more complex and continues to change. Recent reports that historians in Germany are beginning to interrogate the meanings of the Allied bombing of Dresden suggest that further significant scholarship about the war is underway.

Closer to home, this book, which deals primarily with Australia's commemoration and celebration of this fiftieth anniversary and the continuities and discontinuities within Australia's memory and history of warfare since 1788, reminds us that when the memorialising ends, we have to return to the social realities that such events temporarily suspend.

In Australia, continuing avoidance of Indigenous peoples' rights to a place in the national memory appears to remain entrenched. Increasingly however, Indigenous writers, film-makers, historians and others appear determined to explore and extend the meanings of their families' involvement in wars since colonisation. They are carrying forward the aims of those who fought in the Second World War as a part of the larger struggle for Indigenous rights.

This book could not have been written without the assistance and encouragement of others, whom I acknowledge and thank.

The Centre for Australian Indigenous Studies at Monash University has provided a congenial space from which to carry out the research and writing of this book. I also wish to thank the Arts Faculty of Monash University for providing study leave during which I completed revisions of the manuscript. I also gratefully acknowledge a small research grant from the Arts Faculty that enabled me to conduct some of the necessary research. The Monash University Publications and Grants Committee also provided a subsidy for the publication of the book, for which I am most grateful.

The Department of Veterans' Affairs, Canberra, provided access to its library newspaper collection relating to *Australia Remembers 1945–1995*, without which I could not have gained a sense of the popularity and ubiquity of this commemorative program, nor of the intense commitment of individuals and groups in parts of the country rarely otherwise heard of.

The Hon. Con Sciacca, who as Minister for Veterans' Affairs conceived of and oversaw *Australia Remembers 1945–1995*, has been extremely generous with his time and has remained actively encouraging in the writing of this book. I thank him for his friendship and support and hope that he derives enjoyment from this book.

The family of Ray and Varlie Walsh, whose photograph was used for the *Australia Remembers 1945–1995* logo, have also been generous in their support. I particularly thank their eldest son, Arthur Walsh, for granting permission to use the photograph. I thank them also for their faith in this book and hope that they are not disappointed. Arthur and his wife Shirley also offered wonderful hospitality, and with other family members shared memories and stories of their parents over a very long and delicious lunch. No doubt, from their accounts, Ray might have found the book part of the 'hoo-ha' he tried to avoid, but I like to think that Varlie might have enjoyed seeing it.

Among other friends made while researching for this book, I thank Josie Jones who has urged me on to completion and who will no doubt find things within the book to discuss with me.

Friends and family have heard more than they probably wanted to about both the book and its subject matter. My list of those to thank—by no means definitive—includes Bain Attwood for his friendship and advice; Marie Clark for stimulating discussions of war and memory; Irene and Frances, simply for being there; Lynette Russell, who as colleague and friend has found ways of removing obstacles; and lastly my children, Danni and Rog, for providing constant reinforcement, as always.

CHAPTER 1

Introduction—
Memory and World War II

THROUGHOUT 1995 the fiftieth anniversary of the end of the Second World War was commemorated and celebrated through a variety of events within those countries that had played a major role on either side of the conflict. Such events, like the wartime alliances themselves, were not without tensions and to a significant extent reflected the political realities of the 1990s. For all involved, in different ways, the war itself and the half-century since it ended, provoked contested meanings, and would evoke a series of remembrances that would be employed to construct a history of the war that suited national purposes. Within Europe, ceremonies marking the war's end were shared by four cities, beginning with a religious service in London on the evening of 7 May, followed by a celebration in Paris the following morning, an observance in Berlin that evening, and a parade in Moscow on 9 May.[1] United States President Clinton chose to attend Moscow's functions rather than those in London, a decision that raised anger in some quarters in the US.[2] The first of the victory celebrations, VE Day in May 1995, exemplified some of the difficulties that peace had brought, and that victors and the former vanquished (now allies) had much in common, not the least being a degree of discomfort and uncertainty about how best to observe this anniversary.

Contested remembrances

Particularly striking about the commemorations and celebrations, wherever they were occurring, were the competing voices, only some of which were consciously acknowledged by those involved in the official events to mark the end of the war. Some of the sites of contestation were obvious ones, involving the ways in which 'the war' had become a construct within those countries that had experienced it. Military and ex-service organisations still attempted to 'remember' a war which privileged male endeavour, that is, the glorious remembrance of glorious deeds exclusive to men. It was at local levels of 'remembrance' and within specifically focussed events that people strove to imbue their memories of the war years with particular and personal meanings. At times, as shown by the discussion in this book of the formal commemoration of women veterans in Australia, men's remembrances of women's roles during the war initially threatened to dominate the occasion, and parallel, gendered memories jostled.

Nonetheless, the overall character of remembrance in Australia as well as in the wartime dominion nations, Aotearoa/New Zealand and Canada, was located within the civilian population rather more than the military. Without such a focus, the fiftieth anniversary would not have been able to capture the interest and enthusiastic participation of the public, as there was much more at stake than simply commemorating a military victory and the end of the war. Indeed, at stake was a desire for unmediated contact with the past, through carefully planned programs of remembrance that were to enable the past—or rather a number of pasts—to be imagined. The means to achieve this was the creative reconstruction of the past, through visual representations of the home fronts and the battle fronts and through the memories of 'ordinary people' that were conveyed in packages prepared as a part of each nation's commemorative literature.

Australian remembrance and *Australia Remembers 1945–1995*

This book is about remembering World War II within Australia during 1995, using the commemorative program *Australia Remembers 1945–1995* to focus on the relationship between history and memory. I examine how nostalgia for the past was the means through which the nation was imagined as it was during the wartime period and in the present. This commemorative program illustrated the ways in which 'memory is socially and culturally constructed'[3] and central to this was the use of images ranging from the logo to posters designed to promote memory of a particular aspect of the war, and events that visually recreated the sights and sounds of the wartime period. These and other (re)creations of memory throughout 1995 suggested ways in which the transmission of images as a means of representing the past fosters memory, rather than being a means by which memory itself is transmitted.[4]

I analyse the gendered nature of remembrance and representations of men's and women's wartime activities, as well as the inclusion and exclusion of Indigenous Australians. I show the ways in which a memory of Australia's war was created by *Australia Remembers* through events which not only commemorated and celebrated key moments fifty years earlier, but which employed a range of strategies, particularly that of spectacle, to manufacture an end-of-century nostalgia for a past whose remembrance was under construction.

Situating this book

This book contributes to existing literature on war and memory, remembrance and commemoration, and on the gendered nature of memory, especially in relation to wartime. The *Australia Remembers* program's place is considered alongside other commemorative moments in Australian history since 1788. It managed to avoid many of the worst aspects of the 1988 Bicentenary. This was partly because 1995 provided a more neatly contained remembrance, but also because of a number of other key factors such as more modest aims and a more democratic structure and funding formula. In deconstructing *Australia Remembers* I also suggest some continuities in how the nation is imagined through commemorative programs. Some of these, dating from the first commemoration of the nation in 1888, include the 'normalising' of the nation as white. This continuity exists regardless of the ways in which inclusion of Aborigines and other non-Anglo whites was attempted in 1988 (Bicentenary), 1995 (*Australia Remembers*) and 2001 (Centenary of Federation). The continuing search for a definitive national identity was a key feature of *Australia Remembers*, suggestive of a further link with other commemorative moments, each of which sought to articulate Australia's national identity.

Key themes

Nostalgia, memory and commemoration are key themes of this book, which I explore in the context of national identity and its articulation throughout the *Australia Remembers* program. I also examine the role of spectacle as the means through which nostalgia was expressed and the past (re)inscribed in the nation as imagined within commemorative moments.

The following chapter considers the manner in which Canada, Australia and Aotearoa/New Zealand influenced each other's remembrance of the war as the occasion when they 'grew up' as nations, as well as specific focuses within their respective programs.

Around the theme of 'uses of the past', chapter three discusses memory and remembrance of women's wartime roles, and demonstrates how women at key moments sought to speak for themselves and in the process provided gendered accounts of the meanings of the war.

This discussion leads into a consideration of, in chapter four, the manner in which VP Day was celebrated on 15 August 1995, with spectacle providing the vehicle for nostalgia. The past and memory remained contested at such moments, which chapter four investigates.

Chapter five seeks to situate the contemporary desire for a national identity within its historical context, and I examine the manner in which remembrance of the war provided a unifying theme, through the use of stirring events such as pilgrimages to sites of memory.

The final chapters consider the legacy of *Australia Remembers 1945–1995*, and how it was assessed by its organisers and the Minister for Veterans' Affairs. As well, I speculate on the program's relationship with ongoing desires for a clearly defined national identity and ways of framing this in a multicultural nation that in 1995 sought to include women and Indigenous peoples in its celebrations. I consider the extent to which these inclusive aims were achieved and the possibilities these suggest for future national commemorations.

Australia's 'story'

Commemoration of past military glories, including the glorified debacle of Gallipoli, has been something which Australia has enthusiastically embraced. In the process, our past has been not only glorified, but a narrative about ourselves has been created. The Anzac legend has been crucial to this national imagination. Prime Minister Keating, when speaking in 1992 at the seventy-seventh anniversary of Gallipoli, evoked the ways in which the spirit that arose from this event had 'become the canon of Australian life', providing the values and ideals to which Australians aspired, as well as shaping and 'twist[ing]' Australia's history.[5] The legend, Keating continued, was not static, and *Australia Remembers* sought to ensure that the dynamic nature of Anzac was further enhanced through a series of pilgrimages and other events that demonstrated its links between the generations. This was drawing upon earlier symbolic occasions that included a pilgrimage by First World War veterans, to commemorate the seventy-fifth anniversary of the landing at Anzac Cove in 1990, followed by the dedication of the Australian Vietnam Forces Memorial on Canberra's Anzac Parade in 1992. In the following year there was a pilgrimage to the Western Front, to commemorate the end of the First World War, and in the same year 'an emotion charged interment of the Unknown Australian Soldier on Remembrance Day'. In spite of a suggestion that women had been included in these constant reminders of 'the debt owed to ex-service men and women',[6] these events had remained primarily rituals to honour the deeds of men.

Other Australian commemorations

In 1888 the Centenary of colonisation was 'celebrated as an Australian event',[7] even though the inhabitants of the various colonies were yet to achieve federation, the nature of which was still in dispute. As Lyn Spillman has noted, such celebrations were unabashed in their racism, Indigenous people in Australia being excluded (as they were to be when Federation occurred) beyond providing the visual 'other' to non-Indigenous Australia's self-congratulatory moment.[8] Such exclusion and/or appropriation was no longer possible in 1988, counter-celebrations of Indigenous peoples' survival and revival being staged through the 'Invasion Day' march variously estimated at between 15,000 and 50,000 attendees.[9] These events were supported by many non-Indigenous Australians who were determined to ensure that the 'Black History of White Australia'[10] was not erased from the national consciousness or conscience by the official Bicentennial. In both the Centenary and Bicentenary celebrations of white Australia, activities aided the imagination of the nation. Importantly, though, in these and *Australia Remembers* and the Centenary of Federation program, the nation continued to be imagined as white. 'Australia' continues to be a linguistic signifier of 'whiteness', the normative nature of which has not been destabilised, but arguably strengthened, by events and visual representations that 'included' Indigenous peoples in these commemorations.

In terms of organisation *Australia Remembers* was more modest than the Australian Bicentennial Authority (ABA) which had a longer organisational lifespan, having been formed in 1980 following discussions with the state governments two years earlier.[11] Whereas the 1988 Bicentenary was 'widely criticised for the often crude chauvinism of the events which took place under its aegis',[12] and the perhaps cruder commercialisation epitomised by the Coca-Cola logo on the sails of the First Fleet re-enactment ships, *Australia Remembers* managed to avoid such pitfalls. Indeed, the failure to attract significant corporate sponsorship was one of the few negatives in the overall assessment by the state organisers. Not that Veterans' Affairs Minister Sciacca was particularly perturbed; rather, he turned this into a positive attribute, seeing it as ensuring that *Australia Remembers* belonged to the people rather than to corporations.

Similarly, perhaps because of much shorter lead-in time and considerably less government funding, *Australia Remembers* managed to avoid the political in-fighting and prime ministerial heavy-handedness that were a feature of the Australian Bicentennial Authority.[13] This factor distinguished *Australia Remembers* from the debacle regarding bipartisanship in the Bicentenary. On that occasion, despite Labor opposition leader Bill Hayden's eager protestations of bipartisan support in April 1978 when the Bicentenary celebrations for a decade later were announced, this did not endure.[14] As the following chapter suggests, a yearning for the past can be less problematically accommodated when organised around a grand theme such as that offered by the Second World War, possibly the only war about which Australian schoolchildren, for example, are taught.

Whereas the official commemorations might have been seen as 'the last hurrah' of a Labor government in its thirteenth successive year, this was not the lasting impression of *Australia Remembers*. Labor lost the election shortly afterwards in a landslide defeat, and the Minister for Veterans' Affairs lost his seat of Bowman, attributed by many to the intensity of anti-Keating sentiment and in spite of a significant veteran component within Sciacca's electorate.[15]

The sexual division of warfare

Of fundamental importance to the *Australia Remembers 1945–1995* program was the ubiquitous logo, a photograph taken by an army photographer on the day of the return of Patrick Anthony Raphael (Ray) Walsh, to his wife and five children. The logo created a celebration of a past in which the male concept of mateship was combined with a highlighting of women's roles at the home front. In what became a formalised division of wartime labour, between the mostly male battlefront and the mostly female home front, commemorative posters, videos and events were created to celebrate and 'remember' the gendered contributions of Australians. Despite a significant focus upon women, attention remained primarily on men, albeit on the 'ordinary men' and on the POWs, whose iconic status was assured by the *Australia Remembers* program. Ultimately then, war remained something glorious which was done by men, but this time by ordinary men, with valuable support from 'ordinary women' who finally received significant recognition, which they had been denied in 1945.

It was ordinary Australian men who went away to fight and die, and to be captured and suffer in Japanese (for the Germans were virtually forgotten) POW camps, whose sufferings were to be woven into the national memory of the war. A key device was the deployment of poignant scenes of former prisoners who in 1995 became 'pilgrims' to sites of suffering such as prisoner-of-war camps and cemeteries. On these occasions men bearing the signs of their age and of their suffering and grief remembered their mates 'as they were then, not as they are now', as one expressed it. Indeed, the concept of mates was to be enlarged, to embrace what has become, officially, a multicultural Australia.

Women's roles during the war received unprecedented attention. The manner in which the concept of 'heroes' was extended to include them, with speeches and other forms of official remembrance naming women's varied roles as 'heroic' was indicative of this. This desire to designate women as heroes nevertheless suggested an acceptance of the inevitability of warfare, and merely made the suffering and loss war produces more evenly shared. That women did not demur from their construction as heroes suggested the extent to which the absence of wartime women within the narratives of the state and nation has been resented by them. Nonetheless, women's roles, and most importantly their grief, remained universalised throughout *Australia Remembers.* As Joy Damousi has observed, there have been few studies of the manner in which 'the experience of mourning [has] affected men and women in different ways'.[16] With a few exceptions that I explore, the particularised nature of grief remained obscured throughout the events of 1995, despite women themselves seeking to articulate the specificities of their experiences.

Australia Remembers commemorated Indigenous people's contribution to the war effort with a poster which included photographs of Victoria's Reg Saunders, who was Australia's first Aboriginal commissioned officer, shaking hands with a white 'mate', and of Aboriginal RAAF pilot Leonard Waters, as well as a number of speeches by the prime minister and others. In doing so, there was an attempt to include Indigenous people in Australia's 'story'. Such inclusion was designed to promote a memory of their participation, but this was problematically contained within the non-Indigenous discourses of the nation. As well, Reg Saunders' representation remained within the tradition of what Marcia Langton has termed an annoying paternalistic tendency 'to focus on the "first Aborigine to …"'.[17] In addition, the privileging of the Aboriginal male veteran over Torres Strait Islanders and Indigenous women reflected a lack of appreciation of the varied roles in and meanings of the war for different Indigenous communities. In this way the practice of homogenising Indigenous people within Australia remained unchanged.

Pacific focus

In spite of the significant involvement of Australian personnel in the European theatres of war, and Australia's historic ties with Britain, albeit redefined during the war, the most important meanings of the Second World War for Australia were located in the Pacific war. This was expressed throughout 1995 not only in the almost exclusive attention given to the POWs of the Japanese, but also by the restrained media attention paid to VE Day as opposed to VP Day. Notwithstanding that VP Day was celebrated as the day upon which the war ended, beyond this the passions that were aroused around VE Day within Britain and Germany about continuing moral issues like the bombings of Dresden, received minimal attention within Australia. Similarly, postwar responses to the war by Germany have received less attention within Australia than those of Japan. The common belief that the Japanese had never 'apologised' for their wartime aggression and behaviour had prevailed for fifty years and was to resurface in sections of the media leading up to 15 August 1995.

As VP Day neared, it became clear that for many, nothing short of an absolute apology from the Japanese would be acceptable, and that for some even this would remain insufficient. Within Australia two contradictory representations of the Japanese predominated, both of which contained familiar racial and cultural stereotypes. These were as 'money-earning tourists' whose former desire to destroy had been replaced by 'a will to communicate',[18] or as 'mealy-mouthed' and unable to be trusted.[19] Some media commentators on the other hand, worried that suggestions of unfinished business with the Japanese achieved little more than encouraging the 'yobbos' within Australian society.[20] The official apology when it came, having overcome obstacles within the Japanese Diet, veterans' groups, and right-wing opponents, expressed the prime minister's 'feelings of remorse and…heartfelt apology', and offered his '…sincere condolences [for the] huge pain and sorrow [caused] to many nations, especially those in Asia…'.[21]

Predictably, however, the apology did not satisfy all. The Victorian RSL President, Mr Bruce Ruxton, with his characteristic lack of subtlety, described the apology as 'half-hearted', and demanded instead an unconditional apology 'for what they did during the war'.[22] Others were more sanguine, suggesting that it 'really is time…the Returned Services League…consulted a calendar…World War II was a long time ago, and Japan should not be expected, having apologized in 1957, to repeat the exercise continuously'.[23]

Unknown then was that soon Australians would elect a prime minister who would also steadfastly refuse to apologise on behalf of the nation for the policy and practice of removing Aboriginal children from their families, and who contested the work of 'revisionist' historians who had exposed massacres of Aborigines on various frontiers throughout Australia.

CHAPTER 2

Small nations remember—
Canada, Australia and
New Zealand remember

'Canada and its people did a lot of growing up in a very short time.'[1]

'...a golden moment in the history of this country... Colleagues, if this doesn't tug at your heart strings, you haven't got one.'[2]

'Maori did not get a good return on their investment in citizenship.'[3]

ON Monday 30 May 1994, Australia's Prime Minister Keating faced interjections from Opposition members regarding his attendance at the fiftieth anniversary D-day commemorations in Europe. He justified his trip by reference to the 2,600 Australian servicemen who had taken part in the landings or related air and sea operations, pointing out that as many as 2,100 RAAF air crews had been involved. Embarking upon what was to become a familiar theme, Mr Keating suggested that 'Australians today cannot imagine the odds these men faced' as they went into battle, citing their 'substantial contribution' to the war effort in Europe. With a clear focus on the nation's contribution to victory in the European theatre of war, he detailed the memorials to be visited and effectively challenged those on the opposition benches to question this trip further. He concluded his response by stating that he was sure that all members of the House and all Australians 'will join me in expressing our thanks to them, to the thousands of other Australians who served with such courage and distinction in that great battle, and to their families and the families of those who died'.[4] Notably absent from Mr Keating's response on this occasion was any reference to the thousands of Australian servicemen who became prisoners of war in Europe, two hundred and sixty five of whom perished.[5]

The minister and the vision

A few months after Paul Keating's strategic deployment of remembering and forgetting, *Australia Remembers 1945–1995* was launched, largely inspired by the vision of the Minister for Veterans' Affairs. For his part, the Minister had been inspired by Canada's commemorative program, following which he provided the impetus for Aotearoa/New Zealand to similarly mark the anniversary of the war's end.

For Veterans' Affairs Minister Con Sciacca, the fiftieth anniversary of the war's end presented 'a golden moment in the history of this country...[to] 'do something big' with *Australia Remembers*, as a way of showing his respect for the wartime generation. This would enable him to express his more generalised admiration for older people which his maiden speech in 1987 had touched on, citing his Sicilian origins and the 'circle of respect' for the elderly in his culture. His son having died of cancer at nineteen years of age, he felt able to empathise with those families who lost young men during the war years. He also admitted that perhaps *Australia Remembers* had enabled him to pursue his 'quest to keep himself busy' in response to his son's death three years earlier.[6]

Born in 1947, in Piedimonte Etneo, a village at the foot of Mt Etna, his family arrived in Australia in 1951, unable to speak English or to read or write their own language, with 'only ... the clothes on their backs', but with the immigrant dream of succeeding through hard work and giving their children opportunities unavailable in their home country.[7] Sciacca became fascinated by the Second World War, partly in response to schoolyard taunts of being a 'wog',[8] his interest perhaps also being inspired by his school, Wavall High, which had Houses named after famous battles. As he expressed it, he had 'always marvelled at our country', which five or six years after the end of the war allowed large numbers of people from former enemy countries to immigrate, and regarded himself as 'a beneficiary of that'.[9]

Sciacca's is perhaps the archetypal multicultural success story. Proud of his Sicilian roots and anxious to dispel any negative images of that community 'because of the unsavoury activities of the very few', he embraced the concept of equal opportunity early, joining the ALP at the age of seventeen, becoming President of the Queensland Branch of Young Labor at the age of twenty-one, and devoting his work within his own legal practice and through his connections with the trade union movement to that principle.

As Minister for Veterans' Affairs, Con Sciacca seemed capable of transcending partisan politics through his enthusiasm for projects such as *Australia Remembers*. He gained respect and affection from diverse groupings and individuals, regardless of their own political philosophies or affiliations. This was evident throughout 1995 during which he was described by the national president of the RSL, Major-General Digger James as 'an extraordinary fellow' without whom *Australia Remembers* 'would never have happened. He deserves high praise'.[10] In August 1995 he was honoured by the New South Wales Rats of Tobruk Association with a reception usually reserved for generals, and was made a life member of many bodies such as the Returned Services League of Australia.[11] In the year following *Australia Remembers* Sciacca was made an 'honorary member for life' of the Naval Association of Australia by its Federal Council, the wording on the certificate confirming he 'gave 100 per cent to the veteran community', as well as being awarded life membership of the British Commonwealth Occupation Forces Association (Queensland

Branch), and honorary life membership of the New South Wales Lancers Regiment Association. As an honorary life member of the Royal Australian Air Force Association National Council Inc., he is in exclusive company with HRH Prince Philip, The Duke of Edinburgh, Group Captain Douglas Bader, Sir Roden Cutler and ten other eminent men. Expressive of his ability also to maintain his cultural links, he is one of 'a handful of Australians of Italian origin' in Australia to be awarded an Italian Knighthood, as 'Commendatore in the Order of Merit of the Italian Republic', the rank of Commendatore being the highest that can be awarded to overseas citizens by the Italian Government.[12]

Sciacca became Minister for Veterans' Affairs on 24 March 1994, inheriting a small budget of about one million dollars set aside for the fiftieth anniversary commemorations, half a million having been earmarked for an education kit, and about half a million for two major ceremonies at the War Memorial in Canberra on VE Day and VP Day. His vision, however, was for something more substantial, and *Australia Remembers 1945–1995* was launched in federal parliament in August 1994 as a nationwide program to commemorate and celebrate the fiftieth anniversary of the end of World War II. In spite of having to fight the perception that this was a political stunt by the Labor government, he gained the essential bipartisan support to ensure the program's success, and visited numerous coalition electorates handing out *Australia Remembers* certificates because it was 'too important for the Australian community and the spirit of Australia' to be partisan.[13] Indeed, he visited more non-Labor electorates than those of his 'own mob' as he termed it, and was enthusiastic in his praise of his Opposition counterpart, the Hon. Wilson Tuckey, 'one of the toughest shadow ministers possible [who] to his eternal credit' supported the *Australia Remembers 1945–1995* proposal.[14]

Structure of *Australia Remembers 1945–1995*

Described in a media release in November 1994, as the 'largest series of commemorations in Australia's history', it was clear that the program was to be presented to the public as unique in both form and content, as well as offering job opportunities for 'about 700 unemployed Australians' via a 'unique initiative [to] restore many of the nation's ageing war memorials, remembrance driveways and memorial parks'.[15] The program was implemented in ten phases, ranging from national and state launches to what were termed 'reinforcement activities', such as the provision of radio and television segments throughout the year, culminating in a major national VP Day event in Brisbane on 15 August 1995. Almost every community participated in some way, and the VP Day events in all capital cities, regional cities and towns were attended by 'multiple thousands of participants and spectators' and received 'unsurpassed press, radio and television coverage'.[16]

Structurally, the Minister himself headed *Australia Remembers 1945–1995*, with a taskforce established within his department. There were state and territory chairpersons, and *Australia Remembers* electoral committees in each of the 147 electorates, with their own subcommittees. From an overall budget of twelve million dollars, each electoral committee was provided with $20,000 as 'seeding funds', regardless of the size of electorate. This no doubt made it easier to allocate the funds, but also would have assisted considerably with ensuring that the program was genuinely bipartisan. Three 'pilgrimages'—to Britain for VE Day, and to Borneo and New Guinea—cost approximately two to three million dollars, but were regarded by the Minister as 'worth it because they marketed' the *Australia Remembers 1945–1995* concept. The major national event in Brisbane on the night of VP Day, 'The Flame of Freedom', took up two million dollars, and the education kit for every school in Australia, through which the program was 'sold…to the youth' accounted for approximately half a million dollars.[17]

The minister later joked that his taskforce had worked such long hours promoting the commemorative program that they would be hoping that 1996 was the year that 'Australia forgets',[18] and indeed it seems their task was gargantuan, with the immediate goal of making the public, as well as key organisations, aware of the significance of the fiftieth anniversary of VP Day on 15 August 1995. Thus, 'a comprehensive community communications strategy was put in place', the key objectives of which included the encouragement of all ex-service organisations to 'associate their activities with *Australia*

Remembers', and the encouragement of all communities to participate in events. The involvement of all Australians 'including various ethnic groups', and the education of the young about 'events leading to the coming of peace and to promote the *Australia Remembers* education kit throughout the country' were also major objectives.

The communication strategy/plan was developed so *Australia Remembers* would become part of every Australian community's planned events throughout 1995, with the logo playing an integral part. Ten 'broad phases' in this plan, which were focused heavily upon the media, included 'issues management to minimise any criticism or controversy', promotion of planned race meetings, ex-service activities, sporting and cultural activities as *Australia Remembers* events. Short videos and radio segments were provided, as was a daily 'On This Day' feature for newspapers, radio stations and community organisations. In addition, there was 'constant reinforcement through media liaison involving the Minister for Veterans' Affairs and provision of a talent bank of older people for talkback and interview programs', most of which were carried out by a small public relations and media team within the *Australia Remembers* taskforce.[19]

Target audiences

Whilst the target audience for *Australia Remembers* was the whole nation, specific groups were identified as 'target publics', most of whom were fairly predictable, such as national, metropolitan and regional media, ex-service and community organisations and local government officials, educational institutions, state and federal politicians and ethnic communities. Eighteen- to thirty-year-olds, identified as 'the lost generation' were specified as one of these 'target publics', and it is interesting to consider the meanings of this identification of what is a key age group in times of warfare. In the years immediately prior to the Second World War, this age group, along with older men and women, had experienced the deprivations and traumas of the Great Depression and the social and political divisions that it highlighted within Australian society. Fifty years later youth unemployment was higher than for other age categories, for which the economic policies of the Keating government were directly blamed by many in the community. The targeting of this age group also suggested a desire to ensure that a 'memory' of the war was instilled, to be enacted throughout their lives as a continuing manifestation of the 'Australian identity'.

In presenting his ministerial statement on the *Australia Remembers* program to the House in February 1995, Veterans' Affairs Minister Con Sciacca enthusiastically spoke of its aims: the three overseas pilgrimages by veterans; his desire to honour the role of Pacific Islander people; and to work with the Aboriginal and Torres Strait Islander Commission (ATSIC) in finding surviving Indigenous veterans and appropriately recognise 'the special—and often unacknowledged—role played by these people in the defence of Australia'. A Department of Employment, Education and Training (DEET) initiative, whereby unemployed young Australians would be employed to refurbish or create new war memorials, was touched upon, as was the necessity to educate the young, with the provision of an education video and kit to all secondary schools. Controversy had already threatened to arise over whether the climax of the *Australia Remembers* program on 15 August should be termed Victory in the Pacific (VP) Day or Victory over Japan (VJ) Day. Sciacca was anxious to avoid further controversy, and quickly dismissed this in one paragraph, with the remark that '… at the end of the day, the expression used is peripheral…and I do not intend to engage further in a debate which distracts from that anniversary'.[20] In this he was largely successful, maintaining bipartisan support despite some on-going dissatisfaction, mainly from veterans' groups, about the term 'VP Day' instead of 'VJ Day'. Nonetheless, this was a major achievement on the part of both sides of federal politics.

Selling the concept was the minister's next major success, meeting with the editors-in-chief of most of the Murdoch newspapers 'that the people in the street read',[21] except in Western Australia 'where they were not interested—if you were Labor, but they had to come on board later on'. The concept was then marketed to the other media, allowing the television stations to use the program's logo. The fact that it was the minister himself 'selling' the concept seems to have been what impressed people.[22]

The *Australia Remembers* logo

Of fundamental importance to the commemorative program was the ubiquitous logo, a photograph taken by an army photographer of Patrick Anthony Raphael (Ray) Walsh on the day he returned to his family. Among other things, the logo solved any problems associated with the perception of many Australians that their flag is anachronistic. While banners bearing the logo often flew alongside the Australian flag, their immediate identification with the commemorative program enabled Australians of all ethnic and political backgrounds to engage in the collective act of remembering the war, regardless of their objective relationship to it. The logo was 'carefully chosen' to reflect the theme of remembering the veterans who served in the war, and the 'Australians who remained at home and kept the home front running', with the children representing Australians of the future, 'those who benefited from the sacrifices of the veterans and the efforts of Australians who remained at home'.[23] In fact, the logo was suggestive of much more; it was a gendered representation, which, because of its composition, spoke to the viewer in specifically gendered ways. It showed Ray Walsh, his arm around his wife Varlie's shoulder, kissing her, while two of their children, Jeanette and Barry, were framed on the other side. Barry was held up high by Ray, and was wearing his father's slouch hat, suggestive of the male bond of warfare. Ray Walsh would not have countenanced such a connection himself, however, having remarked 'I'll have you out of that (uniform) tomorrow' when he first saw his eldest son, Arthur, wearing his own Army uniform.[24] Daughter Jeanette was looking on, in the female act of watching, so closely associated with warfare. Varlie's gloved hand—a sign of respectability—was holding onto Ray's lapel. Because Ray's was the only figure facing the camera, he became the immediate visual focus, in keeping with the representation of warfare as something that men do. Thus attention was upon the man returning, more than on the wife who waited, and who in a differently gendered reading of the photographs, was herself one of the true 'heroes' of the war.

Con Sciacca had a vision of the image he wanted for the logo—of the men who were away, and the women who carried the burden at home, and the children who thought on their fathers' return that they hardly knew them, and how this represented the whole war experience. He was initially shown about seven photographs which seemed to fit his vision, and made his choice, only to find a few days later that it was of a Vietnam veteran and his family.[25] The story may well be apocryphal, but it seems that he then briefly flirted with the idea of having a professional photographer recreate the scene he was seeking, using some of the staff of the Veterans' Affairs Department in Canberra, only to have this idea scotched on the grounds that those he had in mind to be the 'models' for this photograph could not be made to look authentic, being bigger and stronger-looking than most returning soldiers in 1945.[26]

Figure 1: The *Australia Remembers 1945–1995* logo, featuring Ray Walsh reunited with wife, Varlie, and two of their children, tapped into the desire to commemorate women's wartime roles as well as reinforced gendered divisions between the 'home' and 'fighting' fronts.

The family behind the logo

The *Australia Remembers* publicity information supplied about Ray Walsh and his family suggests a series of happy coincidences, from a Labor point of view, in the choice of this photograph. Ray Walsh was the archetypal Australian 'battler', the son of an engine driver. Upon leaving school in his early teens he had worked as a general hand around his birthplace, Cowra, in New South Wales, after which he moved to Newtown, where, like many of his generation and class, 'he picked up what relief work (such as road maintenance) he could'. Here he met Varlie who was working in her parents' fish-and-chip shop, and after their marriage he worked at several jobs in various factories. He enlisted early, on 15 December 1939, at Newtown, joining the 6th Division AIF,[27] assigned to the Royal Australian Engineers. His eldest son suggested that he probably joined up because 'it was more permanent [and] the money was regular'. Even though at the time he had a full-time job at the Wonorora Dam, there are also strong memories of 'chasing any jobs he could get; doing gardening, doing anything at all to get enough to survive on'.[28] He sailed on the *Orcades* to the Middle East in January 1940, and was captured in Crete on 1 June 1941, spending the remainder of the war as a prisoner of the Germans in various camps. Liberated by Soviet troops,[29] although many prisoners had been marched away to the west beforehand in difficult conditions along frozen roads with inadequate food and mostly brutal treatment by the accompanying guards,[30] he arrived home on 28 July 1945, and was discharged on compassionate grounds in September 1945.[31] There had been no tradition of military service in Ray Walsh's family.

It seems the fact that Ray Walsh had been a POW was coincidental to the choice of the photograph and remained irrelevant as he had belonged to that category virtually ignored by *Australia Remembers*: the prisoner of war of the Germans. Nor was his working-class background a factor in the choice of the photograph, but rather was regarded as typifying the armed forces.[32] Nevertheless, it seems hard to imagine that had *Australia Remembers* been a program sponsored by a Coalition government, such a serendipitous choice might have occurred. Indeed, to complete the picture perhaps, a touch of the larrikin was added when it became known during the *Australia Remembers* program that Ray Walsh's return had been accompanied by some uncertainty, as he was a week late, having been 'celebrating with some mates at a pub and miss[ing] the boat from New Zealand', as daughter Jeanette recalled.[33]

Ray Walsh's incarceration after mid-1941 had a profound effect on the family, and his wife, Varlie, typical of the female 'heroes' of the war, became involved in activities for the Red Cross, as well as carrying the sole responsibility for their five children. Eldest son, Arthur, recalled that as a result of the 1930s Depression, the building of their house was unfinished, verandahs yet to be added, and that their mother 'threw herself into doing that', mixing concrete and so on; as soon as she got the money, it went into finishing off the house. Both Arthur and Jeanette remarked upon the social differences of fifty years ago, when there were no counselling services for families, and that Varlie Walsh had coped well, being a 'very strong woman who held the family together'. Arthur recalled the harsh conditions of life then, of the washing being done outside in a wooden copper, and of leaving for school in the morning when his mother was already in the back yard washing, and coming home to find her still there at the task. Like many of her generation, she was able to 'make something out of nothing'; for instance, when Arthur and Shirley married during the war, there was only one dress made up for the bridesmaids, so Varlie Walsh made the other one to match, and made the hats also.[34]

The children of Ray and Varlie Walsh, including Robyn, who was born after the war, agreed that their parents would have been very proud to have been honoured by the use of their photograph for the logo, and that their mother would have loved being involved in the *Australia Remembers* events, whereas Ray Walsh would have said 'you can stick this, I'm off' after a couple of weeks of 'all the hoo-ha'. All of the Walsh children expressed the universal regret that we realise too late that we should have listened to the stories of our parents' experiences. The youngest, Robyn, probably heard more about Ray's experiences than the others, being around their parents more after Ray's return. Like many veterans, Ray Walsh did not like to talk about the war, but did often relate funny stories, one of which involved a missing donkey and a soup.[35] This reticence on Ray Walsh's part was not surprising, given that he had been incarcerated for much of the time in Stalag VIIIb at Lamsdorf, near the borders of Germany, Czechoslovakia and Poland. Conditions in Stalag VIIIb were reportedly described by Ray Walsh as 'very bad',[36] an understatement, although it seems there was a hierarchy of hardship and brutality within this camp, with misery and starvation being the obvious aims of the Germans, the Russian POWs being treated worse than other nationalities, and starved to death.[37]

As was the case throughout numerous prisoner-of-war camps, including those of the Japanese and those in which women were incarcerated, the prisoners developed their own ways of transcending the conditions in order to survive. Within Stalag VIIIb, an 'excellent university' was conducted, where men of many nationalities studied for the Bachelor of Arts, Law or Engineering, being instructed in Law by a Melbourne lawyer, and in French by a POW from Sydney.[38] The Germans encouraged entertainments, and Stalag VIIIb boasted fourteen bands, including two official military bands, three dance bands and a fifty-piece symphony orchestra.[39] The inmates also produced a weekly, four-page newspaper called 'Stimmt' ('Correct'), produced on stolen German official paper, using a German typewriter. This was placed on noticeboards in each compound, attacking the Germans and explaining which prisoners ran which 'rackets'.[40] Perhaps Ray Walsh's name might have been mentioned in this newspaper, as he was a barber, for which he was paid in cigarettes, the universal currency of prisons. As he had been the family and neighbourhood barber before the war, with kids 'coming from everywhere' for a haircut on a Sunday in those hard pre-war times,[41] it may be that Ray not only benefited from this role in the camp, but also felt some kind of connection with his home life as he employed this skill.

Escapes were rare from Stalag VIIIb.[42] Undeterred by this, Ray Walsh escaped twice with his brother-in-law Jack Byrne, with whom he had met up in Crete when they were taken prisoner, spending the remainder of the war together until Jack Byrne was repatriated in a prisoner exchange about eighteen months before the end of the war. Ray Walsh was badly beaten for these escape attempts, which caused a lot of pain later in his life, but refused his wife's pleas to apply for a TPI pension, always pretending he felt fine whenever he went for an examination with the Repatriation doctor.[43]

In spite of the hardships, separation from his family, and the beatings with their painful legacy, Ray Walsh, like many POWs, was not embittered by his experiences, remarking after the war that the Germans had been as badly off as the Australians during that time. All he wanted, it seems, was to put the wartime experiences behind him, and to immerse himself in family outings such as picnics, although Shirley Walsh recalled that her father-in-law always ate his food quickly after he returned, and liked to have a piece of roasted meat available in the refrigerator at all times. He was not inclined to the 'mateship' syndrome, and did not keep in touch with men from the war, nor march on Anzac Day, although his daughters recalled that later in his life he occasionally went to the Dawn Service, after being invited by a relative through his daughter's marriage, who had been a prisoner in Changi. Although he was a member of the Bankstown RSL, he did not participate in its activities. Similarly, he was uninterested in the trappings of warfare, giving his medals to eldest son Arthur, because he also had worn the uniform, before which they had simply been thrown into a shoebox on the top of the wardrobe, only being taken down when one of his grandsons wanted to look at them.[44]

When interviewed, the Walsh children and their spouses agreed with the view that their father had been 'a character', with 'a touch of the larrikin' about him, which seemed to shine through in the photograph of the logo. There had been some initial disagreement about this photo, the photographer falsely claiming that it had been staged. The entire family was present when Ray Walsh and his wife were finally reunited in that embrace which was to become famous fifty years later, and the photographer in fact happened to come along at that moment, taking one photograph only, when the rest of the family was still standing back from this first embrace. The War Memorial Archives had authenticated this version of the event.[45]

They all remarked upon the enthusiasm of Veterans' Affairs Minister Sciacca, and the way he would always call them his 'other family' when they attended *Australia Remembers* functions. In a telling commentary on the thin line between fantasy and reality generated and encouraged by the modern media, they recalled people approaching them with the questions, 'Are you the Walshes?', 'Are you a real family?' and so on. Robyn recalled people frequently asking whether their father had been an officer, and seeming surprised when told he was not, while Shirley said a lot of people had thought the logo was a posed photograph.[46]

Situating 'memory'—the launch of *Australia Remembers*

Launching *Australia Remembers 1945–1995* at the Australian War Memorial, Canberra on 14 August 1994, Prime Minister Keating used a broad brush to tell Australia's story, as he liked to call it. That the launch was held at the War Memorial was inevitable. This site of memory and commemoration, or 'storehouse of our collective memory and…icon of our faith', as he termed it, seemed to shape Keating's story, as well as providing a motif for the sometimes competing voices within the commemorations and celebrations. He cited the War Memorial as the public building to which his duties had predominantly taken him over the past two-and-a-half years leading up to the anniversary of the war's end. Such events, Keating suggested, were proof that the 'sentiment that emerged from Gallipoli, the Western Front and the Middle East in the First World War does live on', and that the tradition of Anzac—not forgotten by the nation—would 'inspire and unite us through the next century'. These would provide 'powerful symbols of…an enduring Australian faith' for new generations. The 'heroic generation' of the Second World War, born of those 'who had endured World War I and the Great Depression, and who had been denied so many of life's opportunities by those tragic events…were nation builders'. Not only ensuring our freedom, they passed on ideals and faith for us to live by, as well as 'the principles of mateship, and the conviction that wherever we come from on this vast continent, whatever divides us, we are Australians'. Thus we are compelled 'not just to remember…but to pass on the lesson to *our* children'.[47]

An inclusive hierarchy of commemoration was articulated by Keating; 'the focus' of *Australia Remembers* would be 'on Australia and Australians: the veterans of battles'. As well, the nation would remember those left behind to grieve, as well as those 'who served at home, in factories and on farms', and those who came as refugees from Europe and 'who by doing so made all our lives so much richer'. With characteristic desire to transcend what might be perceived as parochialism, Keating hoped that *Australia Remembers* would 'add to our nation's understanding and confidence about our place in the world and our capacity to play a creative and humane part in it', including a greater recognition of 'how important it is for a nation to believe in great ideals—to have them at the forefront of our ambitions', and to 'believe in ourselves'. And finally, Australian women were to be 'involved as never before in such a commemoration'.[48] This aim was pursued in a number of ways sometimes at odds with the continued iconographic memorialising of the Anzac tradition. Although, as discussed elsewhere, *Australia Remembers* compensated for the inadequate representation of women in the 1988 Bicentenary, early events in the year's program provided a gendered focus on some key themes.

Influences and themes—remembrance in Canada, Australia and New Zealand

Having gained bipartisan support for his quest to honour the wartime generation, Veterans' Affairs Minister Sciacca sent some of his staff to find out what other nations were doing to mark the occasion. Dissatisfied with British and US plans, it was Canada's proposed commemorative program, already in planning for four years, which impressed the minister. He decided to adapt the title and incorporated some of the key ideas outlined in the brochures of *Canada Remembers*, in line with his overwhelming priority that Australia's commemorative program be 'people-based'. Once settled upon the name and the format for *Australia Remembers 1945–1995*, the minister went to Aotearoa/New Zealand, only to find that there was nothing official planned there, nor was there any government funding allocated for a commemorative program. Disappointed with this state of affairs, Sciacca went on radio in New Zealand, lamenting the absence of a commemorative program funded by the government of the 'other half' of the Anzacs. *New Zealand Remembers* was born. The departmental head of the Australian Veterans' Affairs Department and other personnel then furnished their New Zealand counterparts with literature and other promotional materials from *Australia Remembers*.[49] The superficial similarities in the three countries' commemorative programs and literature are thus explained, but of more interest is the differences that these exhibited.

Perhaps the single most striking difference was to be found in the centrality of the Anzac legend to *Australia Remembers*. In spite of Con Sciacca evoking this on New Zealand radio, there was a distinct absence of interest in this experience as a defining aspect of identity on the part of *New Zealand Remembers*. This was explicable largely because New Zealanders have never taken the Anzac experience as seriously as the Australians[50] and perhaps because the bulk of New Zealand's personnel and investment in World War II had been in the army in the Middle East and the air force in Europe.[51]

A common theme within each nation's commemorations was the desire to assert the present-day significance of their countries, and to relate this to the ways in which the Second World War had changed them. Con Sciacca, for example, spoke at the launch of *Australia Remembers 1945–1995* of the ways in which every family within Australia had been 'touched in some way' by the war. By doing so he was able to include those families like his own, who brought a variety of wartime experiences and often traumas with them when they came as refugees or as part of the postwar immigration schemes. Australia, Sciacca said (ignoring the history of the significant Indigenous population in his own electorate), had been 'a still young nation confidently finding its natural place in a modern world'.[52]

The effects of war upon Canada were asserted as even more profound, having 'fundamentally altered the structure of Canadian life'.[53] The war had been the most exciting time of 'a great many' people's lives, 'when Canada and its people did a lot of growing up in a very short time'.[54] According to the Secretary of State for Veterans, those who returned from the war however, 'quickly put the war behind them' and got on with taking advantage of the peace. Indeed, Prime Minister Chrétien in his introduction to the *Canada Remembers* publication ($4.95), saw Canada's transformation to a 'strong and united [nation] with a major new role in world affairs' as 'a miracle'. Moreover, this 'miracle' was something which Canadians were destined to 'achieve over and over again' as they faced new challenges.[55] The themes of remembering and imagining, so central to the *Australia Remembers* commemorations and literature were apparent also within the *Canada Remembers* publications, it being stated that 'now, half a century later…it is sometimes hard for the younger of today's generations to imagine the lives and times of the last world war'.[56] An additional dimension to this theme within Canadian remembrance was its linkage to the Cold War from which the world had recently emerged, and the 'overarching shadow of nuclear weapons'. This perspective arguably reflected the geopolitical closeness of Canada to the United States from whom fifty years later, as much as from Great Britain in 1939, *Canada Remembers* was wont to demonstrate independence and a separateness of identity.

Much was made of Canada's 'first and only' independent declaration of war on another country in 1939 despite acknowledging the ties of empire that had been reinforced by a visit a few months earlier by the King George VI and Queen Elizabeth. Whereas Canada had followed Britain into battle in World War I, it being 'unthinkable to do otherwise', its independent declaration of war on 11 September 1939 was accepted fifty years later as both a mere gesture and as 'a sign of the growth in Canada's view of itself'.[57] *Canada Remembers* noted that Canada had been ill-prepared for war, with run-down armed forces further affected by budget cuts aimed at coping with the economic depression. In addition, fifty years later, *Canada Remembers* chose to highlight and perhaps imply some blame on a prime minister who had supported Chamberlain's Munich agreement and who apparently believed that a thorough understanding of Wagner would enable one to deal with Hitler. Indeed, like the US, Canada's foreign policy had been one of isolationism and its leaders had silently watched the victories of fascism throughout the 'thirties. Said by a *Canada Remembers* article to have 'remained firm in his delusions', Prime Minister Mackenzie King had feared that the ties of empire might ensnare Canada once again into a war that would further divide the already seriously divided society. The Depression had left Canadians not only impoverished but 'divided and angry'. Of particular concern at the time had been the increased popularity and power of parties of the left, including the banned communist party, which, like its (legal) Australian counterpart, was busy building support within the trade union movement.[58] Elsewhere, *Canada Remembers* created a 'memory map' of Canada's war. Whilst acknowledging that much more was omitted than included, this revealed much about Canada's uncomfortable relationship with both Britain and the United States, each of which in different ways had dominated Canadian affairs, history, and identity. The memory map enabled Canada to assert itself apropros the US. Observing that 'if you read the American books, we're minor players, lumped in with the British', the memory map notes were keen to assert that 'the truth is [that Canada's role] rivals that of any other nation', adding that for most of the war Canada's army had been a volunteer one 'made up of the cream of Canada's young men and women'. Another aspect of Canada's leading role was that it 'armed an astonished world'[59] when the war came. The change from an agrarian to an industrialised country—albeit still in the grip of the Depression, with fifteen per cent unemployment among unionised workers in 1939[60]—had resulted in Canada becoming the fourth-largest Allied producer of war materials. Fifty years later, *Canada Remembers* felt confident in claiming that in terms of per capita output Canada had been possibly 'Number One'.[61]

Remembrance of Canada's war also necessitated (re)positioning the country's relationship with Britain. Reminiscent of wartime propaganda techniques, to this end was a bold type headline to the effect that in January 1942 'Canada made an outright gift of one billion dollars to Britain, enough to meet her needs for a year'. Ambivalence pervaded much of *Canada Remembers* material, however, and reflected a tension between wanting to remember (and emphasise as much as possible) Canada's close fighting relationship with Britain while at the same time wanting to argue for an independent and important wartime role. The memory map for the last years of the war offered better opportunities for *Canada Remembers* to create a memory of a central role (like that of Australia and New Zealand in their respective remembering) in the Allied victory. The memory map informed not only of the Canadian participation in D-day, but that of all of the Allied forces the Canadians made 'the furthest incursions inland...thrusting deep into the lines of the 21st German Panzer Division'.[62] Furthermore, history had been made in July 1944 when the 'major Canadian objective [of Caen was] taken [by] the first army-sized field force in Canadian history'.[63]

Similarly the memory map was able to boast of the return to Dieppe two years and two weeks after Canadians had suffered defeat there. Even though there had been no German resistance this time, German troops having withdrawn, the event was regarded as sufficiently significant to be included elsewhere in the book with 'before and after' photographs of this defeat and then glory. In writing about the front line during the war, a sense of Canadian superiority over the British way of life, British rations, weather, food, 'in jokes' and coarse humour in their entertainment for service personnel,[64] and perhaps even British servicemen was projected.[65] While Canada has never had the 'lucky country' mentality that has sustained Australia's sense of itself when seeking to assert its perceived superiority over Britain, there were perhaps elements of a similar mentality in this Canadian remembering of the past. Indeed, the fears of being perceived as unworthy or unsophisticated colonials were evinced by the 'memory' that Canadians were not without worldly experience, proof being that 'even in 1939, the majority of Canadians lived in cities and large towns'. While Canadians served in Malaya and Sumatra, and some even in 'faraway places like Australia', the majority 'passed through the old country', providing many with the opportunity to 'broaden themselves or to search out their ancestral roots'.[66]

Canadian women and the war

It was women whose home front work had enabled the war effort to continue, and, as elsewhere, this affected their lives in fundamental ways that resonate in the present. Celebrating 'Rosie the Riveter (every woman worker was a Rosie, whether she riveted or not) as the nation's darling',[67] because the 'Rosies' of the war had 'blazed the way for working women of today', it was noted that many women gave up their jobs at war's end, 'often regretfully'. 'Rosies' became contested, however, another article arguing that 'not even many women seemed to mind returning to housework to make room for the "boys" coming home'.[68] A disclaimer at the beginning of this publication, to the effect that the views expressed belonged to the authors rather than the Canadian government or the Clair Group (which had assisted in the drafting of the document),[69] indicated that the manner and meanings of the war would be contested, which was a unique feature of *Canada Remembers* program. Both *New Zealand Remembers* and *Australia Remembers* tended to present a more homogenised view of the war in their official publications.

Whereas in 1939, 569,000 Canadian women were in paid employment, mostly in clerical jobs, five years later 960,000 worked in war and civilian factory jobs with a further 800,000 working on farms. As was to be the experience of Australian women at times, this was praised with a touch of paternalism fifty years later. That 'fully half of [these women] were doing what once was deemed men's work, and doing it well', indicated that women's efforts were to be measured against male standards. However, volunteer women, whose Voluntary Service organised housewives for a variety of war-associated tasks, were apparently deemed to be the 'unsung heroes', perhaps because they had not actually left their primary role as housewives.

Remembrance of Canadian children

Canada Remembers was unique in its inclusion of children's contributions to the war effort. Children's patriotic roles were highlighted, for example, by their subsistence on 'white' comics (caused by the cessation in production of colour-printing comics and the cost-saving banning of US imports), and their collection of materials for the war effort, as well as their memorising of enemy aircraft in case of a stray coming their way.[70] Children were represented in the text as having 'eagerly caught the spirit of the times, vying for savings stamps and collecting mounds of junk'.[71] The inclusion of the information that the author of this article had been a teenager on the 'home front' in the early war years suggested that his own memories of such activities remained vivid. Thus the remembrance of children may have been a unique feature more because of an authorial idiosyncrasy than a clearly formulated intention on the part of *Canada Remembers*.

Unlike Australia, Canada did not debate the terminology to be employed when naming the day of victory, 15 August, 1945. This was 'VJ Day', and there were no apparent concerns about offending modern-day Japan by so naming it. Perhaps because Canada had not engaged troops in the Pacific theatre of war there was less importance attached to this day, which for *Australia Remembers* was momentous.

'Ordinary' Canadians' memories

Like *Australia Remembers*, Canada sought to locate important memories within those it termed 'ordinary people'. To this end, the reminiscences of six Canadians and their reflections on 'what it's been like since the Second World War' were published. These men and women represented a careful mix of civilian and military memories, and gendered as well as class backgrounds. 'Sara Johnson loved the military life', and the war presented a 'marvellous release from poverty and drudgery', as she put it. All her memories were positive ones, arising perhaps from the extreme material and resultant intellectual poverty of her youth. She was adamant that women had been far happier than men in the services, attributing this to what she regarded as feminine inclinations: 'we were good at making our own nest'. The 'sheer paradise' of the war, as she termed it, had clearly changed her from a provincial into a Canadian, and she remembered the end of the war as 'one of the worst moments I've ever had'. This was because she was to be discharged from the air force, a possibility that had never occurred to her although she went on to use the skills and confidence it had given her.

Another woman joined the navy because like 'virtually every young Canadian [she] was imbued with a wartime sense of duty'. Her adventurous streak and impatience to 'get out and *live*' were other factors her memory selected, and she benefited by not only having a good time, but from a postwar education which 'freed her from the steno pool'. Agnes Brunning had been a 'Rosie' who enjoyed the 'good' money offered by working in the biggest munitions plant in the British Commonwealth, a move which took her much further than 100 miles away from her family's farm (the furthest she'd ever been until the war). A dutiful daughter who spent all her spare money on her family, she married a fellow worker, and remembered the war as 'happy years, that's for sure'.[72]

A rare insight into the complexities of memory was offered by a Royal Canadian Air Force member who ended up in Bomber Command who had the good sense to observe that 'after fifty years it's hard to separate fact from fancy, and to remember what I actually felt'. After reflecting upon the moral dimensions of what he believed to 'be a necessary war', he seemed to gain a memory after all, not only for himself but for 'most ex-servicemen', and concluded with certainty that they 'remember the war as one of the greatest experiences of their lives. It was for me'. Edwin Henry, on the other hand, had a quiet war, having joined up enthusiastically at eighteen, as soon as he finished high school, and ended up a paratrooper private, being denied the necessity to use his training for the Pacific war, as 'the atomic bomb ended that'. Unlike the others, the war had no particular resonance for Edwin, it being 'a distant memory' in spite of keeping in touch with his wartime friends.

This publicity material concluded by posing a number of questions and reflecting on 'the war [that] changed everything', suggesting that Canada had more to celebrate than mere victory because 'it had loosened up, lightened up and become a kinder, gentler place'. Initially asking whether it was worth losing 47,000 lives and thirteen billion dollars and perhaps replacing 'one evil empire' with another, or merely fighting 'to restore corrupt capitalism', it then berated those who present such questions in university classrooms. The Second World War was 'the one good war…quite literally a struggle between light and darkness'.[73] The democracies, including Canada, for all their faults, had simply been forced to fight against the Axis powers, the only regret being that 'unfortunately it took them so long to draw a line and defend it'.

Canadian troops had come home 'to a changed nation, an industrial giant, poised on the brink of a boom in everything from suburbs to babies'. Indeed, this final summing up of the effects of the war revealed the underlying theme of *Canada Remembers*: the national trauma of the Great Depression, in which the country was still 'trapped' in 1939, with almost a quarter of families having the 'humiliation' of accepting welfare payments. In a very gender-exclusive remembering, it was the sons who were singled out for their plight in having to seek work and shelter anywhere they could, whilst couples postponed marriage, and farmers watched the devastation of their crops and people starved. The war had taught defence workers the value of trade unions and had provided the tool for the lifting of wage levels. Other welfare benefits included a baby bonus to be paid directly to the mother. Provision of free university educational opportunities for veterans had arisen from a pragmatic as well as grateful motive, as it helped to rescue the economy.

Perhaps most importantly, Canada was now no longer a backwater, completely overshadowed by its powerful neighbour. Not only had its agricultural and industrial growth been 'immense', but as 'a major military power...the Great Powers [now] had to listen when Canada spoke...the little, isolationist Canada of 1920–39 had grown up'.[74]

For its part the tourist industry took the opportunity to attract visitors to Ottawa. Advertisements featured pretty photographs of some of the three million tulips that flower in Spring. This clever marketing was linked to Crown Princess Juliana of the Netherlands who had fled to Canada during the war, after which as Queen, she sent 10,000 tulip bulbs to Ottawa as an expression of her thanks. Other advertisements seemed entirely commercial, with no connection made between their product and the war. One can only assume that these were among corporate sponsors and simply taking the opportunity to get in on the act.

Providing the model—the logo

Canada Remembers provided a model for Australia and New Zealand with its logo which was designed to 'visually represent the aims of this national program'. Featuring a gold maple leaf to symbolise Canada celebrating war's end, a foreground red poppy in remembrance of Canadians who served and died overseas, and a background red poppy which commemorated those who died in Canada and providing a reminder of 'the wives, husbands, children and all those who played a vital supporting role at home', the three elements of the logo were intertwined to symbolise 'the unity and strength of Canadians

Figure 2: The *Canada Remembers* logo provided the model for others. Designed to symbolise the unity and strength of Canadians, it also evoked national(ist) sentiments of Canada's 'enduring values'.

and their loyalty, dedication and sacrifice—enduring values that will sustain Canada in the future'.[75] With the positioning of the battle front poppy in the foreground, this front—mostly associated with male endeavour—was privileged over women's mostly home front activities, reinforcing the sexual division of labour in warfare. Nevertheless, the *Canada Remembers* logo did not offer the richly textured gendered readings of the *Australia Remembers* logo, and to a lesser extent the *New Zealand Remembers* logo.

Commemoration of indigenous participants

Australia Remembers' commemoration of Indigenous peoples' contributions clearly arose from a genuine desire to honour them, yet remained problematic, whereas *New Zealand Remembers'* discussion of Maori involvement in the war appeared to reflect a more inclusive dimension to race relations, in spite of criticisms that this evoked. *Canada Remembers* chose to commemorate indigenous involvement in the war through a separate booklet entitled *Native Soldiers, Foreign Battlefields*. This format signified that indigenous Canadians were more comfortably accorded such recognition through being maintained as 'the other' in public memory. Indeed this conceptualisation was exemplified by the cover of this booklet, with a photograph of recruits from Saskatchewan's File Hills community posing with elders, family members and a representative from the Department of Indian Affairs (DIA) before departing for Great Britain during the First World War. The framing of this photograph placed the camera's focus on the seated DIA representative flanked by four men in 'traditional garb, two of whom wore head-dress, one resplendent with buffalo horns'. In the front row two men exhibited various stages of assimilation, wearing a combination of suits, collars and ties, earrings and long plaited hair. The two back rows contained men in army garb. All the men were solemn in expression except for the DIA representative whose hint of a smile suggested perhaps that he alone was at ease. Indigenous veterans were situated as both 'modern' and 'traditional' and quoted as seeing their role as simultaneously defending civilisation and 'show[ing] the bravery of our warriors of old'.[76]

In the booklet's introduction, the Canadian Minister for Veterans' Affairs spoke of the quick and impressive response, whose 'strength [was] unexpected', of Canada's indigenous population during the three wars of the twentieth century, with more than 3,000 serving in World War II,[77] mostly in the infantry, as was the case in World War I. Their efforts had been publicised at the time by 'countless articles' in the newspapers, and five hundred died during these three wars, 'defending values that were meaningful to all Canadians'. They brought home 'incredible memories' as well as cultural influences from the British, and in some cases, British war brides.[78]

It may well have been comforting for the minister to express the Native war effort in those terms, and clearly such sentiments fitted nicely within the overall *Canada Remembers* perspective. However, as was revealed elsewhere in this booklet, support for participation in World War I had been far from unanimous, some band councils linking military service with demands for British recognition of their status as independent nations, which was not granted.[79] Such demands were similar to those made of their government by Australian Aborigines for civil rights, which remained similarly unmet. Elsewhere it became abundantly clear that some Native Canadians responded for reasons more directly relevant to them than those preferred by the minister in his introductory remarks, including a long tradition dating back to the eighteenth century, of fighting on the side of Great Britain. Most importantly, the Second World War provided the opportunity for Natives who had otherwise lost contact with their fighting traditions and identities to again be 'warriors in a proud tradition stretching back over thousands of years into the dim past [as we] travelled by ship, by plane…and mostly on foot'.[80] Other cited motivations included ideological concerns about Nazism, economic hardship and feeling pressured to volunteer.[81]

Canadian Natives earned at least seventeen decorations for bravery during World War II, and participated in every major battle and campaign. At least sixteen Indians and Métis became POWs of the Japanese, nine of whom died. As was the case with Torres Strait Islanders and Aboriginal Australians, on the home front Canadian Natives also made important contributions in coastline surveillance and the war industries and agriculture.

New Zealand Remembers

Having arrived at the idea of a national commemorative program in 1995, based largely upon the models provided by *Canada* and *Australia Remembers, New Zealand Remembers 1945–1995* shared a number of similarities, but was distinctly more low-key. As in Australia, the New Zealand program consisted of official government-sponsored events at the national level and local events arranged and sponsored within their localities in association with RSA branches. Total funding was $995,000, $370,000 of which was seeding funding for the seventy-four local authorities' use. Lottery grants provided an additional $885,000 for the completion of the Carillon housed at the National War Memorial. As in Australia, corporate funding was not forthcoming, but Mobil Oil sponsored the Veterans and Civic Parade in Wellington. An education package and video was also produced,[82] as in Australia.

The objectives of *New Zealand Remembers* reflected those of Canada and Australia but were more narrowly focused, reflecting a greater interest in peace in the present and future. Four aims were identified: to 'recall the sorrows of sacrifice and the joys of victory'; to enhance understanding of the causes of the war and to learn from that understanding; to provide 'a reminder of the importance of keeping the peace in our world'.[83] To assist in achieving these aims, *New Zealand Remembers* featured two separate packages of maps: 'theatres of war' and 'the world at war 1939–45'. The 'theatres of war' chart included a time line of events with the top two thirds detailing 'Germany—Axis Power', beginning with the Battle of the River Plate in December 1939, and ending with 'Soviets take Berlin' in May 1945. New Zealand's desire to establish the independence of its declaration of war mirrored that of *Canada Remembers,* whereas this had not been an issue within *Australia Remembers* literature. This was more at pains to demonstrate the crucial role of Australia in the war as well as the ultimate necessity, to take control of its destiny and defend itself against the Japanese. It was within these expressions that the meanings of Australia's war were located.

Promotional material

A sixty-three-page book, *New Zealand Remembers the Second World War*, featuring photographs and text on the theatres of war, details of the various VJ Day events around the country, as well as the symbolism of the *New Zealand Remembers* logo, was published by the Department of Internal Affairs Te Tari Taiwhanua. The cover of this was redolent with gendered meanings. Against a sepia background of joyful looking young women obviously celebrating news of the war's end fifty years ago was a colour photograph of 'Cameron Taylor wearing his great-grandfather's medals [as he] assists Kerikeri RSA President, Keith Weeds, to lay the Association's VJ wreath'. In the background to this photograph were older women, of the wartime generation, watching.

Unlike in Australia, but similarly with Canada, the nomenclature of VJ Day was 'never a matter of serious debate'. Whilst there 'was sensitivity within government circles at not wishing to upset relations with Japan', the veterans organisations made it very plain that VJ Day was the only acceptable term, that 'history could not be rewritten'. This effectively 'forced the government to acknowledge and accept the use' of the term.[84] That the New Zealand Prime Minister did not share Australian Prime Minister Keating's passion for defining Australian identity as well as its place and role within Asia may have also influenced this decision.

The message from Prime Minister Bolger, outlining the national ceremonies of the program, which would begin with Anzac Day and end with VJ Day events, spoke of the threat to civilisation posed by the Second World War and the 'tribute to the human condition' which victory demonstrated. Evoking the distant theatres of war in which New Zealand men and women had stood 'shoulder-to-shoulder with allies', Mr Bolger was keen to assert the pre-eminence of his country's effort, as were his Canadian and Australian counterparts. He assured New Zealanders that their country's 'contribution to the final outcome was as significant as any nation in the world', and that the 'initiative, the humour, the strength of resolve and the courage of New Zealanders in battle is legendary'. The other 'ordinary people', those at home, could 'only stand and wait' but were 'absorbed in the storm of war' which 'decimated' a generation, dislocated society and left an 'indelible imprint' on society. The aim, he said, was for reflection on the lessons of war, as well as 'to recall' New Zealand's fighting forces far away and near to home, to 'pay tribute' to 'those who kept New Zealand functioning in those dark days' and to 'remember' the refugees who came after the war, and who 'added to the tapestry of our country'.

For his part, the language of the Minister of Defence and Minister of Internal Affairs, the Hon. Warren Cooper, indicated a confusion about the nature of history and its relationship with memory. The war, Mr Cooper opined, was 'history [for young New Zealanders], whereas for other generations it was an experience', and indeed there would be many 'poignant memories' throughout the year. In his view, *New Zealand Remembers* was primarily to remind everyone of what was happening fifty years ago, and to focus on the armed forces 'of course'. In articulating this he appeared to privilege the paradigm of warfare as the (gendered) site for the most important meanings of war and its remembrance. That his portfolio included Defence may partly explain this, and in any case, the 'Ordinary People' series diluted his somewhat militaristic focus. His acknowledgment of the importance of the home front was expressed rather lamely, stating simply that 'we should remember them, too'. To this end, television programs would 'tell these stories', and schools would receive education packs.

New Zealand Remembers acted upon the belief that the local program of events would be where 'the best perspective…and understanding' of the war years and their meaning would be gained. The local level was where 'the collective memory resides', for which the government would provide 'some funding to begin the process of remembrance, both solemn and in celebration'. Thus it seems, memory and remembrance were one and the same thing, and memory therefore would become something that was not only created but also organised and controlled through the program of events. In spite of this, *New Zealand Remembers* did not convey the overall impression of *Australia Remembers,* that memory of the past was being created as a part of the process of imagining the nation. While more modest in character than *Canada Remembers* or

Australia Remembers, New Zealand Remembers seemed determined to assert a rather dubious superiority over both countries' wartime records. In a brief 'Did You Know' column, New Zealand's casualty rate was compared both ghoulishly and favourably, depending on one's perspective, citing twenty-four dead per 1,000 New Zealanders compared with nine per 1,000 Canadians and thirteen per 1,000 Australians.[85]

The logo

The *New Zealand Remembers* logo was designed to be appropriate to the three services, as well as 'representing those who stayed at home'. Spatially encased by two fern leaves, 'distinctly New Zealand symbol[s]' which gave 'the form of a military badge', were three central figures from the statue in the Hall of Memories in the National War Memorial in Wellington. These figures were to 'symbolise those who were left behind, and so represent the efforts of the home front and the families of those who did not return'. The motif as a whole was 'strongly symbolic of the crisis of war and its effects on citizens, but also of the nation's relief at a just victory'.[86] Arguably, however, it contained more meaning than that simply intended and described above. The central figure was a woman who shielded/held to her side a figure of a boy, standing erect, with her arm around his shoulder. A smaller figure, of a girl leaning into the woman as if for protection, was also shielded/held by the woman's other arm and the woman's head was inclined towards the little girl. It offered a gendered representation of the home front, where the young boy was being portrayed as male and stronger whereas the younger girl, being feminine, required greater protection and was the one with whom the adult female/mother figure was more closely identifying. In line with common practice, but also reflecting the significant inclusion of Maori within the commemorative program, the logo was inscribed with the Maori words: 'look back to remember'.[87] The final photograph in *New Zealand Remembers the Second World War* was of a young Maori serviceman in the act of remembering. The foreground of the photograph showed Chief Petty Officer Steve Paul of the Royal New Zealand Navy, in civilian clothing kneeling reflectively at the grave of a twenty-three-year-old Maori member of the NZ Infantry at Suda Bay, Crete. It was a pretty, coloured photograph, which clearly showed the blue daisies growing around the grave. Chief Petty Officer Paul's right forearm rested on the top of the headstone, the other hand—in which there was a handkerchief—was cupping his chin in classic reflective pose. Opposite him behind the graves stood two men of the wartime generation, their figures slightly blurred. One was wearing a jacket on which there were at least five medals and a couple of other badges. The photograph was suggestive of the desired link between the generations in terms of homage and remembrance.

Figure 3: The *New Zealand Remembers* logo, designed to be appropriate for the three services and those 'at home', incorporated distinctly national(ist) imagery and also reinforced warfare as gendered.

Concerned with reaching young people, *New Zealand Remembers* funded an education kit which targeted third- and fourth-formers, i.e. fourteen- to sixteen-year-olds. The aim here was 'to make history real' to young people. The only way this could be achieved, it seems, was through the device of oral history, with these students being encouraged to 'embark on oral history projects' with their own families by researching the impact of the war on the various generations within their families.[88] In this, *New Zealand Remembers* was as cheerfully oblivious as its Australian counterpart about the complexities of oral history and questions of methodology involved in conducting this kind of research. Young people were perceived as eager if perhaps somewhat intellectually limited receptacles of 'history'. Therefore, videos were regarded as an essential part of any education kit about the war.

A documentary series of six ninety-minute episodes 'New Zealand at War', screened early in May to coincide with VE Day, presumably aimed to bring the war to New Zealanders 'in a way never seen before', focusing on 'what really happened' and what it was like to be there. This account of what its producer described somewhat effusively as the 'most epic event of the century' included previously unused archival material. The inclusion of 'the personal memories of those who fought' was said to overcome for the first time the 'Kiwi characteristic [of being] modest about achievement', as well as the disinclination 'to remember' on the part of the men who went to war, but who fifty years later were 'ready to talk'. For this documentary series over 700 people were interviewed and 150 veterans recorded on tape, much of which was described somewhat superfluously as 'very emotional'.[89] The emphasis of this video series was clearly the fighting war and the 12,000 New Zealanders 'who gave their lives', with the ten researchers involved having worked with defence historians to 'uncover...the story of a nation at war'. The 'darker side of war' was not avoided but the stories of 'incompetence and betrayal...looting, hard discipline and drinking [were] put in context [in an attempt] to come to grips with both the horror and the heroism of war'.[90]

An 'Ordinary People' package was designed to 'make history...meaningful to young people' or 'to bring history alive', and was a gift to all secondary schools from *New Zealand Remembers*, with the aim of making it clear to them that the war touched all people and not just the military. Including a ninety-minute video of a selection of 'New Zealand Weekly Review' newsreels screened in cinemas between 1942 and 1945, as well as facsimile headline pages of major newspapers, a booklet on the United Nations and maps of the theatres of war, it was hoped that the 'diverse range of personal stories' in these kits would encourage students to discover the impact of the war on their grandparents and other family members.[91] It was hoped that the young would come to 'appreciate that history is not just something that happened long ago and in far away places'. Laudable as this aim was, and impressive as the preparation of these kits at very short notice was, it was inevitable that students would gain little more than 'bites' of information and as a result a limited understanding of the actual nature of the struggle. This was compounded by the tone and content of some of these stories that were so ordinary as to border on the mundane. For example, Ian and Ngaire Darby related their very ordinary meeting and how their frequent correspondence after he was sent to Britain and America for training led to them becoming 'serious' about each other. For Ngaire the war had been depressing in many ways but 'in the end life went on and you made the best of it'. This prosaic theme was to be a frequent one, which competed with other voices that remembered the war as the best time of their lives and of the formation of enduring friendships both male and female.

Another 'story' by Nan and Heath Simcox, farmers near Otaki, photographed in the present with Nan wearing a medal expressed a continuing antagonism towards the Japanese—or 'Japs', as they both were wont to express it. Heath remembered the 'great relief at the news of the atom bomb…[which he chose to believe] saved more Japs [sic] than it killed', whereas Nan was keen to conclude her 'story' with the comment that 'whatever our grandchildren might think about the Japanese, we've got other ideas'.

Maori couple Grant and Heather Maninui who lived near Masterton, told of their experiences in the air force and the land army.[92] Indicative of constructions of 'the other' in New Zealand at the time, Grant had been considered a 'lost cause' by his school teachers because he spoke only the Maori language. He was rejected outright by the NZ Navy and his application in 1937 to join the air force was seemingly conveniently misplaced, leaving only the army. He remembered that it 'didn't make any difference to me, whether it was the Maori Battalion or anywhere as long as I got in', and that the war had been a profoundly unsettling experience, recalling that afterwards 'it took having children to straighten me out'.[93] Heather's memories suggested a political consciousness at the time, having had secret elocution lessons resulting in a 'very plum-in-the-mouth accent' in order to pass the nursing interview. Her memories of the slights Maori had endured seemed sharper than Grant's, observing that 'in those years Maori weren't really educated', that the men had to look for work in the towns, and the women were 'cut adrift because there was nothing in the towns for them'.[94] The war had enabled her to take the advice of her 'very black humble father', by making the 'Pakeha system work for us'. Wikitoria Te Huruhuru Whatu Nee Katene did not recall experiencing the same difficulties in being accepted as a young Maori woman, albeit as the only Maori, in nursing training at the Wellington Hospital and being sent overseas which she really loved, regarding herself as 'lucky' to visit places like Italy and Palestine. Her brother George, an officer of the Maori Battalion, was killed in Italy but she 'did not feel bad about it', having met up with him and seen some places together. Her memories of feeling lonely after the war and of not wanting to continue with nursing were mingled in her remembrance fifty years later with gratitude for being 'well-off in our country'.

New Zealand Remembers and peace

Celebrating peace emerged as a key theme throughout the country, providing a character that was quite distinct from either Canadian or Australian remembrances with their more overt desires to instrumentalise the war for contemporary national purposes. Peace was identified as 'an issue of real concern to young people',[95] with many local events seeking to cater especially for that generation in an attempt to make the fiftieth anniversary 'relevant to them'. As its contribution to this aim, the Te Awamutu RSA announced on VJ Day the establishment of two Peace Scholarships of $1,000 each to assist local students embarking on tertiary studies.

Peace provided the focus of the National Service in Celebration of the Fiftieth Anniversary of the End of World War II at Wellington Cathedral of St Paul on Sunday 13 August. Arranged in partnership between the Cathedral, Heads of Churches and the *New Zealand Remembers* Office of the Department of Internal Affairs, this had as its title 'Reconciliation, Hope and Thanksgiving'. With much of the proceedings printed in the Maori language and verses sung in Maori, the emphasis of this VJ Day commemorative service was upon reconciliation. Governor-General of New Zealand, Her Excellency Dame Catherine Tizard, began her reading with the reminder that reconciliation derives from forgiveness, when 'the question of who was right and who was wrong ceases to matter'. Elsewhere in her message to the nation, which opened the official commemorative book, Dame Catherine spoke of being able to 'remember both VE Day and VJ Day clearly' and of the challenge within the *New Zealand Remembers* program of paying tribute to the wartime generation without glorifying war itself.[96] While the New Zealand national anthem concluded the ceremony, including a verse sung by the choir in the Maori language, earlier in the proceedings all present sang 'God Save the Queen', suggesting that there may not have been a strong need on the part of *New Zealand Remembers* to proclaim a separate identity, almost in opposition to Britain, as was the case with *Canada Remembers* and to a greater extent, *Australia Remembers*. Also unique in New Zealand's program and commemorative publications were photographs the Queen. Whilst *Canada Remembers* had advertised that its video contained a special message from the Queen, New Zealand's book featured a solemn photograph of the Queen at the commissioning of the second of the new bells, Peace—Rangamarie—at the National War Memorial,[97] during her recent visit to New Zealand. Perhaps more important for New Zealand was its assertion that the Second World War represented 'another step towards independent nationhood...[being] no longer Anzacs but...now Kiwis...'.[98] In other words, the war had enabled New Zealand to emerge from the shadow of its closest neighbour, Australia, much in the way that *Canada Remembers* asserted that it had shaken off America's dominance. Perhaps as a result of this, *New Zealand Remembers* on the whole seemed more inclined to focus on contemporary issues. To a significant extent also, this was consistent with New Zealand's leadership in the campaign against French nuclear testing in the Pacific during 1995. The tone of the prime minister's speech to the Parliament after the VJ Day parade carefully urged against complacency on the part of the younger generation, saved by the sacrifices of their elders. He then focused on New Zealand's contribution to United Nations peacekeeping forces in Bosnia and elsewhere and most importantly, on 'our campaign fifty years after Hiroshima to bring an end to nuclear testing'.[99]

New Zealand Remembers and spectacle

The VJ Day Commemorative Pageant, a sound and light extravaganza on the forecourt of Parliament at twilight, 'provided a striking culmination to the day's commemorative activities'.[100] Broadcast on prime time television later in the evening, this included the bands of the three services in full ceremonial dress, 'combining in a dramatic and musical presentation'. A 'powerful [and] very meaningful' haka performed by the Maori culture group drawn from members of a Landforce Group based in Palmerston North, represented the prestige of past unit members and enabled the young to show their respect.[101] Photographs showed the singing of Vera Lynn's 'We'll Meet Again', backed by the army Maori cultural group, some in army uniform and others with their chests naked but for traditional bone carving around their necks and face tattoo patterns. A feature of the pageant had been the haka performed by the present day army Maori cultural group against the backdrop of the parliamentary buildings. This reinforced the greater respect with which Maori—unlike Indigenous Australians or Canadian Natives—have been positioned in the nation's imagining of itself, in spite of their continuing struggle for recognition and implementation of the terms of the Treaty of Waitangi.

Commemoration of women

A similarity with *Canada Remembers* and *Australia Remembers* was
the ways in which New Zealand women were commemorated. *New
Zealand Remembers* literature examined how the war had been 'A
Turning Point for Women', 228,000 of whom by 1943 were in employment, with a further 8000 in the armed forces. Photographs were
featured of Country Women's Institute members in the Wellington VJ
parade, and of three female wartime science technicians at a reunion
of 'Man Power' [sic] women conscripts held at their laboratory in
Lower Hutt. Describing women as 'the unsung heroes of the war
effort', their experiences half a century earlier were linked to present-
day equal opportunity measures. Indeed, Women's Affairs Minister
(and later prime minister), the Hon. Jenny Shipley, spoke of the debt
of today's women to the wartime generation of women 'for their courage, determination, and fortitude [urging] that their contribution be
remembered'.[102] Thus, in the remembrance of New Zealand women,
as in *Australia Remembers,* women were to become heroes, and the
problematic aspects of this designation were to remain unexamined.
Doubtless there were many New Zealand women of the wartime
generation, as well as their children, who remembered the hardships
their mothers endured, who were happy to be accorded this status,
as was the case in Australia.

Although not a part of the official 'remembering' of Aotearoa/
New Zealand women's wartime experiences, the screening of 'War
Stories Our Mothers Never Told Us', also published as a book
accompanied by a six-page study guide, provided a rare occasion
for women's voices to be heard, in ways which remained unique to
New Zealand's anniversary events. These stories transcended the
more commonplace representations of the war as a turning point for
women. 'War Stories' was a collection of nine women's stories from
the war, and as Judith Fyfe noted in the preface to the book, she had
grown up hearing stories of the war as she sat 'under the kitchen
table while the women talked'. Their conversation had never been
about battles or bombs, but rather, always about the relationships,
'dislocated and wrenched apart or, sometimes worse, forced together
again because of that time called "during the war"'. The men's stories,

she continued, 'were very different. Not only in context, but in the telling...loudly with a beer in one hand...army yarns for public consumption'.[103] Both she and film-maker Gaylene Preston were 'war babies' who had developed a particular interest in the voices of their female relatives. Prompted by the imbalance in research on the impact of the war on their mothers' generation and therefore also upon their own generation, they had initiated a major oral history project which aimed to explore the ways women felt about the war period, rather than what they actually did in that period.[104] In-depth interviews with sixty-six women followed, with the intention that these interviews would provide the resource for the film and book. These interviews revealed that the war had specific meanings for women, among which was the 'milestone' in New Zealand women's lives provided by the presence of 100,000 American troops between mid-1942 and mid-1944. 'War Stories' enabled women to overcome fears about their wartime conduct, and indicated a range of ways in which the war shaped their lives. A theme that emerged was the sexual ignorance of young women at this time, which had often resulted in unplanned pregnancy.

Canada Remembers, *New Zealand Remembers* and *Australia Remembers* assess the present

As occurred in Canada and Australia, the fiftieth anniversary celebrations provided the occasion for *New Zealand Remembers* to evaluate the progress of the nation over the past half-century. In doing so it became apparent that it was less complicated for these nations to engage in such self-examination, given that the war was believed to have provided an important boost to their separate identities and self-esteem. For the major nations of the wartime alliance on the other hand, remembrance was more complex and tied to questions of wartime morality and postwar status.

In assessing New Zealand's progress, the Rt. Rev. Manu Bennett, the retired Bishop of Aotearoa and a patron of *New Zealand Remembers,* who had been Chaplain to the Maori Battalion during the war, chose to focus on race relations. At a ceremony to open the

NZ Army Marae at Waiouru, the meanings of Maori involvement in the war became contested. Chief of General Staff, Major Piers Reid, described this event as 'another milestone in the development of the partnership between the two dominant cultures...Maori and Pakeha'. Indeed, Maori participation in the war had not been accorded specific, separate, attention as had been the case with Indigenous commemorations in Canada and Australia, but rather the wartime Maori Battalion had been 'accorded recognition' at national and international levels and Maori veterans on the whole had attended within 'mainstream activities'.[105] Nevertheless, on this occasion, the Rev. Manu Bennett provided a differing view on this 'partnership', by reflecting upon the encouragement to join up which had been provided by eminent Maori politician Sir Apirana Ngata 'who said that their participation was the nation's price of citizenship'.[106] However, Ngata's dream had been imperfectly realised according to Rev. Bennett. The awareness of issues relating to the Treaty of Waitangi and heightened consciousness that the nation did indeed comprise two peoples, had not been sustained. Speaking very much from the political perspective of the 1990s, he suggested that the existence of the Maori Battalion had expressed the true concept of partnership, 'whereby Maori as a people and a Treaty partner could fulfil their obligations to the nation'. This was a nation which at the beginning of the war had 'not emerged completely from its colonial shrouds and the formation of the Maori Battalion had therefore been a significant milestone', whereas on reflection fifty years later, 'Maori are still struggling to maintain their identity as a Treaty partner'. Indeed an examination of Maori representation in parliament, as well as the poverty level indicated, Rev. Bennett argued, that 'Maori did not get a good return on their investment in citizenship'. Nevertheless, he concluded his remarks on a positive note, expressing the hope that the present 'stress and tension' in New Zealand around Treaty issues would be resolved in the future.[107]

New Zealand Remembers' more open discussion of the wartime and contemporary relationship between the state and Maori was unique among the three nations examined here. Whereas, as we have seen, Australia and Canada went to considerable pains to *include* Indigenous peoples in commemorative literature and events, there was little acknowledgement of *their* perspectives then or fifty years later. A significant additional factor was the presence of Maori spokespersons within the nation, occupying positions such as bishoprics, whereas in Australia and (to a lesser extent) Canada, such inclusiveness is rare.

As did Maori in New Zealand, Australian Aborigines and indigenous people in Canada had enlisted for a variety of reasons, not the least being that their fathers and grandfathers had served in World War I. There was also a strong political dimension to Australian Aborigines' enlistment, whereby it was linked to pre-existing campaigns for citizenship rights. As well, the Second World War provided the opportunity for Aboriginal men and women to gain employment and to provide a support role in the war industries. As discussed later in this book, Aborigines and Torres Strait Islanders did not attain their desired rights as a result of their war efforts, but rather their second-class status was magnified once they returned home and took off their uniforms.

As suggested, of the three nations, Aotearoa/New Zealand was inclined to concentrate more on the present and the resolution of outstanding issues in the future. *Canada Remembers* for its part had revealed considerable continuing interest in analysing the ways in which the nation had been divided and overshadowed by both Britain and the United States prior to the war, a situation which was largely remedied by the vital role it was perceived as playing in the war. *Canada Remembers,* like *Australia Remembers* was quite self-conscious in its attempts to be inclusive of all elements within Canadian society. *Australia Remembers* for its part had a more extensive and comprehensive program of events during which it indulged Australians' penchant for defining their national identity. There was also an emphasis on encouraging Australians to imagine themselves in ways that enabled the multicultural nation to share in sustaining national legends such as Gallipoli. Nostalgia, evident in the programs of the three nations, but most palpable within *Australia Remembers,* encouraged the belief that the past could be retrieved through a range of recreated events, styles of dress and so forth. Through these devices, what one generation 'knew' because of being alive at the time, could be 'imagined' by the generations who followed the war. Thus, terrible as the loss of lives and suffering of different kinds on the home and battle fronts were, the Second World War was presented in different ways by *Canada, Australia* and *New Zealand Remembers* not as a grand and tragic adventure like the First World War, but as an occasion for growing up and attaining a true sense of self.

CHAPTER 3

History and memory:
Australia Remembers 1945–1995
and uses of the past

Women made '…a massive contribution to the story of Australia'.[1]

'The government committed aggression; our husbands were its victims.'[2]

THE celebratory and commemorative events of *Australia Remembers 1945–1995* occurred between the 1988 Bicentenary and the Centenary of Federation in 2001. While sharing a number of common features, most notably perhaps that of seeking to employ 'the past' in order to imagine the present, *Australia Remembers* was, in significant ways, qualitatively different from both of these. A key reason for this may be that the Second World War is something with which each generation has some familiarity, whether because of direct experience, learning about it at school or university, through oral histories, or from popular film and documentary. On the other hand, the 1988 Bicentenary commemorated a history that has become increasingly contested, as well as being something about which many Australians remain lamentably uninformed. The war, on the other hand, may have had a greater resonance regardless of cultural heritage or political inclination.

With regard to the Centenary of Federation, it was unfortunate that this occurred so soon after the Olympic Games in September 2000, which had provided a focus for many people's pride in Australia, boosted by International Olympic Commission officials' declaration that the Sydney Games had surpassed all others in the history of the modern Olympic movement. As well, the spectacle of the opening and closing ceremonies, the grand new venues, the self-congratulatory national pride in the achievement of an individual athlete who won a gold medal had momentarily enabled many Australians in the era of 'Reconciliation' to delude themselves that race relations in Australia were not problematic. All of these things added to a generalised 'hype' about Australia throughout 2000. By the time the rather lacklustre task of commemorating—or more still, celebrating—the Centenary of Federation came around a few months after the Olympics, there was little energy let alone enthusiasm, left within the Australian public. Similarly, the media appeared less than inspired by the anniversary, appearing more to report dutifully on activities than to find anything particularly dynamic about them.

A further problem was that a somewhat dour formula for politically uniting the disparate Australian colonies in 1901 was never likely to capture the national imagination. For a nation whose population largely remains disrespectful, if not suspicious, of its politicians, the Centenary of Federation did not appear to have generated the excitement of *Australia Remembers*. Nor did it generate the contestations and sense of unease on the part of non-Indigenous Australians who throughout 1988 were unable to ignore that 'white Australia has a black history'. As Federation had constitutionally excluded Australian Indigenous peoples from the nation, its centenary similarly did not ignite public interest in contemporary race relations, in spite of the changes that have occurred since then. Nonetheless, the strategically timed launching of Treaty papers by Aboriginal and Torres Strait Islander Commission (ATSIC) chair Geoff Clark on 8 May 2001, provided a momentary reminder that Federation remains an exclusive moment in Australian history.

The Centenary of Federation

The Centenary year opened with a 'New Dawn' at Alice Springs, said to be 'the heart of the country', on 1 January 2001, with a message to be 'sent to Sydney inviting all Australians' to travel to Alice Springs in September for the Yeperenye Federation Festival.[3] This ceremony signalled two problematic factors, one of which was the continuing non-Indigenous Australian search for an authenticity based upon the appropriation of Aboriginality. The other was the centring of Sydney as the nation's focus, compounded on this occasion by the fact that the formal Federation ceremony had occurred in Melbourne. The Sydney focus suggested a continuity with other celebrations of the nation, most notably the 1888 Centenary and the 1988 Bicentenary.

It became clear in September, however, that Indigenous people were firmly in control of the Yeperenye festival. Beginning with a welcome from an Arrernte elder on whose land the event took place, the compere of the event, Aaron Pederson, followed with the opening statement that those present and television viewers were about to 'witness the biggest demonstration of Indigenous ceremony ever performed in this country'. From all over Australia, Aboriginal and Torres Strait Islander people had come to 'dance on our land and represent their nations'. These performers had brought their law, dance, song and spirit to share. Pederson's opening remarks were followed by an enactment of the Yeperenye caterpillar creation story, performed by 2500 children, telling of the journey of the caterpillars from five regions across the desert to the place named Alice Springs by the colonisers.

Yothu Yindi followed with their song *Terra Nullius*, which they had also performed at the Sydney Olympic Closing Ceremony. This provided a smooth link with Aaron Pederson's commentary in which the 1901 Centenary paled into insignificance in comparison with the Indigenous federation that had existed 'for many years before that'. During this period, '390 Indigenous nations made up this country that was, and still is, the first federation'.[4] For Indigenous people, acknowledgement of the Centenary year meant that they looked 'back at the past so that we can have a strong vision for the future'. As the style of Pederson's compering became increasingly like a rallying cry of pride, he reminded all present of:

Australia's history of 60,000 years, of bloodlines span-
ning 2500 generations, [that] over one billion people [had]
walked this land prior to 1788. This is our inheritance as
black and white Australians, and this is our story.

The Yeperenye Festival was the occasion for the most clearly
articulated response to the meanings of 'federation'. Such a response
was indicative of an on-going process whereby Indigenous peoples
in Australia engage in 'speaking back' to the colonisers. Whereas the
Centenary of Federation program had provided the occasion and the
funding for Yeperenye, its commemoration was clearly framed and
controlled by Indigenous people. Equally clear was that insofar as
the federation of white Australia had significance one hundred years
later, this was only as a point of comparison with the much longer
and more dynamic federation of hundreds of Indigenous nations
prior to the arrival of the British. Indeed, what was effectively being
asserted at this moment was the continuing Aboriginal sovereignty
of the land.

The Centenary of Federation events followed the pattern of
the 1888 Centenary, the 1988 Bicentenary and *Australia Remembers*
in 1995, by staging a nationwide program of events that included
state, territory and local activities. Its 'highlight events' web site
contained fifty-seven pages of what it termed 'centrepiece events'
aimed at attracting 'Australia-wide and international interest'. These
were so varied as to include a Federation trophy for croquet players
throughout NSW, the opening of the National Museum of Australia in
Canberra, celebrations of the centenary of the Australian army and a
Federation River Procession involving hundreds of 'specially designed
boats and barges as well as Indigenous, multicultural, community
and arts groups each displaying their history and culture to explore
themes of relevance to Australia'.[5] Despite these efforts, the Centenary of Federation did not spark the kind of national engagement
of either the Bicentenary or *Australia Remembers*. As mentioned,
this may largely have been due to a kind of saturation following the
Olympic Games and the possibilities these provided for basking in
self- and international congratulation. The somewhat uninspiring
nature of the political compromises between competing Australian

colonies a hundred years earlier remained for many a virtual non-event. For this reason, it is the events of 1988 and 1995—and their mass participation—that are discussed here.

1988 and the Bicentenary

The task of the 1988 Australian Bicentenary Authority (ABA) was always going to be larger than that of either the Centenary of Federation or commemorating the fiftieth anniversary of the end of the Second World War. Whereas both federation and the war were focused on specific events and, in a sense, contained by the timeframes woven around them, the ABA had the task of trying to evoke a national character that was relevant for the entire nation and spanned the two centuries of non-Indigenous occupation of Australia. The very nature of this unresolved occupation meant the proposed celebration of the nation was going to be a conflicted one. As David Lowenthal has observed, the past has become both 'an ever more foreign realm' and 'increasingly suffused by the present'.[6] This became particularly evident throughout the lead up to 1988 and throughout that year. The establishment of the Australian Bicentenary Authority a decade before the anniversary was indicative of a sense of unease about the task ahead, given the increasing prominence of Indigenous peoples' voices in national discourses of land rights and sovereign rights and renewed demands for a treaty. Added to these were the legacies that remained from recent divisive events such as Australia's involvement in the war in Vietnam, conscription, and the sacking of the Whitlam government in 1975, as well as the absence of any particular attachment to the 1788 founding moment or its annual observance.[7] A further underlying theme has been the desire for a republic, a desire that has been articulated erratically but consistently since colonisation began in 1788. The intensity of these debates has varied, but the hope to emulate the American republic inspired many supporters—and frightened their opponents—during the first half-century of white Australia's existence.[8]

As was to be the case with *Australia Remembers*, and less self-consciously so with the Centenary of Federation's program of events, two major unifying themes were those of the young (in European terms) nation and its sense of self as well as its place in the world, and the multicultural character of the nation, particularly in the last half-century. The benefits of the latter at times meshed with the consistency of a foreign policy that sought both to be and be perceived to be independent from Britain's.

It was only the Bicentenary, however, that both generated and experienced prolonged controversies. This was due to a number of factors, not the least being the long lead-in time and conflict within the ABA itself. This had not been foreseen by Prime Minister Fraser in 1978; indeed, when initiating the ABA, which was legislated as a private company,[9] both he and the Labor opposition leader united behind the theme of unity.[10] Perhaps inevitable sources of the problems that beset the ABA may well have been precisely this decade-long lead-in, as well as the payment of officials to organise events drawing on their expertise within the commercial sector. Included among these was the entrepreneur Harry M. Miller who was replaced in 1979 by the chairman of James Hardie Industries, John Reid (who was also a director of BHP at the time). This was in sharp contrast to the extremely short lead-in to *Australia Remembers* and the equal distribution of fairly limited funds to all Australian electorates, as well as the largely voluntary nature of the work provided in organising and coordinating events nationally and at other levels across the Australian community. In spite of the bipartisan support for the Bicentenary at its inception in 1978, the intervening decade also provided the opportunity for a change of government, the Fraser government being replaced by the Hawke Labor government in 1983. A significant difference between the two commemorative programs was also that of budget, the ABA being promised $166 million by the Fraser government on Australia Day 1983, a promise that was kept by the incoming Hawke government a few weeks later, albeit with a demand for a change of emphasis in the celebrations.[11]

An unprecedented feature of the Bicentenary commemorations was the direct and personal intervention of recently elected Prime Minister Hawke. Among Hawke's motivations, beyond a desire to hose down the political and ideological conflicts generated by the ABA's vision for 1988, was his concern about the extravagant spending of ABA officials. Inquiries about expenditure and staff sackings, and some virtually forced resignations within the ABA throughout 1985, placed the organisation into further public disrepute, prompting Hawke's decision to reform it. To this end he continued the top-heavy corporate presence in the ABA, appointing as its head the chief executive of Esso Australia.[12]

Promoting the Bicentenary—the logo

Central to the promotion of the Bicentenary was the logo, which was selected from 5000 designs entered in a national competition. This was replaced a few months after, on the grounds of being too expensive to reproduce, but perhaps also because of its somewhat uninspiring design. Almost three years later, in March 1984, a third design was chosen for the logo. This less than auspicious experience exemplified some of the difficulties caused by the theme of Australia as a unified nation, logo number two being rejected because it had not included the state of Tasmania. With the change of government to Labor, and the desire of Bob Hawke himself that Aborigines and women should be 'added', the colours of the logo also were changed from the blue and gold of the Commonwealth of Australia to the preferred national colours of green and gold.[13] The stylistic design of the logo in the shape of the continent, whilst instantly recognisable, was arguably somewhat predictable and possibly did not resonate with the public in the same ways or to the same extent as did the deeply personal representation of the *Australia Remembers* logo.

The direct hands-on involvement of Prime Minister Hawke was in stark contrast to that of both Prime Minister Keating in 1995 and of Veterans' Affairs Minister Sciacca. Despite the latter's immense energy and enthusiasm for promoting *Australia Remembers*, he refrained from intervening in the character or direction of the program. Another major difference was in the process of promotion; whereas the ABA spent half of its budget on advertising and promoting,[14] *Australia Remembers*, through the personal commitments gained by Con Sciacca from the media, received free advertising.

Themes of the Bicentenary

As has been observed, the Bicentenary was far from a spontaneous outpouring of national pride, being ten years in the making with lavish funding and largely corporate-savvy consultants and advertisers also assisting. The final slogan of the Bicentenary, 'Celebration of a Nation', provided the visual and aural core around which much of the promotion revolved. So ubiquitous was this that it has been suggested that the ABA's promotional campaign was almost 'pedagogic…Australians…being *taught* their bicentennial behaviours', the slogan indicated what was expected of dutiful celebratory citizens.[15] While I argue elsewhere in this book that *Australia Remembers* among other things imagined the wartime past for Australians in 1995, my own memory of the Bicentenary and of 1995 is that there was a qualitative difference in the manner in which *Australia Remembers* sought to engage the population in its commemoration and respecting of the wartime generation.

Central to the 'Celebration of the Nation' in 1988 was the theme of 'Living Together', which was also the source of some amusement, as I recall, for its triteness. 'Living Together' was designed to celebrate the notion of the multicultural and united nation. Exactly where Australia's Indigenous peoples fitted into this remained problematic, despite—or perhaps because of—Bob Hawke's directive that they, along with women, should be effectively 'added' to the program.

Adding Aborigines and women

Clearly, if the notion of a nation of people 'living together' was to be realised, those who remained most at the margins—Aborigines and women—needed to be 'brought in'. This, like most efforts that are generated more by tokenism than a concern for using the occasion to examine the reasons behind such marginalisation, was largely unsuccessful.

What Bob Hawke and other ABA organisers failed to comprehend was that Aborigines were not a 'category' of people who would comply with inclusive gestures on their behalf. Rather, Aborigines were drawing on the political actions of their forebears and naming 26 January 1988 as the 'day of mourning', as it had been termed fifty years earlier on the occasion of the sesquicentenary. On that occasion members of the Aboriginal Progressive Association and others gathered at Sydney Town Hall, dressed in black to symbolise the occasion as one of mourning. In the years leading up to the Bicentenary there had been Aboriginal protests that included demonstrations against the Tasmanian government for refusing to grant Truganini's[16] last wish to be buried at sea and demonstrations at Captain Cook's cottage in Melbourne's Treasury Gardens at which Cook was labelled an invader and land rights were called for. On Australia Day the year before the Bicentenary, Aborigines and their supporters gathered in front of the Australian War Memorial in Canberra to mourn what they termed 'invasion day', and laid wreaths and observed two minutes' silence for Aborigines who had died since invasion.

The Bicentenary march of Aborigines from all over the continent (conservatively estimated at 20,000 by Melbourne's *Sun* newspaper)[17] was the largest gathering of Indigenous people in Australia since 1788.[18] This was to protest the invasion and dispossession, and celebrate Indigenous peoples' cultural survival in the face of colonisation and its various oppressive policies. The march was in spite of concerted attempts by Prime Minister Hawke and the ABA, who in their concern about the 'controversies' threatened by Indigenous peoples' protests, increasingly promoted spectacles that highlighted re-enactments of European arrival.[19] Coupled with this was the manner in which much of the media 'beat up' the Indigenous protests. This included formulaic predictions of violence and editorial directives to behave with 'discipline', and attempts to represent the Indigenous organisers as 'divided'.[20]

As has been noted by others, the 'unintended consequence' of the Bicentenary was 'the elevation of Aboriginal rights in the national consciousness of social policy imperatives'.[21] Such interpretations have some validity but continue to centre white Australia, whereas the most important consequence of centring Indigenous peoples was that this unsettled the notion that social policy was an adequate response to the two centuries of colonisation. Indeed, what was highlighted was that there have been ample such policies, each of which has had disastrous results, still felt today. Rather, what was at stake was nothing less than an acknowledgement on the part of non-Indigenous Australians that their celebrations of the Bicentenary were based upon illegal occupation of sovereign Aboriginal land.

This was made explicit on 12 June 1988 at the Barunga Festival, where Prime Minister Hawke was presented with the 'Barunga Statement' by the Chairperson of the Northern Land Council, Galarrwuy Yunupingu, and the Chairperson of the Central Land Council, Wenten Rubuntja. This Statement sought to enshrine the principles of Indigenous autonomy and self-determination, and drawing upon the Universal Declaration of Human Rights and other international covenants and conventions, called upon the government to enact laws providing a framework, among other things, for national land rights and recognition of Indigenous customary laws. The most fundamental demand of the Statement, however, was in its final paragraph that called upon the government to 'negotiate with us a Treaty or Compact recognising our prior ownership, continued occupation and sovereignty and affirming our human rights and freedoms'.[22] In other words, it was Aborigines who were determining the terms for their relationship with the non-Aboriginal nation.

Perhaps overcome by the occasion, or the heat, or the audience of 10,000 people, Hawke's response to this document, framed by a bark painting as was the Yolngu people's 'Bark Petition' of 1963, was to promise a treaty. This was a promise that was soon revised by Hawke and is yet to be acted upon, despite numerous similar calls for a treaty both before and since the Bicentenary. Nevertheless, in assessing the 1988 Bicentenary overall, it may be argued that Indigenous people negotiated the spaces opened by this celebratory moment in white Australian history, and presented on their own terms, their accounts of their histories since 1788, as well as their ongoing demands for rights culminating in a treaty.

When seeking to 'add women' to the Bicentenary commemorations, a similar set of intellectual barriers seemed to exist. Jill Julius Matthews has suggested that one of the reasons that historical works that sought to situate Aborigines within the two hundred years under observation were beset with difficulties resulted from a failure to 'deal[ing] with the politics of race'. In Matthews' view, for the same reason, writers were unable to 'deal with the politics of gender'.[23] The underlying problem was an inability to conceive of the historical relations between Indigenous and non-Indigenous people as characterised by complexity and by Indigenous agency. Similarly, Matthews argued, Australian women in 1988, whether Aboriginal or non-Aboriginal, continued to be regarded as secondary to the 'real business' of men.[24]

Australia Remembers **and memory**

Australia Remembers organisers were faced with an easier task than those of the Bicentenary, as were members of that undefinable construct, the Australian people. Whereas the anniversary of two centuries of non-Indigenous occupation of the continent was by definition imbued with unresolved questions of (il)legitimacy and 'race', the fiftieth anniversary of the end of World War II did not evoke such extreme anxiety or self-doubt. *Australia Remembers* was blessed with the task of remembrance of a short, dramatic, and containable period that many members of the public had some interest in, even if only possessing passing knowledge drawn from Hollywood versions of the war. As noted elsewhere, the Second World War is most likely the only conflict with Australian involvement about which schoolchildren in 1995 had been taught. In commemorating the Second World War, which had involved that generation's parents or more likely, grandparents, members of previously enemy nations were also embraced by their inclusion in the act of remembering a period that had created the society which they now shared.

The program of commemorations suggested that there was 'a memory' of the war, or of different aspects of it, and the program of events seemed aimed to ensure that such a memory would become one that all Australians shared. Australians were urged to remember the past, but in reality it often seemed that the past was being remembered for them, or that the past was being created. The past 'remembered' through *Australia Remembers* was designed to become the national memory. In terms of the official commemorative events, a new narrative of Australia's recent history and the identity of its people was being made.

Prime Minister Keating, in an addresses at the National Commemoration Service on VP Day in Brisbane, spoke of the inability of those who had not been 'in' the war to appreciate what it really involved. They had a 'duty to try', so that the children of the present could apprehend the meanings of wartime deaths at the time, as well as in the present. Keating enumerated burial sites of Australians in Papua New Guinea, Asia, Europe, Britain and the Middle East so that the present generation could learn of these graves and 'recognise the profound truth of the ties that bind us as Australians. These are Australians like ourselves'. Throughout this 'story' of Australians who 'so loved this country…[that] they defended it to the death', Australia was resolutely the focus, the war was entirely about defending Australia. Similarly, Keating's address on the same day to the *Australia Remembers* National Youth Forum at Brisbane Girls' Grammar School aimed to assist their imagining of the war by pointing out that their age cohort had been the ones 'sitting there in that tropical environment facing the strongest and the best combat troops the Japanese could throw at our country', and that it was these young Australians' faith in their country which had helped them through the battles to victory. Australia was a 'smaller, much more innocent place than today', and the sight of 'our dead relatives, laying around the battlefields of East Asia and Europe…had to mean something' fifty years on.

For Veterans' Affairs Minister Sciacca, in announcing the choice of Brisbane as the national focus for the commemoration of VP Day, deemed this fitting because of its significance during the war as the headquarters of Australia's General Sir Thomas Blamey and United States General MacArthur, Commander-in-Chief South East Asia, it was important for people from all over the state and from other parts of the country to travel to Brisbane for the occasion. He noted, however, that accommodation was heavily booked already. With rain clouds hovering over Brisbane for the first time in weeks, the Minister declared that the parade would proceed regardless of the weather that could not 'stop Australia from paying tribute to the generation that secured our way of life and denied our shores to the enemy'.[25] Acknowledging some inconvenience to city workers caused by the ticker-tape street parade at 10.00 am, 'expected to be one of the biggest ever through central Brisbane', he suggested that workers could remind themselves that any such inconvenience would 'pale[s] in comparison to the hardships, the sacrifices and the suffering endured by those' who were being honoured on that day. Another attraction drawing visitors to Brisbane was a 'Home Front Exhibition' of 'the sunniest smile in the AIF', the Queensland Beach Girl of 1941 and 'hundreds of other World War II memories captured on film', which had been visited daily by up to 1,500 people since opening on VE Day. In what must have been a very appealing exhibition because of the personal, ordinary nature of its memorabilia and other features, Bill Morgan, now seventy-seven laughed when recalling the 'fifty quid' as well as the teasing he got from his 'mates' when, as a twenty-four-year-old lieutenant in New Guinea, his picture won a competition in mass circulation *Pix* magazine for the most appealing digger's smile. Unknown by him, his photograph had been submitted to the magazine by his sister.

Children as metaphors of the future was the major theme of the Northern Territory's commemoration of VP Day, with an estimated 6,000 turning out to a Tattoo at Football Park on the eve of VP Day, televised by Channel Eight Darwin. The event was reported as primarily an attempt to educate the young 'about their ancestors' efforts…[and to] remember not only those who carried arms, but those that remained behind'. Thus, according to local *Australia Remembers* director, the ceremony was 'as much to recognise our future [sic] as it was to remember our past'. The accompanying photograph, however, made one wonder what kind of future he had in mind, featuring as it did a two-year-old boy, wearing a slouch hat and waving an Australian flag,[26] suggesting that the gendered dominant paradigm of warfare and its inevitability remained intact.

Australians were urged, wherever they were at midday eastern standard time on VP Day, to observe two minutes' silence, to enable the nation to:

> reflect on the achievements of those men and women
> between 1939 and 1945 who were united for the common

cause of protecting Australia's way of life, our institutions and striving for peace.

It was particularly 'incumbent upon' those Australians born after the war to 'remember' these men and women. Such observation was less than perfect and extremely erratic in its execution, however, the plea from the Minister supposedly being ignored, for example, by 'the big Australian BHP, the national carrier, Qantas, and the industrial group CSR'. Neither the Japanese Embassy in Canberra nor the consulate in Sydney, or the Japan–Australia chamber of commerce observed the two minutes' silence, but some Japanese companies such as JAL and the Nikko and ANA hotels reportedly directed their staff to respect the call for silence at midday. Mr Yoshi Hosaka, the founding president of the Japan Club of Sydney took part in a two minutes' silence at his workplace at AGL, but the club itself did not have an official commemorative service, he said, because of the Australian festivities, adding that 'of course, we are very sorry for the regrettable things which took place but we don't want to upset the celebrations here in Australia'. The ABC continued to broadcast the VP parade in Brisbane[27] and was thus unable to observe the silence, providing reaffirmation of the importance of the mass media in the creation and transmission of national memory and, on this occasion, of the use of spectacle. The ACTU's call to union members to remain silent at midday was mostly heeded, whereas lectures continued as normal at Sydney University, but like McDonald's restaurants, their flags were flown at half-mast. Many state primary schools held official ceremonies, but some state and private high schools had no official events because final-year students were taking part in Higher School Certificate trials. A lone cartoonist chose to portray the irony in the situation, picturing a couple at their breakfast table, the man reading the newspaper announcement of a two-minute silence for VP Day, and asking the woman 'I wonder if we'll be able to hear them fighting in Bosnia'.[28]

The overriding message on the eve of VP Day was expressed on the 'Four Corners' television program, in which the tone was set with the introductory remark that these 'ordinary soldiers' who had fought back and defeated the Japanese at Australia's doorstep had not been appreciated by their superiors. Their average age was twenty-one and their story had to be told, 'because it tells us what ordinary Australians can do'. One of the diggers featured in this program, Jack Manol, provided a poignant reminder of the horrors of warfare, when he spoke of finding a photograph of a Japanese soldier he had killed. This photograph, of the man and his wife and children, still seemed to haunt Mr Manol half a century later, as he fought tears while the camera lingered on his face. A Japanese soldier's memory of seeing a young Australian soldier at Kokoda, wearing shorts and naked to the waist, running towards the Japanese, grenade in hand, and the comment that the Japanese would not have expected that of their men, added strength to the image of Australians defending the nation at all costs.

The first edition of Melbourne's *Herald Sun* on 15 August 1995 was at pains to teach readers about 'the day that peace came', differentiating between the official ending of the war at 9.08 am fifty years earlier, and the unconditional surrender by 'two top-hatted and frock-coated Japanese leaders...to the ten victorious commanders' on 2 September 1945 on the *USS Missouri* in Tokyo Bay. One of these was General Sir Thomas Blamey whose words to the Japanese at the time, that he would not recognise them as honourable or gallant foes, were contrasted with more than a touch of xenophobic consistency, with the perceived irony that fifty years later Japan was Australia's major trading partner and 'Japanese cars get parking spots at RSL clubs'. The Japanese Ambassador, however, had more positive links between the two countries in mind in his VP Day message that spoke of the 'scars that are painful even today' which had been caused by Japan's actions throughout the war. Expressing his 'most sincere feeling of apology to those who suffer from Japan's past actions', he highlighted the 'encouraging' scope and depth of Australian–Japanese relations.[29] Such fine sentiments, however, did not prevent a new outbreak of dissatisfaction over the term VP instead of VJ Day. Those wanting to revise the name were forced to acknowledge that the term 'VP Day' had indeed been used in 1945. This did not prevent them from 'remembering' that the expression was probably 'out almost before it was in', and that VJ had 'the right resonance for Australians, who had spent four years fighting the Japanese'.[30] For politically conservative columnist Piers Akerman, the use of VP Day signified the gulf between the thinking of the government and the 'philosophies of the men and women who actually fought for this country'. Even though he was forced to acknowledge that Prime Minister Ben Chifley's August 1945 speeches had referred to VP Day, Mr Akerman chose to believe that 'VJ Day appears to have been the title of choice of great numbers of ordinary Australians who were in the front lines during the conflict. Perhaps Canberra has always been one removed from the national sentiment'. This unpleasant piece of journalism was unashamed in projecting an image of 'several thousand Japanese tourists seeking koala colonies and directions to Bondi Beach [who will] today learn that, not only did their countrymen fight against Australian forces in the last war, but that their countrymen were also beaten', such knowledge coming as a shock to Japanese who have been kept ignorant of their past. Similarly, others interested in maintaining anger saw the divisions within Japan over the issue of an official apology as evidence of a 'sizeable chunk of present-day Japanese society [which] thinks Japan's behaviour in World War II was justified', and that, like the neo-Nazis who deny the Holocaust, they were 'too numerous for us to ignore'. Thus, this argument ran, a preference for the term VJ Day was justified because it 'reminds Japanese and Australians alike of a valuable lesson in the past. VP suggests we have forgotten it'. Posing the sufferings of civilians and POWs as arguments against concerns about the fire bombings of Japanese cities and use of the atomic bombs, expressed by those who fought that 'we were the victims of war and they were the aggressors', the article concluded that such 'ghastly measures were necessary to end the war, not to start it' as the aggressive Japanese had done.[31]

Other newspapers were more inclined to try to evoke the atmosphere of 1945. Brisbane's *Courier-Mail*, for example, featured a front page photograph from 15 August 1945, with the face of nineteen-year-old Joan Underdown circled, and a photograph of her in 1995. This was accompanied by her reminiscence of that day fifty years ago when she had arrived at work at the milliners where she made uniforms for the air force, and was told she could go home. Out in the street she had been carried along on the wave of 'spontaneous burst of unfettered relief' by the population of Brisbane that 'had poured out onto the city streets in rapturous celebration, a spectacle unrivalled to this day'. She remembered being tossed about in the crowd of 'soldiers, civilians, women, even grannies and grandpas—they must have heard it on the radio and come in to town', and she had waved to the camera, the memory of which, even after fifty years, still evoked a wellspring of emotion in her.[32]

The desire to engage with the nation's narrative of the war years may have partly accounted for a feature of *Australia Remembers* which was that the smaller towns and communities were often the most enthusiastic in the ways they sought to reconstruct the war years. This may also have reflected a time when such communities were indeed more genuinely tightly knit and economically viable, and when things seemed certain in ways which can only be imagined now. The 'small, sleepy' township of Delegate on the NSW–Victorian border provided a vivid example of a desire to reconnect with the past and to imagine its meanings. A town 'riddled with stories of war service', having been the starting place of the legendary 'Men from Snowy River' recruitment marches for both world wars, in 1916 and 1940, and boasting the smallest RSL sub-branch in the country, complete with 'outside loo' built by 'the World War I blokes', Delegate honoured the district's seventeen surviving World War II veterans and the six who did not return. In the months leading up to VP Day the country club was transformed into a World War II museum, with locals collecting memorabilia, making costumes, learning 1940s songs, researching history, ordering sweets and making casseroles. Indeed, the sense of community remained so strong in Delegate, or perhaps the desire to imagine and recreate this community, that within five minutes of the 'Delegate Remembers' dinner being announced, the 102–seat venue was booked out, requiring a second dinner to be organised to meet the demand.

Sites of memory

As Raphael Samuel has suggested, memory is 'historically conditioned, changing colour and shape…stamped with the ruling passions of its time',[33] and far from being something that is inherited by each new generation, it is changed in the process of generational transmission. Individual memories were to form the focus of many of the most evocative and symbolically significant events within the *Australia Remembers* program. In this way they were to take on the function of what Pierre Nora has termed 'guarantors of social continuity'. These he regards as increasingly important in the modern world that has seen the disappearance of the 'environments of memory',[34] which had provided the loci of pre-modern collective life.

Throughout the commemorative program, a number of 'sites of memory'[35] were constructed. A 'site of memory' provides a 'meaningful entity of a real or imagined kind, which has become a symbolic element of a given community as a result of human will or the effect of time'.[36] 'Sites of memory' include national flags, memorial buildings/monuments, honorific dates, commemorative events, and exhibitions, all of which have the function of evoking a set of values.[37] *Australia Remembers* provided a focus for these symbolic elements in a variety of ways. Not only was Australia's national flag very much in evidence throughout all events, but the *Australia Remembers* flag on which the green-bordered, sepia coloured photograph of the logo stood out effectively from the satiny white background, presenting a sign of the idealised past. War memorials and places of significance such as former POW camps and occasions such as Anzac and Remembrance Days acquired the status of 'sites of memory', these places and days of national commemoration already being regarded as sacred.

The '1945: War and Peace' exhibition at the Australian War Memorial in Canberra, mounted especially to coincide with the fiftieth anniversary commemorations, presented private, public, military and prisoner-of-war memorabilia as well as relics from Hiroshima, creating a very evocative site of memory. Visitors to this exhibition were advised, if they had not 'been there'—that is, alive during the war years, and therefore able to 'remember'—then they should 'imagine' the war and its experiences. On entering the exhibition, visitors confronted a Japanese bunker, 'reconstructed...[from] detailed drawings captured in fighting in New Guinea and the islands'. The audio guide urged visitors to:

> Imagine you're the forward scout of an Australian patrol.
> You're creeping up a jungle track. Ahead, the ground
> slopes upwards....What's that? Hidden beneath the trees
> and tangled foliage...maybe a bunker...maybe full of Japs
> [sic]...maybe not.

Imagining oneself in a captured bunker was aided by the description of an Australian soldier, which dwelt on nauseating filth and stench, the audio guide concluding, 'this was the reality of war. You can smell the jungle...and imagine'.[38] Remembering, therefore, became more than 'the re-excitation of innumerable fixed, lifeless and fragmentary traces [but also...] an imaginative reconstruction, or construction'.[39]

It has been suggested that 'sites of memory' play an important role in the construction of 'the Nation', upon which social cohesion and identity rest.[40] The *Australia Remembers* events were, effectively, a celebration of the nation, in which the gendered virtues believed to be uniquely Australian, pre-eminently mateship (men) and stoic determination in the face of hardship (women), were carefully constructed as the backdrop to the 'story' of the war years, as Prime Minister Keating liked to frame it. The celebratory and commemorative events conveyed a desire for a collective Australian memory. Such a desire is not unique to Australia. Jay Winter and Emmanuel Sivan note in their work on war and remembrance, 'the terms "memory" and "collective" appear with such frequency and ease' as to create the false impression that there is 'a scholarly consensus about what [they] mean' whereas 'nothing could be further from the truth'.[41] Instead, as Maurice Halbwachs has argued, there exist many 'communities of memories', and what binds individuals into a collective is their 'adhesion to particular representations of the past'.[42] Indeed, insofar as individual memories exist, this occurs when they 'are localised in the past by linking up with the memories of others', that is, that one only ever remembers as a member of a social group.[43]

Australia Remembers enabled various groupings within Australia, as well as the government of the day at certain key ceremonies, to imagine an idealised past. This was done through the act of 'remembering'. The positive public reception of the 'shared activity of commemoration',[44] offered by the *Australia Remembers* program suggested that people were, to a considerable extent, united by these acts of commemoration at the time that they were experienced. This appeared to be more important than members of the public necessarily being familiar with the events behind them. The crowds that filled the streets of all the major cities and towns throughout Australia on VP Day provided a clear example of this process. The people in these crowds were clearly united by many things, not the least being the sheer excitement of the spectacle. For many of those of the wartime generation, the commemoration of war's end fifty years earlier would not have had a single meaning, as was at times implied by the commentaries. Similarly, there may have been a limited knowledge of the larger issues thrown up by the war both at the time and in the half-century since. Nevertheless, this did not render the occasion any less significant for all those who attended and 'remembered' the ending of the war. The commemorative occasions and year-long retelling of the war illustrated ways in which memory, being discontinuous, fades and even disappears altogether, but becomes acute at other times, often being reactivated by interaction with others whose memories are 'at the same time unique and independent'.[45]

It can be argued that *Australia Remembers*, among other things, may have sought to use remembrance as a tool with which to 'come to terms with the past'.[46] The multiplicity of pasts and of the meanings ascribed to those pasts by the various *Australia Remembers* events served as a reminder that systems of meaning and interpretations of artefacts/memories/texts from the past do not remain fixed, but are continually evolving, that meanings 'do not simply mirror or represent but actually constitute or create the reality experienced by human beings'.[47]

Remembering women—an overview

The most significant social change since the war has been the status of women, which provided the backdrop of much of what was written and said about the war and women during the year of remembrance. International Women's Day, 9 March 1995, provided the opportunity for Australians to be urged 'to reflect on the important role women played during World War II and the precedents they set in carving out a niche for women in the workforce', for which purpose the month of March had been designated as 'Homefront month'. It was hoped that this would promote awareness of the important contribution of civilian women to the war effort. The Minister for Veterans' Affairs used the occasion to highlight the fact that:

> hundreds of thousands of women [also] stayed home during the war, bringing up young children on their own and keeping the home fires burning while their loved ones went off to war.[48]

Women were honoured with separate *Australia Remembers* posters, one of which commemorated their presence in the defence forces, the other the Australian Women's Land Army. With these posters, the division of the war between home and battle fronts, traditionally also a gendered division of wartime labour, signified the ways in which women were to be included in the story of the war, 'filling the place of men' as it was expressed.[49] The Land Army poster celebrated a particular construction of (white) Australian womanhood that tapped into earlier images of the female companion of 'the battler', portraying a smiling woman, stacking sheaves of oats at the Victorian Government's experimental farm at Werribee in 1944. This was an idyllic representation of a tanned and smiling young woman at her home front work, suffused in a golden light that evoked a clear, hot, immediately 'Australian' summer's day.

In addition to these two posters, there was a special commemorative ceremony in Canberra, devoted to remembering the women who served in the defence force. Billie Melman has explored the ways women came to be remembered in the nineteenth and early twentieth centuries. She has questioned the kinds of narratives that were invented in order to include women in what she termed 'the collective memory', and whether these meant women gained a belonging to and participation in communities from which they hitherto had been excluded.[50] Melman has suggested that women's exclusion from the public memory—from religion, law and custom,

Figure 4: One of the *Australia Remembers*
commemorative posters, featuring a photograph of a
Women's Land Army worker infused with distinctly
Australian, golden hues. AWM Neg. No. 140342

as well as from the battlefields—resulted from the 'long androcentric tradition in Western thought [which] had naturalised women and placed them outside history'. Furthermore, historically, women had not been treated as active agents of change, but as 'feminine, as the helpmates paired with "world historical men"'.[51] Much the same could be said for the ways in which women had been remembered after the Second World War, at least until the second wave of feminism began to interrogate women's roles and life experiences, including those of wartime women. Through *Australia Remembers* women gained a place *within* Australia's history, but this place remained contingent upon their representation as providing essential material and moral support on the home front. This celebratory inclusion of women ensured that the war itself simultaneously remained male-centred. This can be seen, for example, in the exclusion of female POWs and the proclamations of the valour of the men who went away and fought. The familiar trope of male warfare was reinforced by the visual representation of soldiers returning to the women who waited for them.

Ken Inglis has written extensively on the historically problematic inclusion or representation of women in Australia's remembrance of wars.[52] Among explanations suggested by Inglis is the manner in which the word 'Anzac' became synonymous with maleness.[53] *Australia Remembers* sought to find ways in which women would be included in the 'story' of Australia's war years, that is, to incorporate women into the nation's narrative, by 'remembering' their participation. As Prime Minister Keating said in his opening address to female veterans, his government 'wanted women to be involved in the commemorations to an extent that women have never been involved in…major national commemorations before'.[54] This was successful in that women did become a part of the 'story' of Australia, however the 'memories' that were used to achieve this were often constructed or at least orchestrated within the format of official events. What the official commemorative events often seemed to ignore was that memory is gendered and an important consequence of this was that the specifically gendered meanings of women's experiences were often overlooked because of the desire to ensure that women were honoured for their support of the war effort. Even though men and women shared wartime experiences, notably as prisoners of the Japanese, it is clear that these have been remembered in different ways.

Thus, a sexually exclusive reading of the war was maintained fifty years later, enabling it to remain 'a crucial site where meanings about gender [were]...produced, reproduced, and circulated back into society'.[55] The fiftieth anniversary of the war's end presented the opportunity for such gendered representations of the war to be reworked, for the paradigm of remembrance to be shifted away from tales of conflict and glorious suffering, associated with men's endeavour on the fighting fronts. Instead, women were constructed as heroes also, equal to the men in their contributions of labour on the home front. This extension of a heroic status to women simply added another layer through which their voices struggled to be heard. By calling them heroes, the meanings of the war to women remained obscured, and this label had a homogenising effect. In this way, the more personal and detailed memories of women were often lost. Such memories, when collected by women in a British compilation, for example, recorded the ways it had felt during the war when it was realised that the children had vanished, having been sent out of London over the weekend in 1939,[56] or of 'conscientious parents' making the 'heartbreaking' decision to send their children to the dominions, following the fall of France.[57] Other more seemingly mundane aspects of women's wartime memories had included 'being measured for my conductress' uniform', or 'tractor driving', as well as accounts of 'such a struggle to get an onion...a victory indeed!' and the difficulties in obtaining sanitary towels.[58] Similarly themes of female sexuality were freely explored and recorded by women during the war, such as the view that it was 'an ungenerous heart that does not give itself in wartime, when men's mere physical hunger for women is so great', and discussions of the desirability of contraceptives being made available for the Wrens (Women's Royal Naval Service).[59] After victory, such views were excluded from the official accounts of the war.

Gendered experiences and perceptions of war crossed national boundaries and indicated similarities in the ways in which, historically, women have suffered from the sexually exclusive meanings of warfare. The historical division of labour between home and battle fronts has functioned not only as 'the consequence of war but [has] also been used as its justification'.[60] A seventy-five year old Japanese war widow, who had endured the hardships of being left pregnant ten months after marriage and having her house destroyed in an air raid, fifty years later attacked the continuing insistence by the Association of the Families of the War Dead and politicians opposed to a Japanese apology for its wartime behaviour, that Japan had been fighting a war of self-defence, against its will. The experience of Japanese women, she insisted, had been that:

> our husbands were persuaded by the militarists that they were dying for the Emperor and for the country, and were herded into battlefields without knowing they were engaged in an invasion. The government committed aggression; our husbands were its victims.[61]

Remembering women in the armed forces—men's voices

Women who served in the Australian armed forces during the war were honoured in a separate ceremony and with their own commemorative poster. The *Australia Remembers* ceremony to remember women who served in Australia's defence forces in World War II, held in Parliament House, Canberra, demonstrated in subtle ways that, when they were permitted to speak, women gave specific meanings to the war, but had great difficulty in having these meanings acknowledged on occasions such as this. This ceremony was one of a number of official *Australia Remembers* events to be produced on video by the Office of the Minister for Veterans' Affairs and the *Australia Remembers* taskforce. Following women marchers from the present defence forces, the female veterans were filmed marching, a little more slowly, to music provided by the Duntroon Military Band. A few of these women were dressed in their military uniforms, and many wore medals. Nearly all were dressed in warm skirts or suits, rather than the trousers their daughters and granddaughters might have opted for, and this was clearly an occasion for which one dressed up, although not ostentatiously. A few women used walking sticks. The camera, after panning their faces and medals, then focused on their feet. This seemed both cruel and full of pathos, as the aged and, in many cases, somewhat puffy feet looked vulnerable, but the women's faces suggested, instead, strength and pride. As they marched past, a man of their generation raised his hat to them, and the women were clapped by Con Sciacca and groups of school-children waving *Australian Remembers* flags, although the applause, in the main, was restrained, as if the spectators were unsure of their role. Some of the women talked with each other, but the march was a very solemn matter, with some obviously feeling self-conscious when the camera's lens rested on them.

Ex-servicewomen from around Australia had been urged to participate in this ceremony, so that their 'often unsung heroic efforts' could be recognised. The Minister for Veterans' Affairs, in publicising this event in May 1995, spoke of how in the past the focus had been on 'deeds of valour, mateship and sacrifice of our ex-servicemen'. While taking nothing away from their obvious and important contribution to Australia's war effort, he hoped Australians would also 'reflect on the lesser known contribution made by our ex-servicewomen', pointing out that in 1939 there had been only two women's services, but by 1945 there were nine services within the army, navy and air force.[62]

The Hon. Michael Beahan, president of the Senate opened the ceremony with the understatement that it was 'not new to say that history has underrated the role of women, not only in war, but in settling and building the country'. He was pleased that this first major event in parliament was one to honour women, without whom Australia could not have sustained the effort needed for victory. There was also no doubt, he continued, that these women had been the 'catalyst for social change', for better recognition of their rights, and access to employment, of which many young women are beneficiaries. The banners of the various forces, behind which the women had marched, were then brought into the assembly by young defence force women, to enthusiastic applause from the audience. At the end of this, there rose a quiet cheer from the women present, as if, finally, this semiotic mélange was something that was recognisably theirs.

When the Minister for Veterans' Affairs was introduced, the applause was particularly strong, and it was evident at other parts in the ceremony that the women strongly identified with him as the man who had made their recognition possible, whereas the Prime Minister was politely received. Later in the program, the President of the Australian Women's Armed Services Association, NSW, Coral Farrelly, OAM, spoke of Con Sciacca's evident sincerity being 'known and understood by all present', and indeed there was applause from the women whenever Sciacca's name was mentioned throughout her speech. For his part, Sciacca ensured that the women's preferred term, 'female veterans' was made known, as he spoke of watching the pride on the faces of the women as they had marched past him outside parliament, urging the women to 'feel free to be proud and shed the odd tear' if they felt like it. Careful to include all women in his praise, the minister spoke of how those who did not serve overseas had been vitally important at home, doing jobs 'as good as the men and…[proving] they were worthy and part of the entire war effort'. Thus, despite the undoubted sincerity of his praise, his gendered 'remembering' of what the women did remained tied to the model of male endeavour, whereby they were judged to have performed as well as men.

For the women themselves it was often everyday things that they inclined to remember about 'their' war and which gave it meaning. This involved life-changing moments, such as the account of Joan Hockins, Secretary of the Ex-Servicewomen's Association, Gympie Branch, of her initial desire to join the navy being thwarted by her mother, who had been concerned about sailors having 'girls in every port', so she joined the Australian Women's Army Service (AWAS). Upon being sent to Lae, she and other women there 'gradually improved the barrack compound with flower and vegetable gardens'. Precautions against malaria, and seasickness on a trip out with the navy,[63] were among other simple but quite fundamental memories, which seem to speak more of the patterns of everyday life, albeit in a quite different environment, which women may have been more attuned to than the men.

Women were also able to look back on their unequal relationship with men with humour and a strong sense of pride in overcoming this. Jean Haughton-James and Sheila Manley, whose close friendship fifty years later had resulted in a joint biography of the war years, had to overcome 'wild stories' about Women's Auxiliary Australian Air Force (WAAF) workers being 'scarlet women'. After joining the Royal Air Force, they were transferred with six other women to the transport section of the RAAF base at Evans Head where for nearly two years they 'battled against a unique blend of good-natured chauvanism [sic] and recalcitrant trucks to pave the way for women to be accepted as a vital cog in the Australian military'. They proved their worth through their conscientious work, recalling the shapeless uniforms they had to endure as well as hard physical labour. Their fondest memories, they said, were reserved for 'the camaraderie shared among the [4000] men...and the handful of truck-driving women'.[64]

Such personal memories, however, were excluded from the carefully prepared format of remembrance of servicewomen on this occasion. Prime Minister Keating spoke of his delight at the warm reception that the *Australia Remembers* program had received within the community, wanting to make it clear that events such as this were 'not simply some kind of pageant'. Rather, the government had felt that the sacrifices in World War II 'had to mean something fifty years later [so we] all remember...and celebrate'. In a rare reference to this dimension of women's wartime sacrifices, he reminded the audience of Australian nurses who died in the fall of Singapore or as internees of the Japanese; that fifty-five Australian Army Nursing Service members received decorations, including two George Medals, and a further eighty-two were mentioned in dispatches. In addition to nurses, 27,000 women served in the Women's Auxiliary Air Force and worked in seventy-two of the 120 air force trades, and that 'the WAAF changed the role of women in wartime'. Seven thousand women donned the uniform of the Women's Land Army, which, while not one of the defence forces, meant that they were 'subject to discipline and learned to take orders', and their labour covered the loss of 100,000 farm workers to the defence forces. Furthermore, by 1944, 250,000 women were working in factories, and over forty per cent of munitions workers were women, much of this work being 'hideously monotonous and harmful to their health…but they made a huge contribution to winning the war…they made a massive contribution to the story of Australia'.[65] Women's experience, Keating ventured, 'is inseparable from our military history, our national legends and traditions, and the inspiration and values we draw from these things'. He touched on 'stories of heroism' such as Sister Vivien Bullwinkel, the only female survivor of the 'Vyner Brooke', as well as the experiences of nurses captured at Rabaul and sent to Japan, and nursing staff killed in the bombing of Darwin. Women in other medical units were not to be forgotten either, Keating ensured, such as the physiotherapists in the Middle East and the Pacific, and on hospital ships, and he reminded the audience, that 27,000 women had received only two-thirds of the male rate of pay. Women, then, had not only given great service in wartime, but had provided an important example in the peace, claiming the right to play a part, from which they had been previously excluded. Thus, in Paul Keating's account, women were to be made a part of the total story, to be included in the military history of the nation, hitherto a male domain. In this way Keating sought to remedy the inequalities women had experienced, by making them heroes also. He remained, nonetheless, tied to the problematic notion that there was a single story, and that this was one that was located within the male paradigm.

By the time the next speaker began, the Chief of Defence Forces of Australia, General John S. Baker, AC, it was clear that the 'lady veterans' as he somewhat quaintly called them, were going to be told more about themselves. This included his view that they had been 'pioneers, serving home and abroad, [who] changed the face not only of Australian defence forces, but society at large'; they had 'answered the call'. The use of this phrase, very much associated with male military endeavour, suggested that his desire to understand and to demonstrate his appreciation of women's involvement could only be achieved if mediated through employing male military imagery.

Remembering women in the armed forces—women's voices

When Lieut. Colonel Mary Douglas, OBE, rose to speak next, on behalf of all the ex-servicewomen, many women in the audience rose to give her a standing ovation. One could perhaps be forgiven for wondering whether this was in part because at last the men had ceased instructing the women about their wartime past. Clearly it was protocol that had dictated the order of speakers, beginning with the prime minister, but this suggested once more, the ways in which a differently ordered ceremony might have facilitated a paradigm shift in the ways in which warfare is remembered. Such a shift, potentially, could change the mentality with which warfare itself is regarded, and the fiftieth anniversary of the war's end arguably provided the ideal opportunity for this to be attempted. Introducing a different note and, in the process, ignoring the almost ritualised observance of women's changed roles during the war years, Miss Douglas emphasised that she was talking for all the women who had already died, and 'who we miss very badly today', some of whom she then named and provided brief personal details about. The memory of the war that she seemed interested in sharing was of meeting a lot of interesting people and having a 'jolly good time'. Similarly, she was more interested in remembering ways in which women had continued to do lots of 'very useful jobs' after the war, such as being involved in numerous organisations like the Girl Guides, and 'the most important job of bringing up their families'. By-passing the more clichéd remarks of the male speakers, Miss Douglas was more inclined to focus on the lived experiences of women, welcoming the numerous books recently published about the women's services. She also praised the choice of the song of women prisoners of war, the 'Captives' Hymn', for this ceremony, expressing her 'greatest respect for women who were prisoners and also in places like Darwin'. Her remark that most of the other women, like her, can remember what happened fifty years ago 'a jolly sight better than what happened last week' brought instant recognition and point of contact between her and the other women present.

Prayers followed, beginning with a somewhat curious, rambling prayer led by the Principal Chaplain, which almost seemed to be reminding God of the contributions made by those women at home 'in maintaining the flow of food and industry', and 'filling the place of men'. Also important, the prayer continued, were women's other home front activities, which 'helped maintain the morale of the men close to the fighting and those held prisoner, by their knitting and writing letters and sending food parcels'. This prayer mirrored Paul Keating's aim of including women in the 'story' of the nation at the same time as reinforcing the traditional situating of women as providing support to the men.

Throughout this ceremony, women sought to reclaim the meanings of their own experiences. Following the laying of wreaths, led by Mr and Mrs Keating, the presentation of the 'Oath' by Mrs June Stone, Chairman of the Council of Ex-Servicewomen's Association, NSW, was used to 'remember our friends, and those magnificent women who were our leaders, who shaped the rest of our lives'. A sense of continuity was provided by the granddaughter of a woman who had served in the Australian Army Medical Corps, who spoke of the treasury of memories of the war that she had inherited from her grandmother. This inheritance included knowledge of the hard life, dangers, and improvisations in treatment when supplies ran out, but also light-hearted memories of the lasting friendships formed.

This ceremony was reported in the media the following day as 'The grandmothers of Australia marched through the freezing cold and into the Great Hall of Parliament House...to take their place in the country's history. Heads held high, aged faces beaming'.[66] Other reports were more inclined to take up the points made by the prime minister in his speech to this occasion, for example, the *Australian* headlined its report, 'War women welcome a belated salute', having been:

> underpaid, overworked and burdened with the responsibility of keeping Australia's military machine ticking...Many lost their lives and their health', but unlike the men, 'have been largely shunned by history.[67]

Memory and the search for history

Pierre Nora has suggested that 'the quest for memory is the search for one's history', and that what we call memory is actually already history, thus the 'task of remembering makes everyone his own historian'. Sites of memory, therefore, are created because of the absence of 'spontaneous memory, which drives us to 'create archives, maintain anniversaries, organise celebrations, pronounce eulogies', because such activities no longer occur naturally.[68] Representation occurs through a process of 'strategic highlighting, selecting samples and multiplying examples'.[69] A reunion of war veterans, according to Nora, belongs in the category of 'sites of memory' because of its ritual nature, which furthers the aim of stopping time, blocking 'the work of forgetting'. This is the 'most fundamental purpose' of sites of memory.[70] The ceremony to commemorate women in the defence forces constituted such a moment.

Gendered remembrance of male POWs

Australia Remembers engaged in all of these strategies in its quest to imagine Australia, not the least in its highlighting of the prisoner-of-war experience. Over thirty thousand Australian servicemen were captured during the war, 22,376 of these becoming prisoners of the Japanese, two-thirds being captured early in 1942. Of these, 8,031 died, this figure representing half of Australian deaths in the Pacific war. Of the 8184 Australians held prisoner by the Germans, ninety-seven per cent survived the experience.[71] While the degree of harshness experienced by prisoners in German camps varied, all prisoners of the Japanese were placed in extreme conditions of deprivation and brutality, which accounts for the death rate of thirty-six per cent of Australian POWs. In addition, the Japanese upon capture killed hundreds of Australians including women.[72]

Despite an apparent fear that their experiences would pass into obscurity with their deaths, rather than being incorporated in Australian history,[73] it has been suggested that the POW experience has become 'a distinguishing experience'[74] that forms part of the

Australian psyche. This has been attributed to the high number of prisoner deaths in relation to other nations engaged in the war against Japan.[75] Literature about the POW experience has sought 'consciously to integrate their experiences into the…Anzac legend', in the process providing one of the 'few opportunities for mythologising' the Second World War.[76] *Australia Remembers* further facilitated this process by firmly situating the Japanese prisoner-of-war experience at the centre of the narrative of Australia's war.

The privileging of the 'memory' of prisoners of the Japanese, in spite of the fact that Ray Walsh, featured on the *Australia Remembers* logo, had been a prisoner of the Germans, mirrored the comparative historiographical neglect of the German or Italian prisoner experience.[77] Indeed, it is only recently that the German prisoner-of-war experience has begun to receive attention from historians, such neglect having been painful for these former prisoners, aware that when fellow Australians learn of their POW status, it is assumed that they were prisoners of the Japanese.[78] The federal government's decision in 2001 to make a payment of $25,000 to men who had been prisoners of the Japanese[79] suggests the continuing focus on this experience in the national imagination.

Women similarly have been excluded from the POW 'memory', a trend that largely remained, throughout *Australia Remembers*, whose commemorative POW poster reproduced a photograph of skeletal Australian men, former prisoners in Changi. The very name Changi resonates with horror and evil treatment, slave labour and starvation, and is also a gender-exclusive name, associated only with men. The poster's photograph was aptly chosen, showing the men, who appear to be naked apart from lap-laps, sitting together, their faces turned towards the camera, with rib cages exposed and stick-like arms and legs which look barely more than flesh-covered bones. One man has a cigarette stuck behind his ear, and all look solemn, with their expressions suggesting that the horrors they had witnessed and experienced were still with them. The photograph was cropped in such a manner to exclude the non-European man sitting next to an Australian prisoner of war, thereby denying recognition that other nationalities, particularly indigenous populations, had also suffered in camps such as Changi. It is interesting to note that the

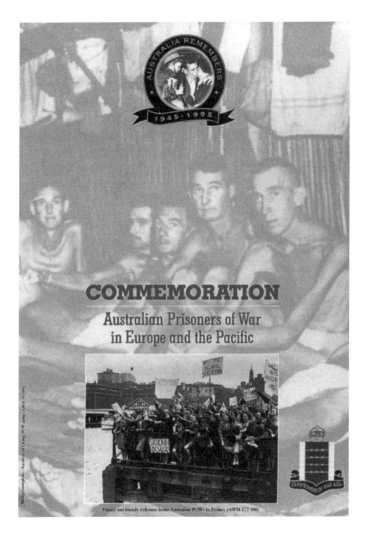

Figure 5: The *Australia Remembers* prisoner of war
commemorative poster featured a photograph of Changi
prisoners from which the non-Australians had been
cropped, thereby obscuring the local experiences of
Japanese occupation. AWM Neg. No. 019199

high status of Changi and the Burma–Thailand Railway as sites of
memory is in spite of the fact that for all its horror, 'the railway was
not as terrible as the lesser known camps on Ambon and North
Borneo, where death rates of seventy-seven per cent and almost 100
per cent occurred'.[80]

The POW poster had an inset, as did most, showing a crowded
wharf in Sydney, with family and friends welcoming the men home.
Inevitably, most of the members of this crowd were women, many
of whom were holding up placards bearing 'welcome home' messages. Thus, while the poster declared it was in commemoration of
'Australian Prisoners of War in Europe and the Pacific', it actually
commemorated men from Changi. The female-dominated welcoming
crowd at home represented the ageless theme of women waiting
for their men to return, after which the temporary changes in their
status and roles would be returned to 'normal'. This situating of the
waiting women had the effect of reinforcing the gendered division
of roles in warfare.

Gendered remembrance of female POWs

This was not the only way in which gendered representations
inhibited a genuine appreciation or inclusion of the female prisoner-
of-war experience. Postwar photographs reveal the skeletal frames
of women who had also been incarcerated by the Japanese,[81] and
who had shared many of the experiences of diseases usually associated in the public memory only with the male prisoners. Postwar
reflections by women who had been in the Japanese camps were
gender-specific, and related to their pre-war status. For example, one
felt that because they had:

> no men to help us it was only our strength and nobody
> else's. I learnt that women can be very brave, very tenacious.
> If it had not been for that we would not be here now.

Another, who before the war had not been 'too keen on
women's company...came away from the camps liking women and

respecting their resource'.[82] Of the seven hundred women held in a camp at Muntok, on Banka Island, half died,[83] but the significance of Muntok remained confined to those who had known it. Knowledge of women's experiences at Banka Island has been limited, generally speaking, to the massacre that occurred on the beaches. Women also experienced the fact that being European became a stigma[84] throughout Japanese-occupied Asia, where some 30,000 Europeans had lived among four million Malays and Chinese, as well as several hundred thousand Indians, a large population of Eurasians and about 1,000 Japanese before the fall of Singapore. Women from all of these ethnic groupings, as well as different nationalities among the European population, were banded together in the prisoner-of-war camps.[85]

By virtue of their pre-war gendered roles, women POWs had the additional burden of caring for their own as well as orphaned children in these camps, and suffered deeply upon liberation, when these 'adopted' children were sent to live with relatives they had never met.[86] These incarcerated women set about establishing some semblance of civilisation in their midst. It seems that music was their chief mainstay, and ultimately an 'orchestra' performed works by Beethoven, Chopin, Brahms and Ravel, all drawn from the memories of the women.[87] These were to be presented to a worldwide audience two years after the *Australia Remembers* commemorations through the film *Paradise Road*. Such concerts were not unique to female prisoners, also being a source of strength and pleasure for men in both Japanese and German camps. In Changi, for example, the Australian concert party began rehearsals by the second day of their incarceration.[88] Finding comfort through music was only one way in which the women sought to transcend the inhumanity that surrounded them. Largely for the benefit of the children among them, they sought to recreate, as far as possible, the lives and patterns of behaviour they had left behind. To this end, the women gave 'gifts' for birthdays and anniversaries, and to all outward intents, maintained normal life, which included holding jumble sales, where pathetic items of tattered clothing were simply redistributed amongst themselves.[89]

Women's gendered suffering in the camp included the disappearance of menstruation, which was for many a relief, given concerns about the lack of hygiene, but others worried about the implications of this when they were reunited with their menfolk and wished to become pregnant.[90] In addition, it was difficult for many women to cope with the visually dramatic changes to their bodies, as well as the general filth in which they were forced to live. One woman recounted how she was torn between relief and affronted vanity when one of the Japanese guards—as was their wont—suddenly appeared in the washroom, leered at her nude body for a few moments, then laughed loudly and walked out. At other times, women who had once put a great deal of effort into their appearance now competed with each other to appear as unattractive as possible, when faced with the Japanese demand that they 'entertain' them.[91] Enforced labour of inhumane proportions was not unique to male prisoners of war either, with women being forced to cultivate the land with inappropriate tools and in extreme weather conditions, in order to grow their own meagre rations. In spite of these hardships, there were only two known suicides among the hundreds of women, perhaps because, as one of them said of that time, 'For all the hardships...there was time to think, to work out what kind of person you really were...I found myself there'. There were occasions, however, when some women simply abandoned hope, or 'turned their faces to the wall'.[92]

Largely absent from the women's camps were problems of theft and disharmony which had been prevalent in the men's prison nearby, where one of the inmates recorded that:

> as a community we were disintegrating. We had forgotten how to play or study or relax...In the struggle for self-preservation too many men adopted the attitude of survival at any cost.

So severe were the problems in the men's camp that a list of laws and punishments had to be devised, and a private gaol established by the inmates. Possessions became so important that executors had to be appointed to administer the estates, such as they were, of those who died.[93] After the Japanese surrender, Major Gideon Jacobs of the Royal Marines, who had been sent to Sumatra to find the camps, described conditions in the women's camp at Loebok Linggau as the worst he had come across. He had been consistently appalled by the state of prisoners of war, especially the women and children.[94] The POW death rate among men was considerably higher than that for women, and Major Jacobs expressed 'a great admiration for these women and the heroic role they had played in the camps', suggesting that their morale was higher than that of the men. He speculated as to whether the women were 'more adaptable or had greater inner resources than the men, but they seemed to withstand the rigours of imprisonment more stoically'.[95]

For the women, as for the men, assimilation to freedom was not easy at first, although it seems the nurses found it less difficult, by virtue of the continuity offered by their profession. Some women's marriages failed, while others made quick marriages, often to men who had been POWs. For the women, an 'extraordinary sisterhood' remained when they were reunited.[96] Vivien Bullwinkel later recalled how much the women missed each other, largely because they:

> felt that nobody talked the same language. We felt that nobody really had any idea. They were saying, "Yes, how awful, how terrible", but they really didn't know. We wrote to each other, we went visiting each other.[97]

As well as the direct experiences of women as POWs, there were other gendered ways in which the war impacted. Wives, sisters, girlfriends, and so forth of men who were known to be POWs were severely affected also, regardless of where their menfolk were incarcerated. For example, Jeanette Watkins, eldest daughter of Ray and Varlie Walsh, recalled that it was about four or five months before receiving notification that Ray was in a German camp, and a further wait of about five months until the family received a letter from him through the Red Cross. Fretting about her father had caused her to develop a heart murmur, and talking with her fifty years after her father's return, it was clear that she still felt deeply emotional about that period.[98] Not that the women's worries were over, necessarily, when the men were repatriated from the camps, as the legacies of their husbands' ordeals impacted on their lives, so that when the wives of ex-prisoners met they often found themselves exchanging stories of anti-depressant drugs, and of how they tried to help their husbands emerge from nightmares.[99]

When the Australian women ex-prisoners returned to Australia, they had received a gala welcome, unlike their British counterparts, who seem to have been something of an embarrassment, their homecoming receiving no press coverage, and the Home Office requesting their families not to meet them when the ships docked.[100] Nevertheless, the women were soon forgotten, it seems, there being no memorial in Australia to those who died, apart from the military nurses. The winner of the *Australia Remembers* National Play Competition, John Misto, donated that prize and another from the NSW Premier's Literary Awards, to a fund for the building of a memorial to Australian nurses killed in war.[101] Civilian wives of Service officers were re-buried in the war cemeteries of Java, under the jurisdiction of the Commonwealth War Graves Commission, while others remain in their shallow, quickly overgrown jungle graves.

The obvious personal desire of the Minister for Veterans' Affairs, and of the organisers of the various *Australia Remembers 1945–1995* events, that women's contributions to the war effort be learned, acknowledged, and valued is indisputable. It seems clear that to a significant extent, women were genuinely included in Paul Keating's 'story' of Australia. Equally clear was that when they were able to express their memories of war, these were gendered memories that provided pride, solace and a continuing sense of connectedness with other women of their generation.

Mediating memories—the Gala Concert

More often, though, women's memories were mediated through more conventional processes of 'remembering', whereby they became part of an entertainment. The Gala Concert on the eve of VP Day, before a capacity crowd including the Prime Minister and Mrs Keating, in the Palais Theatre, St Kilda, and televised live by the ABC, was the major occasion upon which this occurred. That it was televised shaped to a significant degree the ways in which the Concert was presented. This was evident from the opening scenes, where the use of black and white and colour blurred the distinctions between present/past and memory/remembering. As Pierre Nora has suggested, in an age where memory is 'intensely retinal and powerful', representation of the past proceeds through 'strategic highlighting, selecting samples and multiplying examples'.[102] Television is perhaps the principal medium for this.

Indeed, by starting the Gala Concert outside the Palais Theatre, it appeared that the televised version may have been more important than the live event inside the packed theatre. Immediately, the audience at home in living rooms (and those in the Palais, on closed-circuit TV) was captured by the familiar sound of a Melbourne tram clanging its bell as it passed a car parked outside Luna Park. Inside, a couple, both in military uniform, were necking. The swing music on the car radio was interrupted by an 'important announcement', causing the couple to stop kissing and sit up to listen. Then the voice of Prime Minister Chifley informed his 'fellow citizens [that] the war is over'. The couple quickly embraced, then leapt joyfully from the car. In the background was the sound of cheering and then other hugging people were seen, including two women, alone, hugging in their kitchen. A long conga line of civilians and uniformed soldiers and sailors formed outside Luna Park, while another, balloon festooned, car arrived. The original couple jumped onto this car's roof and began an ecstatic dance. The colour in the meantime had changed from black and white to colour, and the spotlight then swung onto the front of the Palais Theatre's billboard, announcing 'Tonight: *Australia Remembers* Gala Tribute'. The crowd danced into the theatre, to a wartime favourite, Glenn Miller's 'In the Mood', and the sound of the audience clapping in rhythm.

As Raphael Samuel has suggested, television uses anniversaries 'as the excuse for revisiting old celebrities and recycling old film footage…[thereby bringing] personal time into historical time'.[103] The Gala Concert combined a primary focus on recreating the sounds, images, and atmosphere of the war years, interspersed with snippets of film footage of battles, enlistment centres, and photographs of individuals who then appeared live on the screen as they were fifty years later, each telling an amusing wartime anecdote. The pain and loss of warfare was equally well orchestrated. A carefully devised re-enactment of the reading of a letter from Tobruk from Corporal John Johnson to his wife Josie and their eight children provided such a moment. Read with a very broad 'Australian' accent, the soldier's letter was essentially a love letter to his wife and the children, seeking to reassure them that he was 'enjoying the show and quite well', and providing mundane details such as what he had for dinner. The woman's letter on the other hand expressed her worries about the news of the war and told of how she got depressed by it all sometimes. The boy then read a brief letter, about how he was going to have a birthday party when his father returned. A photo of the whole family was then on the screen behind the stage, and an official-sounding voice read 'Dear Mrs Johnson, it is with very great regret that I must inform you', that her husband was fatally wounded, details to follow. The husband's photograph lingered on the screen, while the audience applauded this poignant segment.

Being a concert, music such as Glenn Miller's was the main medium through which the end of the war was celebrated and 'remembered' on this occasion, indicating the importance of this 'memory bank' as a means of 'creating a historical narrative'.[104] Another song, 'They're Either Too Young Or Too Old', was sung by a woman to reassure the absent men that she found it easy 'to stay good as gold' because the men at home were either too young or too old. This was no doubt a popular tune at the time, but its inclusion suggested a desire on the part of the *Australia Remembers* organisers to ensure that 'remembering' the war was desexualised. 'Lili Marlene' and 'A Nightingale Sang in Berkeley Square' were other favourites included, and a short segment featured Dame Vera Lynn, who vowed she wouldn't have missed the experience of the war for anything. She knew her songs were a bridge between those at the home front and the 'the chaps' far from home, expressing the words they longed to hear from their loved ones, especially the song 'Yours'—the word they always signed their letters with. Her famous 'White Cliffs of Dover' was sung to footage of Australian troops being inspected by Churchill, and of schoolchildren throwing stones at a cartoon of Hitler. Footage of smaller children at a wartime creche made one wonder about the ways in which the war enabled women to be temporarily excused from the guilt that working mothers have frequently been encouraged to experience in times of peace.

The male experience of warfare was captured in a segment performed by the Meryl Tankard Australian Dance Theatre, where five men performed a dance, their muscled shoulders and arms exposed by singlets, at the end of which they lay on the floor, protecting each other's bodies with very graceful, slow, and solemn movements, which aimed to represent the male, military theme of mateship. The homoerotic dimensions of this dance unconsciously signified the inherent contradictions of 'mateship'.

Indigenous Australians' experiences of the war focused on Victorian Aborigine, Sergeant Reg Saunders, of the Gunditjamara people, the 'first' Aboriginal serviceman to become an officer, who was featured on the poster for Indigenous war service, as discussed earlier. Providing little more than a mere backdrop to the overall aim of entertainment, Reg Saunders' inclusion in the Gala Concert took the form of extracts from letters to his family, read by Indigenous educator and rock musician, Mandawuy Yunupingu, accompanied by snippets of wartime film footage and the sound of a didjeridu. Presumably Yunupingu, a Yolngu man from NE Arnhem Land was chosen because of his high profile as the leading performer in the group Yothu Yindi. A descendant of Reg Saunders would have been more appropriate to the occasion. The Gala Concert was premised on the construction of Australia as a nation united by positive memories of a war which had touched all of its citizens in some way. Obviously it was not seen as an occasion to acknowledge that it was only when in military uniform that Aborigines experience equal rights which were otherwise denied them.

Uses of the past—prime ministerial speeches

Whereas in the years immediately prior to the 1988 Bicentenary, Prime Minister Hawke was intent on using this commemorative occasion as an opportunity to promote his populist vision of a united nation of people living together in harmony, *Australia Remembers*, and particularly its focus on the war in the Pacific, provided Prime Minister

Keating with the opportunity to pursue some of his favourite themes relating to Australia's place in the world. He attacked Britain's support of France's resumption of nuclear testing in the Pacific during 1995, linking his remarks to the benefits of Australia becoming a republic. He argued that, as evinced by Britain's support for France, Britain's interests were 'often very different and even fundamentally opposed' to those of Australia. Even though he was at pains to describe his position as 'not an anti-British one but about the inappropriateness of Australia having a head of state who is not one of us',[105] it remained clear that any misdemeanour such as this would be eagerly seized upon as further proof, if indeed such was needed, of the benefits of republicanism. The subtext of this attack on contemporary Britain linked with Keating's desire to privilege the Pacific war over the European theatres of combat. Given that the Australian government's criticisms of the French tests had been somewhat muted, in comparison with those of neighbouring Aotearoa/New Zealand for example, Keating's political opportunism was more evident here, perhaps, than any particularly strong opposition being provided by his government to the nuclear tests themselves.

Throughout his prime ministership Keating was prone to inspire strong feelings, among other things through his speeches, which tended to be highly articulate and range over historical landscapes in an attempt to educate the public. His speeches have been interpreted as suggesting that there existed 'two Paul Keatings', the 'Bankstown politician (K1), who speaks with his own voice in unmistakable Keatingese and comes on like seventy-six trombones' and 'K2', the Prime Minister who speaks with his own voice, even if articulated by speechwriter and historian Don Watson.[106] Clearly speeches written by Don Watson, such as the Redfern Park speech of 1992, where non-Indigenous Australians were exhorted to imagine their past, and the ways in which colonisation had impacted upon Aboriginal lives and cultures, and a future based upon reconciliation, were suggestive, among other things, of a desire to redefine the nation. Watson's 'taut but stirring language, his elegiac rhythms and…egalitarian nationalism',[107] was perhaps expressed most elegantly at the tribute to the Unknown Australian Soldier in November 1993. Such speeches were regarded by many as indicators of statesmanship, or 'as good as Pericles on the Athenian dead or Lincoln at Gettysburg',[108] but as insufficient counter to Keating's natural inclinations to indulge in 'K1', Bankstown language. Journalists seemed torn between two extremes in assessing the significance of Don Watson's speech writing, on the one hand lamenting the tendency of Keating to spoil the effect through his poor delivery,[109] and on the other accusing Watson of 'readjust[ing] and rework[ing] Australian history to fit Keating's view of the sweep of events'. *Australia Remembers'* focus upon remembrance of Australian military encounters in Papua New Guinea, the Malay peninsula, and the prisoner-of-war experiences on the Burma–Thailand railway, and at Sandakan and Changi was viewed by some as suspect, as evidence of Keating's mistaken belief that Australia had 'fought Britain's wars, rather than for a system of global security'.[110] That these names and places resonated with sacred meanings in what Keating often liked to call 'Australia's story' during the *Australia Remembers* ceremonies was often ignored in the quest by some journalists to capitalise on anti-Keating sentiments within sections of the community.

Australia Remembers events also frequently provided occasions for Paul Keating to pursue other topics close to his heart. The willing involvement of the media in promoting and reporting *Australia Remembers* events meant that his speeches on such occasions received more attention than they might have otherwise, and this obscured the fact that he was, in fact, repeating many themes which had been explored at other times. Indeed, some of his pre-*Australia Remembers* speeches were perhaps more blatantly nationalistic than those presented throughout 1995. One such speech, presented in 1993 as the inaugural Sir Edward 'Weary' Dunlop Asialink lecture, had narcissistic overtones, with Keating quoting a remark by Sir Edward shortly before he died, as evidence that he had been 'a bit ahead of Keating'[111] in his work fostering friendship with Asian countries. Sir Edward's standing in the community was used by Keating as a link that presumably would endow respectability upon himself, and Sir Edward's 'bush' origins and state school education provided further cause for approbation. Whilst a further connection was sought by Keating, in supposing that the 'heroes of [Dunlop's] basic education were the same as those of my generation', there were other important differences which he also chose to explore. These involved the nature of Australia during Sir Edward's youth, when the world was viewed 'through the prism of empire' in which Australia's mainly British and Irish-descended population was 'dependent on Britain', being merely 'an outpost of the British Empire'. While 'Weary' Dunlop's great qualities were identified by Keating as being 'universal', much of 'his character and the values he brought to the appalling human trial on the Burma–Thailand Railway' were claimed to be unmistakably Australian. As such, Keating continued, he knew 'the value of mateship' and his conduct was an 'affirmation of our values, an embodiment of our best traditions', derived from 'the Australian legend, including the legend of Anzac'. In spite of witnessing the appalling physical effects of incarceration, which produced a 'searing hatred of the Japanese', 'Weary' Dunlop had overcome such hatred, seeking instead friendship, understanding and engagement with Asia, as indeed Prime Minister Keating had himself been seeking, against the opposition from many within Australia. Indeed, Keating opined, this was 'one more reason why the story of 'Weary' Dunlop should be known to all Australians', because not only did he embrace change, but 'he imagined a different Australia', in spite of maintaining a love of Britain.[112] Surely the implication of such virtues was that Sir Edward, like Keating, was a visionary who could appreciate the British heritage, but envision a republican Australia. Similarly, 'Weary' Dunlop's far-sightedness demonstrated that he also 'knew where Australia's interests lay',[113] in building trading, institutional and cultural links with various Asian nations. Keating was provided with an opportunity to link his often misunderstood vision of Australia as a part of Asia with one of Australia's icons, whose youth had been spent within the 'monocultural Australia' now transformed, thanks partly to a large number of people from Asian countries, into a multicultural nation. Dunlop's greatness provided 'an irresistible lesson', which was that we should be open to change.[114]

In similar vein Keating's pre-*Australia Remembers* attacks on aspects of Australia's historic relationship with the British were less restrained than speeches on this topic throughout 1995. One such speech, an address to the Asia–Australia Institute, had sought to clarify that what were often construed as criticisms of the British were in fact directed at those Australians who remained unable to imagine Australia's future as separate from Britain's. Former Prime Minister Robert Menzies was singled out as articulating such extreme filial attitudes, and was also made to look like a foolishly naive colonialist quoting Churchill's remark that Australians came from 'bad stock'. Indeed, for Keating, Churchill virtually embodied all that was undesirable about Australia's continued links with Britain, as demonstrated by 'the abject disaster of Singapore and Malaya and the attempt to prevent the return of Australian troops from the Middle East' to defend Australia, which had 'lost 60,000 under the Union Jack in World War I'. This view, according to Keating, was not just his own, but was shared by 'a number of respectable Australian and British historians', whose references he would happily provide, and perhaps more importantly, he claimed, it was a view 'corroborated by fact'.[115] Further, a number of Prime Minister Keating's speeches on the necessity to look to Asia as an independent nation within the region, with its own distinctly multicultural character and social democratic traditions invoked the foresight of wartime Prime Minister John Curtin. By so doing, Keating hoped to encourage Australians to accept his vision of Australia making an important re-orientation in the 1990s and to identify this with the period in the 1940s when Australia was not only at risk, but was making the decision, without prejudice to its ties with Britain, to look elsewhere for protection and security.[116]

It is probable that the *Australia Remembers 1945–1995* program gave lustre to articles marking the fiftieth anniversary of John Curtin's death, with one journalist giving him the status of 'our one political saint', emphasising his common touch, such as sitting with the crowd at the football rather than with officials in the grandstand; his hunger for knowledge which led to him eschewing meals in preference to reading in the Melbourne Public Library, his problems with alcohol; periods of depression and loneliness in Canberra, as well as the stress he suffered during the war,[117] which was generally agreed to have contributed to his death. Even Paul Keating, who had hitherto dismissed Curtin as no more than 'a trier', was forced to acknowledge that 'Curtin's position in Australia's history is completely guaranteed, as it ought to be'.[118]

It seemed that, finally, fifty years later, there was an attempt to ascribe to Curtin 'the heroic stature that many historians feel he deserves', Curtin being ranked either first or second among Australia's prime ministers, with one political scientist describing Curtin's 1942 demand that Churchill allow Australian troops to return from the European theatre of war, to defend Australia, as 'a defining moment of greatness'.[119] While it is generally agreed that Curtin's famous 'Australia looks to America' statement had little real impact on Australia's relationship with Britain, it is likely that for many younger Australians especially, it may have had some currency within the republican debate, and that such an interpretation was not discouraged by Prime Minister Keating.

If, as the *Australian*'s editorial on the fiftieth anniversary of Curtin's death had suggested, such occasions should give pause for Australians to reflect on what remains important to them,[120] then Anzac Day, and the quality of mateship, often associated with this day of commemoration of male valour, seemed to provide the means for *Australia Remembers* to respond to this task. The fact that there had been larger attendances at Anzac Day services in the years immediately prior to 1995, and that this trend has continued since *Australia Remembers,* lends some credence to the somewhat simplistic view expressed in 1996, that 'Patriotism, a virtue that for decades has received a bad press...[is] back in vogue'.[121] If this was so, then the ways in which a national 'memory' of the war was under construction throughout 1995 was an important part of this revision.

CHAPTER 4

Nostalgia unbounded—
VP Day as spectacle

'World War II was the biggest event in Australia's history. Bigger than the First Fleet. Bigger than Gallipoli.'[1]

'...as you get older, these things get more vivid and stay with you longer.'[2]

OBSERVATION of the fiftieth anniversary of major wartime events was characterised by the use of spectacle in an attempt to reach back and reclaim the past. This reflected, as David Lowenthal has argued, that the past remains desirable in itself as well as validating 'present attitudes and actions by affirming their resemblance to former ones'.[3] Nostalgia involves a longing to recapture the past as experience. Such a process remains ultimately elusive, but nostalgia has become a device whereby the present is re-made. It 'transcends yearnings for lost childhoods and scenes of early life, embracing imagined pasts never experienced by their devotees or perhaps by anyone'.[4] Through such longings the past is brought into the present, so that it can be imbued with idealised images and meanings. Nostalgia has become 'memory with the pain removed'.[5]

The use of spectacle for the purpose of evoking nostalgia reflected ways in which *Australia Remembers 1945–1995* sought to look back at the past and bring it into the present. By doing this the generation of the war years could 'revisit' their diverse pasts that were woven around the program of remembering, and the postwar generations could 'visit' the past in their imaginations and their actual participation in the spectacle. This was evidenced through major events such as the VP Day parades and re-enactments of wartime journeys and experiences. Nostalgia was also expressed through the more commonplace but still highly evocative practice of 'dressing up' in the costumes and hairstyles of the period and the use of music and dance, such as occurred spontaneously within the crowds lining the streets for VP Day. It was also more consciously evoked by the celebratory events that were organised for the day. *Australia Remembers* at a national level and through the multitudes of local, community groupings, sought to (re)create the atmosphere and happenings on key anniversary dates. The most notable of these was VP Day, 15 August, celebrated in different parts of the country through the use of spectacle. Spectacle provided the opportunity for those who lived through the war, as well as the young, to imagine living these years, and to yearn for this imagined past. To provide ways of framing this past, the *Australia Remembers* Background Information book suggested a range of activities for local communities to consider. These included restoration of—or commemorative ceremonies at—local war memorials, cenotaphs and churches, concerts, cook books, or victory parades and balls similar to those held in 1945, neighbourhood street parties, invitations to local veterans and citizens who made significant contributions to the neighbourhood during the war, flying flags at half-mast on significant dates, visits to veterans at home or in nursing homes, sporting events, planting trees as living tributes, and memorabilia displays at local shopping centres. Also suggested were student video recording of local people who lived through the war 'to preserve their memories in a unique and timeless record', and school essay writing and other competitions.

A separate list of suggested school-based activities mirrored most of these proposed activities, adding that if the school was old, past students who served in the war might be researched and sought out.[6] These suggestions reflected the importance attached to nationwide commemorations at the local level, whereby genuinely local aspects of 'memory' were not only to be included but also celebrated, and the links between the generations arguably made stronger, at least for the year of *Australia Remembers*. Similarly, this list reflected the emphasis on the ordinary person, the male or female veteran of the war or of the home front. More importantly, perhaps, the activities listed suggested that the sites of (re)created memory need not be any more specific than their geographic locales. This contrasted with the 1988 Bicentenary spectacle, which, despite the intentions of the Bicentennial Authority to make its ' "celebration of a nation" a ritual of national unity', was instead 'a one-off spectacle in one city'.[7]

Nostalgia through spectacle

Spectacle provided a unifying means through which the nation, with the assistance of the direct telecast, celebrated key events in the anniversary of the war's end. That the public embraced such spectacles and engaged in collective acts of recreating the past, therefore, was not surprising. As has been observed, memories continually change through the process of revision, certain events being heightened and reinterpreted 'in the light of subsequent experience and present need'. This usually unconscious process results, often, in exaggeration, and the conflating of events or memories into a 'generalised uniformity'.[8] Through this process, which also involves changing and adding to the past, thereby strengthening the feeling that 'it is all essentially one', history 'becomes larger than life, merging intention with performance, ideal with actuality'.[9]

Within the British press 'VJ Day', as 15 August remained, was presented as an almost exclusively British affair, apart from considerations of the United States' dropping of the atomic bombs on Japan. For some of the media at least, the latest episode in the Princess of Wales soap opera seemed of more interest, however, judging from the Australian edition of the *International Express* for the week 9–15 August. Alongside details of the current scandal was a photograph of the Queen Mother on the occasion of her 95th birthday, with characteristic smile, hat and three strings of pearls, waving a Union Jack flag. An eleven-page special VJ Day edition made only passing mention to Australia in an article on the 'Hell of the death camps', which pictured 'inhuman' Japanese soldiers and their methods of punishment, as well as the infamous bridge over the River Kwai and skeletal prisoners. The photographic images included one also used frequently for Australian representations of the POW experience, of the 'samurai-style beheading of a kneeling and blind-folded prisoner', accompanied by an account of a death camp in North Borneo where 2,000 Britons had perished, the 'full horror [being] recounted by five Australians—the only survivors'. In this way Australians appeared almost incidental to the tale of British suffering, whereas the popular memory encouraged by *Australia Remembers* was of an Australian monopoly on this POW experience. Such is the manner in which 'the past' serves competing national narratives.

Within Australia, celebration of the end of the war in Europe was characterised by significant media focus on the British spectacle through which VE Day was celebrated, combined with re-enactments of aspects of the VE Day celebrations in Australia. *Australia Remembers* at times almost projected the impression that VE Day really belonged to Britain, in spite of sponsoring a number of VE commemorations. Given its somewhat nationalist slant on the war—which privileged the Pacific theatre as where Australia's most important battles had occurred, and its view that VE Day was an occasion for commemoration, whereas VP Day was for celebration—it was not until VP Day itself that the full extent of the use of spectacle by *Australia Remembers* was revealed. Australia's rather constrained celebrations of VE Day in May 1995 suggested a continuity of the view in 1945, that wonderful as peace in Europe was, Australia's war, that is, the real war against Japan, had yet to be won.

Indeed, *Australia Remembers* appeared perhaps a little uncertain about how to relate to a victory that it seemed to regard as primarily of British interest. For example, the commemorative poster, unlike the two for VP Day, contained no scenes of celebrations, but seemed to be finding ways of making the event directly relevant to Australians fifty years later. This poster focused on the VE Day pilgrimage to Europe and North Africa sponsored by *Australia Remembers*, the background photograph of which was of HMAS *Perth* in the Mediterranean. On the right-hand side of this poster, under the *Australia Remembers* logo, were three inset photographs: of a Lancaster bomber of 460 Squadron RAAF with air and ground crews, December 1943; of Australian troops marching towards Tobruk in January 1941; and of Australian nurses from 2/4th Australian General Hospital en route to Tobruk in 1941.

On VE Day and the day of thanksgiving that had followed it in 1945, Australians had 'been glued to their radios to hear the speeches of Churchill, the king, and the Governor-General, and to hear the joy of the London crowds outside Parliament and Buckingham Palace'. Men from the dominions and colonies who had contributed to victory were praised,[10] although women's efforts in these locations did not merit mention. Prime Minister Curtin, who had declared war on Japan independently of Britain, nurturing a 'magnificent obsession' since his announcement in December 1941 that without regard to Australia's traditional links or kinship with Britain, Australia now looked toward the United States, had greeted VE Day with 'gratitude that a terrible phase of the struggle [had] ended'. Nonetheless, he did not believe that celebrations were an appropriate way of behaving when the war against Japan was yet to be won. Similarly, Melbourne's Lord Mayor had announced that VE Day would be an occasion not of a public holiday but of a midday thanksgiving service, with the day being given over to prayer and reflection, fears of possible riots and disorder apparently giving rise to strict police and security precautions which included the closing of pubs as soon as the news of victory was announced. Hence the occasion had seemed to some to be more like a 'funeral procession' than a celebration, and in Sydney 'there was an air of despondency'.[11] Fifty years later, *Australia Remembers* seemed to mirror this attitude in its response to VE Day, which, while joyful, was restrained in comparison with VP Day a few months later.

The ABC documentary screened on the anniversary of VP Day was at pains to make clear that 'in 1939 Australians went to war for Britain, as part of an empire, but in May '45 victory in Europe was not yet a total victory for Australia'. As one of the veterans put it, 'VE Day was not much of a day'; they were pleased about peace in Europe, 'but still had a job to do, and still many casualties to be experienced'.

'Remembrance' of VE Day in Australia was largely conducted via the media, with the ABC's national televising of the VE Day Concert in London's Hyde Park, and newspapers' front-page photographs of the Queen Mother meeting war veterans in London, and of Dame Vera Lynn at the concert, as well as photographs of 'American veterans in a classic jeep' waving to citizens of Pizen in west Bohemia, which had been liberated by General Patten's troops, and of German Chief-of-Staff General Jodl signing the surrender on 7 May in Reims, France.[12] A photograph in the *Australian*, of 'an English bulldog…ready for VE Day celebrations' featured the dog wearing a camouflaged army helmet and draped with the Union Jack with a gas mask around his neck,[13] might have been more at home as a wartime propaganda photograph than a 1995 photograph in a country whose celebrations were resolutely focused on the Pacific war.

Commemoration of VE Day was focused on Canberra, where four thousand people gathered for the day's events. These began in the morning with a special national service at the Australian War Memorial. This included a parade of World War II vehicles, troops in period 'costumes' and a flypast by RAAF FA18 fighters. Churches across New South Wales and in the ACT rang their bells in unison with the carillon from 1.00 pm. The press release which previewed these events expressed the hope that visitors would come from all over New South Wales in particular. Such visitors were reminded to arrive early at events 'to allow for smooth parking and seating arrangements'. This reminder illustrated the ways in which participants in such ceremonies literally may be termed 'tourists' to the past, made a 'foreign country' by nostalgia.[14] On the eve of VE Day a ninety-minute sound and light spectacular, 'Son et Lumiere' reverberated around the War Memorial and adjacent hills and suburbs. The surrounding streets were blacked out in preparation 'for a return to WWII', during which an air-raid siren was sounded and searchlights on Red Hill and

Black Mountain signalled the coming of a bombing run. In addition, 'special effects, wartime music and gun fire transport[ed] guests to the despair of the war years through to the exhilaration of peace in Europe, with fireworks, flowers and streamers'. Guests were urged to bring warm rugs to this free event.[15]

It remained for the prime minister to suggest the meanings of the anniversary of VE Day. This he did by locating the explanation for Australians going to Europe within the Anzac legend. Although 'under fewer illusions about the realities of war', than their parents' generation, those who went did so because Australians had 'decided long ago that they would not forget those who made the supreme sacrifice, and that they would pass on to future generations...the message that sacrifice contains'. This mystical explanation was known to Australians, Mr Keating suggested:

> because our parents and our teachers told us, because we attended ceremonies every 25 April [where] we learned that these men and women had a notion of duty...and loved Australia and believed in its future.

The year 1995 provided the opportunity for young Australians to know that men and women like them had been prepared to join forces with men and women from other countries to defend freedom, and understanding this, young Australians would learn 'what we mean when we talk about courage and perseverance and the immeasurable value of sticking together in hardship'. In paying tribute on the fiftieth anniversary of VE Day, Australians were asked to remember a 'generation whose faith was profound', who had fought to protect Australia, no mention actually being made of the relationship between Australian forces and the British. Indeed, the impression conveyed within this speech was that while Australian troops did participate in the European war, their involvement was primarily a further demonstration of the potency of the Anzac spirit. There was a duty also to learn about the horrors of the Holocaust, and of the dimensions of loss of nations such as the former Soviet Union. For Australians, VE Day fifty years earlier had led to people from other countries, who left their 'shattered lives and devastated homes', to begin again in Australia, the result of which was a population more 'tolerant of cultural differences', because these immigrants had 'in building new lives here...enriched us all'.[16]

A crowd of 3,000 at Melbourne's Shrine of Remembrance was addressed by a twenty-year-old university student who gave thanks not only to those who fought, but also 'factory workers, nurses, doctors [and] entertainers'. This speech was taken by the *Age* to dispel 'understandable fears' of the wartime generation about the direction of today's youth. Injecting a less lofty remembrance of the occasion and perhaps fulfilling the irreverent role of the cartoonist, the shadow of the nuclear future was not forgotten even on VE Day, with a Tandberg cartoon depicting a couple discussing the lessons of World War II, concluding that what had been learnt was 'how to set off a nuclear explosion'.[17]

As was discussed in the previous chapter, the prisoner-of-war experience highlighted by *Australia Remembers* privileged the sufferings of men who had been captives of the Japanese, but VE Day provided the occasion for a rare article in which the experiences of prisoners of the Germans was examined. Pointing out that Australian POW survivors of the Germans were being 'excluded from national history-making', a newspaper article sought to make it clear that prisoners of the Germans had been forced to live with capricious behaviour on the part of their captors and in conditions which were 'a matter of life and death'. In spite of their experiences, many felt discriminated against because of the *Australia Remembers* focus on the Pacific theatre. This was perhaps encapsulated by the 'Weary' Dunlop memorial in Melbourne, dedicated to the doctors of the Burma–Thailand railway instead of all AIF doctors, some of whom, from the 2/5 Australian General Hospital, 'gave up their freedom in Athens to stay with their patients and became POWs'. The problems encountered in creating such public memories were exemplified by the skewed focus on 'Weary' Dunlop, which had ignored the fact that he had served in Europe and the Middle East as well as in Asia.[18]

Editorialising on the day's events, the *Sydney Morning Herald* took up the theme of 'the just war' as reason why, fifty years later the planned mood of the day would be 'triumphal and nostalgic', with the serving of Anzac biscuits by the Salvation Army, a display of World War II military vehicles and the replaying of Prime Minister Curtin's declaration of the end of the war in Europe. Concluding with the understatement that while some actions of the Allies, such as the fire-bombing of Dresden and the dropping of the atomic bombs on Hiroshima and Nagasaki 'have remained controversial events', the editorial sought to avoid engaging with these questions by suggesting that history 'should be read in the context of its times', noting that the ideal of a lasting peace had not been realised. For these reasons, VE Day should be observed with great rejoicing, but also 'a certain amount of contemplation'.[19]

Local level contribution to the Allied victory in Europe provided a focus for Ballarat's *Courier* newspaper, which produced a VE Day commemorative edition, also aimed at enabling readers to 'recall the euphoria' of the moment. One of the few communities which opted for a mainly military style of commemoration, Mackay, reported on about 300 people, including veterans and young Mackay navy, army, and air force cadets, who participated in two commemoration parades. As with the Ballarat press, the occasion provided the opportunity to advise readers of 'special Celebrations' planned for VP Day in August.[20] The particular memories of rural women were rarely represented, apart from a charming photograph, fifty years later, of three laughing local Gladstone women forming a conga line, trying to imitate themselves 'kick[ing] up their heels in remembrance of VE Day fifty years ago'. Their memories, of 'a town flooded with American, Australian and British soldiers on their way to and from combat, with their emphasis on the personal and the micro, provided a welcome contrast to the more tradition-oriented memories featured in most reports of commemorations of VE Day.[21]

Elsewhere, a letter from a Caloundra veteran evoked a vivid visual memory, which he was sure would be shared by three or four hundred diggers, of 'the little girl, aged about eight or nine years old with her mother, standing on the side of the road at Denison Street, between Albert and Fitzroy streets'. The image was particularly noteworthy and nostalgic because of the accompaniment of a piano accordion. They sang patriotic songs to all the diggers as they made their way by train to the unknown North and New Guinea. He suggested that *Australia Remembers* should try to locate the woman who had been that little girl, and ask her to play for the ex-diggers again on the night they stayed in Rockhampton, or on the railway station next morning when they set out on a more peaceful and comfortable journey retracing their movements from Brisbane to Townsville. The plea to retrieve this image became the subject of an editorial requesting anybody knowing the identity of the girl to contact the editor.[22] The potency of a specific location or image in memories of more than fifty years, was indicated also by the precise details of where the little girl and her mother stood.

The media and VP Day—didactic nostalgia

For the media, VP Day provided the opportunity for what I term 'didactic nostalgia', whereby 'the past' was evoked as a desirable time, albeit fraught with danger and sacrifice. The media seemed to regard their role as being guardians of knowledge about the war as well as being purveyors of its meanings to the wartime generation as well as today's. Reflecting variations in quality and with a philosophical bent, sections of the media also indulged in considerable retrospective self-promotion and were not devoid of ethnocentric if not racist discussions of Japan during the war and the present. A Tanner cartoon in the *Age*, for example, showed a man of the war generation speaking to a young child, to the effect that 'we stopped them on the Toshiba track and pushed them back to Yamaha, sank the Daimaru near Sanyo and went on to take Hitachi, Honda, Sony, Toyota, Nissan and Kumagai Gumi'. The *Herald Sun*'s cartoon on the other hand tapped into the deeper xenophobic vein within Australia, depicting two men in the jungle saying 'here comes the Japanese invasion force, lads', one of these diggers then being confronted by stereotypically drawn Japanese tourists with cameras and golf bags, shown in the next frame blinding the hapless digger with the flash from their cameras, the final scene showing a beach, crowded with Japanese tourists but for our lone digger reporting, 'Fifty years on I wish to report our position overrun'. Similarly Brisbane's *Courier Mail* on VP Day, wrote of Australia's 'defining moments in history...Milne Bay and the Kokoda Track...[where]

Australians fought alone and inflicted defeat upon an adventurous and courageous enemy'. Alongside this editorial was a Leahy cartoon, depicting ex-diggers, in their army uniforms standing at a celebration, beneath a VP Day fiftieth anniversary banner, Australian flags in their hands with one observing to another 'hey look at this—in the corner here it says "Made in Japan"'.[23]

Melbourne's *Herald Sun* was also keen to highlight the roles of its two predecessor presses, now combined, and editorialised on the 'heroes who fought for our democratic ideals'. The paper had 'been proud to play its role...by publishing the *Our Home Front* book and yesterday's reprint of the 1945 VP Day *Herald*' as well as other material 'to educate those too young to know the significance of VP Day'. In addition, the editor was 'pleased to help' Veterans' Affairs Minister Con Sciacca and the Victorian *Australia Remembers* Committee in 'ensuring that this is a year which indeed will be long remembered'.[24] Its eight-page souvenir edition on the day before VP Day featured on its cover a photograph of three young women, one, Lois Martin, wearing 'a skin-hugging, red, white and blue hand-knitted jumper' with the words 'VP Day' sewn onto it. This woman had died in 1981 but the photograph had been recognised by her husband who had kept the jumper,[25] which provided the coloured focus of the photograph with a Union Jack flag held by one of the other two women on either side. Behind Lois Martin can be seen part of a coloured Australian flag, and her forehead is covered with the pink letters 'VP' and one cheek has the pink letter 'V' and the other 'P', underscoring that the term VP was indeed popularly used at the time. The caption for this photograph reflected a familiar trope of the *Australia Remembers* program:

> Suddenly, unbelievably, it was over. The boys were coming home. If you were there you would know the elation this girl was experiencing. If you weren't then you can imagine.

The focus of this souvenir edition was mostly on the warriors, women being represented as those who waited, with emotive scenes of a mother greeting her returning soldier son and other women in crowded street celebrations. It concluded with a list of the celebrations for the coming week, complete with a map indicating where to assemble for 'the big parade', and an obligatory look at the ways in which 'Australia emerged from the war a new nation', with the somewhat hyperbolic opening statement that 'World War II was the biggest event in Australia's history. Bigger than the First Fleet. Bigger than Gallipoli'. This was a version of history which would certainly be contested by Australia's Indigenous populations. Reinforcing the Pacific war focus, the editorial concluded with the ambiguous statement that 'our troops learned what some people are just starting to realise now...for better or worse, we are part of Asia'.[26]

The ABC TV round-up of news on the night of VP Day suggested a combination of solemnity as well as the extensive use of spectacle at celebratory events in different parts of the nation. The first item introduced this day of 'joy, sorrow, memories bitter and sweet', as Prime Minister Keating accepted the qualified apology from Japan, for which he could take much of the credit. Viewers were reminded that the day was VP Day, 'the day that helped shape the nation'. Brisbane, the site of national remembering of this occasion, being the base from which General MacArthur had 'led the Allied victory' was covered first, with the image of a young mother in the crowd, child in arms, expressing her thanks to the wartime generation for making Australia 'a free place, a place to have a good life' as she put it. This, viewers were informed, was the chance for the 75,000-strong crowd to give the veterans the homecoming that many had never had. Prime Minister Chifley's voice was then heard announcing to his fellow citizens that the war was over. Other headline events included the parade in Melbourne, with its crowd of more than 200,000, exceeding all expectations. Some old diggers had their brief moment in the glare of the television cameras.

The spectacles—Melbourne

Melbourne's VP Day parade took place on a warm, sunny spring-like day, which doubtless encouraged the larger than expected crowd of 200,000, as well as the light-hearted atmosphere. The suburban train on which I travelled into the city was unusually crowded for eleven o'clock in the morning, and included a group of grade six schoolgirls in their uniforms accompanied by two teachers. It seemed clear from the mixture of medals, pieces of paper containing information about the parade, and the conversations overheard, that most of those on the train, a good mixture of all ages, were on their way to the parade. There was an unusual mood of a quiet cheerfulness, it seemed, and more eye contact was being made than is usual on trains. The parade's assembly point outside the Arts Centre complex on St Kilda Road had been the same site for the assembly about ten days earlier of the coalition of groups and organisations protesting the French nuclear tests in the Pacific and marking the anniversary of the dropping of the atomic bombs on Japan. Among the crowd there were colourful banners of companies, battalions, nurses, women's land army, and others. In quite touching scenes, some of these banners were held on one side by little boys in Scout uniforms with women who presumably were grandmothers, holding the other side. The air was genuinely festive, and it was evident that there were a number of individual reunions taking place. A woman was doing quite a good trade selling badges to raise funds for the restoration of the Mount Macedon Cross, a monument to those from that district who had fallen in the First World War.

Walking along Swanston Street, people were greeted by a hawker from one of the two-dollar shops, spruiking that Australian flags were '$2 today'. Regardless of his somewhat misleading advertising, given that this was the price of the flags on any other day, trade might have been brisk, judging from the number of adults and children who had flags. Over the loud-speakers along Swanston Street Glenn Miller's music, especially 'In the Mood', was playing, and a couple in the crowd spontaneously jived to the enthusiastic cheering and applause of the surrounding crowd, while others chose to clap in rhythm with the music.

At 11.55 am, Vera Lynn's 'White Cliffs of Dover' was interrupted by the announcement that when the Town Hall clock chimes twelve, 'Melbourne becomes the national focus of the *Australia Remembers* parade', that 'the whole nation now joins with us'. The 'Last Post' was then played, followed by two minutes' silence, and then Prime

Minister Chifley's (surely by now very familiar) announcement of war's end. From my vantage point at the City Square, there was a hush as the parade approached, led by the Mounted Police Band. Four fighter planes noisily flew overhead, followed by a single plane, with much clapping from the crowd. The air force band's playing of 'Waltzing Matilda' elicited a comment from a man of the wartime generation near me in the crowd, to general agreement, that this was 'really Australia's anthem'. Ticker tape started to fall, although the fact that this had been specially imported from Los Angeles at a cost of $17,000 plus transport, because there was reportedly no Australian manufacturer,[27] somewhat diluted the impression this had caused on the day. On the other hand, this information provided an illustration of the importance of (re)creating the past, involving a conscious use of spectacle for this purpose.

As the official party then approached, consisting of RSL State President, Bruce Ruxton, (captured in a *Herald Sun* photograph neatly combining images of 1945 and 1995, with his fingers giving the 'V for Victory' salute, the other hand holding a mobile phone into which he was talking), Premier Jeff Kennett suitably attired in a black double-breasted suit and about a dozen other dignitaries, a lone male voice in the crowd called out 'Go home, Jeff'.

Throughout the parade, the music of Glenn Miller and Vera Lynn was played. As marchers appeared with their identifying banner, for example, as 'Ex-POW Europe Far East Japan', they were greeted all along the parade route with loud cheers, whistling and clapping, and planes overhead at this time seemed to provide their own noisy salute. At the rear of the march a character well known in certain parts of Chapel Street, Prahran and Elsternwick—a man with a shopping buggy decorated with small Australian flags and fundamentalist Christian messages—provided an idiosyncratic spectacle of his own.

Watching the entire parade from a superb vantage point atop the Regent Theatre, then in the process of restoration, were workmen who had hung a large banner over the side of the building, which read, in red lettering, 'The Trade Union Movement', and in black lettering, 'On the 50th anniversary of the end of the Second World War, a grateful nation expresses its thanks to working men and women of Australia for contributing to the war effort and the coming of peace', and in red lettering again, 'Sponsored by ACTU CFMEU Building Construction Unions'. This was one of the few visual and explicit reminders that 'the home front' had in fact consisted of men and women workers and trade unionists, who had been a fundamental aspect of the victory.

To add to the spectacle, a dance was held in the City Square immediately following the parade, inside a large marquee made from parachute material, beautifully pleated over the ceiling area. The audience, who sat at tables around the perimeter, was mostly of the wartime generation. Memories of how they had once looked, dressed and danced were prompted by young people hired to perform the entertainment. The men wore service uniforms and the women evening dresses although the hair styles of some of the young men did not look quite authentic, unlike the women's. The master of ceremonies opened the party with the questions, 'Who remembers? Who was there?' reinforcing the disjunction between memory and experience, and enjoined the partygoers to 'enjoy yourselves; remember why you are here'. Dressed in a boater hat and a suit composed of the Arnotts biscuit tins designs, the figure of the master of ceremonies signified the palpable nostalgia within this marquee, mindless of the fact that this national icon had not been Australian-owned since 1994, and had had a chequered history since 1985 when a shareholder, the American company Campbells Soup, was invited in by the Arnotts family to stave off interest from then businessman Alan Bond.[28] Such realities, however, were irrelevant in the context of the nostalgia being manufactured at this dance-party. Rather, the imagery associated with Arnotts, the company having provided biscuits for men at the World War I fronts, as well as creating the popular Anzac biscuit, illustrated the desire to connect with icons around which Australia's national identity has been constructed.

The spectacles—Brisbane

In 1945, '90,000 thronged the streets, and 120,000 danced into the night' in Brisbane, as pictures and articles reminded readers of the *Courier Mail* on 15 August 1995, when 100,000 reportedly 'relived the joy of Australia's garrison city on VP Day'. Fifty years later, the *Courier Mail* turned its attention to some of the more negative aspects of Queensland residents' wartime perceptions that they were living in a 'beleaguered city', a feeling which was exacerbated when they learned of the 'Brisbane Line', an imaginary 'line' north of which would reputedly have been handed over to the Japanese in the event of an invasion. For many of the wartime generation, the 'Brisbane Line' had become tangible and had endured along with other local myths. One of these was woven around the presence of United States troops in Brisbane. This had not only exposed Anglo-Celtic Australians to new cultural influences, but it had also required some 'inventive solutions' to their needs, with brothels now being tolerated. This in turn had led to the creation of the enduring myth about the 'Curtin Special', a trainload of prostitutes supposedly ordered to Brisbane by Prime Minister Curtin. All of this had been avidly reported under the wartime phrase 'over-sexed, overpaid, over here',[29] which had probably been plagiarised from the British.

In spite of their quaint parochialism, none of these themes were present in the *Flame of Freedom* dance performance, produced by Warana, The Brisbane Festival for the Federal Government's *Australia Remembers 1945–1995* program, telecast live across the nation by the ABC.[30] This performance, before a capacity audience at Brisbane's Boondall Entertainment Centre on the night of VP Day, concluded the national celebrations. As the program notes to this performance explained, the opening sequence featured a statue from a memorial to the Unknown Soldier being awakened and performing a ghostly dance of freedom, while the sound of thunder in the distance evoked the sounds of aircraft soon to dominate the skies. As the scene passed into day, a young family—the mother with son, the father with daughter on his shoulders—walked along a jetty, oblivious to the soldier's dance, representing the ways in which Australians at the time thought of the war. To reinforce this point, the boy and girl wore paper hats folded from newspaper upon which news of the war could be seen, and in a gendered representation, the boy carried a paper plane on which the word 'war' was visible. 'The Start of the Second World War', by R. A. Simpson, was read, to the peace-shattering sounds of a plane and a bugle playing a jazzed up version of 'The Last Post'. The family was then torn apart by a wall of fire caused by bombs dropped from the planes, and this scene was juxtaposed with footage from the war. Amid chaotic scenes of civilians and people in uniforms and flame-coloured lightning, the 'flame of freedom' that had been at the feet of the Unknown Soldier was snuffed out. The performance then cut to scenes of soldiers armed and prepared-looking, again privileging the role of the Australian soldiers over members of the other forces, while on another part of the stage stood a group of civilians, with the mother prominent among these. A dance of women then took place, as they folded grey blankets, and sandbags on the stage suggested the defence of the small isolated Australian nation of 1942. This scene, which self-consciously separated the war into the home front and the front line, signified that all sections of society had a role in the war, and the focus on the family showed how 'ordinary' Australians experienced it. Behind the group of women was a wall upon which vertical strokes had been crossed out, representing the passing of the days in POW camps. The man then farewelled his children and wife, giving the boy his watch, followed by dance scenes of battle and death, with the father shown throwing a grenade as the camera returned its attention to the wife, standing with other women, all of whom were reading letters. In a scene that suggested that her husband had been killed, the wife folded her letter and then hugged her husband. The civilian clothes he was wearing suggested her memory of him, whilst the rifle he carried represented the war that had killed him.

The vignette which followed was of 'The Company of Lovers' by Judith Wright, a dance of death which depicted soldiers being wounded and helped by others (their mates), of wives reading letters, symbolic of bad news, with the blankets folded by the women in the previous vignette now being put over the bodies of dead soldiers and around the shoulders of the living, women being represented in this action in their traditional roles as nurturers and those left bereft following the death of male warriors. This was followed by 'A Fox Hole for the Night' by John Quinn, which depicted silent, tired-looking soldiers sheltering for the night, in an evocation of the male theme of mateship, so celebrated by *Australia Remembers* as a unique feature of Australian military experience. Other vignettes represented mateship and suffering among men at Changi and the construction of the Burma–Thailand railway. Then a loud bang represented the dropping of the atomic bombs, and Prime Minister Chifley's voice announced that the war was over.

Following this very visual series of vignettes, with the colour blue and water being the two constant elements, men and women veterans with candles, walked along surveying the scattered bodies of the dead soldiers. Linking the veterans' generation with children of the present, young people walked towards the mother and her daughter and son and then past them, alternately to the right and the left. The soldiers from the dance also moved towards the young people to give their candles light and these were then passed on to other young people, representing the precious gift of peace and security which Australian soldiers had been celebrated as providing.

Immediately after the performance, Prime Minister Keating spoke of how 1945 was a 'great year' as was the fiftieth anniversary, of how 'we have remembered and we do remember…[and felt] the bonds between us and those Australians who, with our allies, fought and won the greatest of victories fifty years ago'. 'VP', he reminded Australians, means 'Victory in the Pacific', which had also been called 'VJ Day', 'Victory over Japan', but he wanted us all to think that the letter 'V' was the really important one.

The spectacles contested

We all 'remember' events at which we were not present, and through memory we give meaning to our past.[31] The 'Dancing Man' at Sydney's 1945 VP Day celebrations has for fifty years provided an image which has become a vivid memory shared by many Australians. On the occasion of the fiftieth anniversary celebrations his identity became a matter of considerable controversy and threatened legal action. In effect, ownership of this memory was being contested, not only by several men claiming to be the 'Dancing Man', but also by those who believed they remembered seeing him. For one journalist, the identity of the 'Dancing Man' was not an issue, because he had 'always known...always will...he's the bloke in the old newsreel'. The 'Dancing Man' was likened in his mind to the 'Unknown Soldier who died on the battlefields of France thirty years earlier, who represents all those who never came home', whereas the Dancing Man represented those who 'lived to dance, to laugh, to celebrate, to give thanks that the war was over'.[32]

Australia Remembers 1945–1995 organisers, however, had a particular interest in seeking to clarify the identity of the 'Dancing Man'. As he had had become 'part of the national memory', the organisers wanted to include him as a special guest in the fiftieth anniversary parade. After some investigation, Mr Ern Hill, a retired electrician from Sydney's western suburbs became 'the official titleholder', a position that was soon challenged by ten others, including friends of a deceased man.[33] A significant aspect of this dispute was that it centred on the memories of those who had 'been there' at the time. This in itself provided a fascinating twist on the 1995 trope to the effect that if you had 'been there' you 'knew', otherwise you could imagine. The most prominent challenger to Ern Hill was Frank McAlary, QC, who though himself rather reticent about the incident, merely claiming that 'For fifty years, I've kept that under the covers', he was pushed into the limelight by his colleagues. A letter from James Poulos, QC, on behalf of the Members of the Eleventh Floor, Selbourne and Wentworth Chambers, Philip Street, Sydney, claimed that Frank McAlary QC, a law student at the time of the photograph, had hung the photograph in the corridors of the law firm 'for several years'. Furthermore, 'evidence...that the man in question is McAlary can be obtained from Chester Porter, QC, who was there when the film (of which the photograph is a still) was taken'. This was backed by the assertion that fifty years later Mr McAlary looked 'a whole lot more like the man in the picture than Mr Hill does'.[34] The identity and individual memories of the 'Dancing Man' became sites of contestation. Eighty-one-year-old Mrs Freda Osborne, who believed that she was the woman also captured in the original picture, looking over her shoulder at the 'Dancing Man', 'said she was certain it was Mr Hill but had not seen the other three men'. Then again, Mrs Noelene Shaw 'thought she might have been the woman'.[35] Other claimants to the identity, after some initial flurry including one seeking the advice of a solicitor and signing a statutory declaration, became 'media shy' about the whole matter, and when VP Day arrived, 'the Dancing Man return[ed] to the streets of Sydney, in the form of twenty-six-year-old dancer Drew Anthony, star of the musical 'Hot Shoe Shuffle', who led the Victory Parade.[36]

Contested memories of this kind were not limited to *Australia Remembers* however, with a similar controversy occurring within the United States over 'one of the most famous images of the Allies' victory...a sailor's celebratory kiss with a nurse in New York', which had been 'exposed as a lie'. This image, a photograph which had appeared in *Life* magazine on 27 August 1945, was alleged fifty years later to have been 'one of several posed shots taken in Times Square' on VE Day. The woman photographed, now seventy-eight-year-old Edith Shain, who had re-enacted the kiss on television in 1994 with another man who had laid claim to the kisser's identity, expressed outrage that she had not been contacted about allegations that the photograph had been staged. Nevertheless, she admitted she was 'still not sure who the sailor was'. Surprisingly, there were no other claimants to the nurse's identity, but like Sydney's 'Dancing Man' fifty years on, memories of the sailor and the nurse—while potent for many who believed they 'were there'—would remain a matter of historical uncertainty. As sites of memory, albeit contested, on the other hand, the continuing significance of these images was assured.

CHAPTER 5

Australia Remembers
and national identity

'...the Anzac legacy goes beyond the British tradition to embrace Australians of all ethnic backgrounds.'[1]

'Even if the Australia of the 1940s was blind to their [Indigenous Australians'] bravery and loyalty, we see it clearly now...It must not be forgotten [as] these are stirring tales.'[2]

'It is my very pleasant duty today to farewell men and women from an heroic generation of Australians who are embarking on a pilgrimage to some of the sacred sites of our history.'[3]

PERHAPS in an attempt to deflate some of the *Australia Remembers*-inspired excitement surrounding VP Day, the national daily newspaper printed a lengthy article on its eve. Written by one of Australia's pre-eminent historians of the Second World War, Joan Beaumont, it reminded readers that before the 'television bites' provided by

Australia Remembers it was the First World War that had 'dominated Australians' memory of war'.[4] Ranging over the profound destructiveness of World War II, the fears and threat of invasion, the changes to family life and politics, as well as the shaking of confidence in Britain, 'though not to the degree Paul Keating would have us believe now', the death rates and efforts involved in both World Wars were compared. Contrary to much recent privileging of World War II, the article concluded that it was only—'and it is a very big only'—in 1942 that Australia can be said to have made a 'decisive contribution to the war against Japan'. This was when Australian troops stopped the Japanese advance over the Owen Stanley Ranges and at Milne Bay in Papua New Guinea. The article suggested that until *Australia Remembers*, the memory of the First World War had overshadowed the memory of the Second, because it gave birth to the Anzac legend. Indeed, Beaumont argued, 'the soldiers of 1939–45 consciously saw themselves as acting within the traditions of World War I, rather than creating new mythology'.[5] In keeping with its contestation of the nomenclature chosen for the occasion, the *Australian* appeared keen to remind readers, through its 'Opinion' page, that:

> for all its recasting to suit the nationalist and republican agenda of the Keating Government, the focus of Anzac remains very much on Gallipoli and the other campaigns of the war that generated the legend seventy years ago.[6]

Australia Remembers and memory and remembering

The *Australian* seems to have ignored Keating's consistent emphasis on the continuity of the Anzac spirit, a continuity that he and others sought to bring into the present. Such a task was assisted by the increased interest in the legend in the years immediately prior to the fiftieth anniversary, a trend that has continued since, leading an editorialist in 1996 to suggest, somewhat simplistically, that 'Patriotism, a virtue that for decades has received a bad press…[is] back in vogue'.[7] That Anzac Day observes with pride one of Australia's greatest defeats, in which over 8,000 men died and a further 19,000 or so were wounded, has often been remarked upon for its strangeness. Because of its sacred status, the nature of observance of Anzac Day itself, as well as the Anzac legend, have been and continue to be sites of contestation.

The brevity of European presence in Australia and the contested meanings of colonisation have been reflected in the ways in which a continual search for meaning and identity has been pursued. As discussed in an earlier chapter, Australians sought to define themselves with a homogeneous identity in 1888, before Federation of the colonies had occurred. A factor in this was the racialised desire for a white Australia. This desire became formalised with the constitutional exclusion of Indigenous people in 1901, coupled with a social exclusion that has lasted much longer. Other non-white populations were effectively locked out of the country by the White Australia Policy. Whereas 'older' nations with recorded national histories have denser mythologies, the so-called 'new' nations such as Australia seem to be driven to 'undertake the process of national formation explicitly, visibly, defensively, and are always caught in the act—embarrassed in the process of construction'.[8] The desire for a national identity has revolved around the need for a national 'story'. This has led to members of non-Indigenous Australian society being particularly 'concerned with defining what a cultural identity is'.[9] One of the ways in which this process has manifested itself in Australia has been through the rituals of remembrance and mourning associated with Anzac Day.

As noted, Prime Minister Keating's more overtly nationalistic speeches had occurred before *Australia Remembers,* in spite of the perceptions of some. Addressing a ceremony in Port Moresby in 1992 to honour the seventy-seventh anniversary of Gallipoli, he had spoken of the 'indissoluble' relationship between 'Gallipoli and the history of the Australian nation'.[10] Keating seemed aware of the importance of debate over the meanings of Anzac when he spoke of the ways in which 'legends bind nations together. They define us to ourselves', but that this should not be the cause of a nation's stagnation. Thereupon Keating enlisted the Anzac legend for his own contemporary purposes. In doing this he extended the meaning of Anzac beyond sacrifice and warfare, harnessing it to assertions of contemporary national interest and autonomy. After a brief mention of some of the particularly resonant battles, which included El Alamein, Tobruk, Greece and Crete, as well as those closer to home, he arrived at the heart of this speech. This was that 'we should also remember the battle fought out in Canberra and London and Washington'. This battle was what made success in Papua New Guinea possible, because 'John Curtin defied those people Australia had never before denied' by insisting on the return of Australian troops from the Middle East, to defend Australia. In making this 'right' demand, Curtin was taking 'the Anzac legend to mean that Australia came first' and therefore the battles in New Guinea were for Australians 'the most important ever fought'. The victories of the Australian 39th and 53rd battalions, later reinforced with members of the 7th Division, 'were the heroic days of Australia's history'.[11] It was battles such as these, as well as political battles fought by Australia's leader that fell within the rubric of 'Anzac'.

Three years later on the eve of Anzac Day 1995, speaking at a press conference at Canakkale, Turkey, Veterans' Affairs Minister Sciacca suggested that 'the Anzac legacy goes beyond the British tradition to embrace Australians of all ethnic backgrounds'. His belief that the Anzac tradition could be extended to all of multicultural Australia arose from the centrality of the deeds of the Anzacs in the founding of Australia's identity.[12] As somebody who had come to Australia as a young boy and strongly identified with its perceived values and beliefs as well as his own cultural background, Sciacca was enthusiastic about embracing and promoting the Anzac tradition. In bipartisan mode, Sciacca and Shadow Minister, Wilson Tuckey, 'mesh[ed] the legacies of World War I and World War II as they reworked the Anzac tradition for a new age'.[13] Unlike Keating, however, Sciacca remained immune from accusations of running any particular political agenda. As well, the involvement of a number of ethnic communities in Anzac Day ceremonies over the previous decade, suggesting that the occasion had 'come to embrace and espouse a broader definition of Australian racial and national identity',[14] made the extension of the legend's embrace less exceptional. Sciacca's universalising of it had the potential to heal the profound divisions it has created[15] by removing it from its military context and extending it to former enemies and descendants of people who had no involvement in World War I. More importantly, Sciacca had decentred the Anzac legend from its location at the core of Anglo-Australian remembrance, offering it as a secular signifier of belonging within the nation.

Prime Minister Keating, in his 1995 Anzac Day speech, was more inclined to locate its meanings within traditional remembrance as commemorating Australia's 'most important and profound day' which had given 'us the creed to live by as Australians and as a nation'.[16] Not that he has been the only prime minister to use Anzac Day to promote his own political views. This was demonstrated the following year when newly elected prime minister, John Howard, used the occasion to reiterate his opposition to any suggestions that Australia's flag be changed. In his Anzac Day statement, equally nationalistic in its own way, Mr Howard identified the occasion as 'a key component of Australia's national identity' and promised to protect 'our great national symbol' from change, calling upon young Australians to 'reflect with pride on how lucky we are to be Australians and to focus on the things which unite us'[17] rather than on what he regarded as divisive issues such as the replacement of a flag. Portrayed by a cartoonist at his desk, holding up the Australian flag, with the caption 'I wouldn't hide behind anything else', it was Mr Howard's turn to be criticised for associating Anzac Day with his political agenda.[18]

Central to the idea of the Anzacs is 'that spirit of mateship', born of the 'courage of Australian soldiers showing a sense of humour [which has] become known around the world—that spirit of what it means to be an Australian'.[19] Always associated with the day is the ways in which veterans intone the same theme, that 'Anzac Day brings back the memories of mates...who didn't make it back with us'.[20] Those who had experienced the horrors of warfare appear to harbour no doubts about the existence and efficacy of this peculiar form of male bonding. Ex-Burma–Thailand railway prisoner Ernie Toovey was sure he and others would not have survived 'if we had not had mates', and their vow to keep in close contact after the war was something that 'only death will break'. It was this 'spirit of Anzac' that was the most important thing to be honoured on

Anzac Day,[21] and this remained so during *Australia Remembers.* The similar survival strategies of female POWs who spoke of their reliance on mutual support and comfort as well as their life-long friendships, remained separate from the male discourse of mateship. Clearly mateship was not a concept to be challenged by *Australia Remembers,* rather it was elevated and redefined in ways designed to embrace sections of the populace formerly excluded from it. Mateship was identified in 1995 not only as a quality which bonded men, but as a characteristic which set the nation itself apart from, and superior to, the British, in whom the absence of this desirable attribute provided the explanation for their unwillingness to join in the Commonwealth nations' condemnation of the French nuclear tests in the Pacific. Indeed, not only were the British lacking in the qualities of mateship, but also were no longer seen as being tied by the bonds of kinship.[22]

Periodic suggestions that Anzac Day should become the national day of commemoration rather than Australia Day, suggest a continuing unease about a persisting focus on colonisation as the defining moment in the nation's history. The suggestion rests upon the arguments that Australia Day has become increasingly irrelevant to contemporary multicultural Australia, as well as being insulting to Indigenous people. Anzac Day, on the other hand, is allegedly a unifying moment, although the continuing absence of Indigenous people from the legend itself arguably destabilises such an argument. Such arguments for making Anzac Day the nation's day are highly gendered, however, the legend being based upon men. Such elevation of Anzac Day would effectively formalise women's status as second-class citizens, 'military combat as the pre-eminent form of national service' having excluded women. Furthermore, the elevation of the almost spiritual significance of the Anzacs 'has rested on a disavowal of the value to the nation of the work of nurturers, carers, conciliators, negotiators and peacemakers' and on the fact that gendered responsibilities have meant that 'men bore arms [and] women bore the babies'.[23]

The most potent representation of the Anzac legend resides in the memorials to the men who died in the First World War, later extended to embrace other wars. Memorials are also expressions of nationalism, the nation being 'imagined as a community', which regardless of factors such as inequality or exploitation, is always conceived of as 'a deep horizontal comradeship'.[24] Such a community has in the past been the subject of gendered imaginings in which the comradeship produced by male endeavour such as warfare has been paradigmatic. Tombs or other memorials to unknown soldiers have remained the most powerful nationalistic symbols, being void of identifiable remains and therefore 'saturated with ghostly national imaginings'.[25] Nowhere has there yet been a memorial to the unknown women whose comradeship and sufferings have been as deep as those of the men who fought, and whose pain and loss have been even greater perhaps, by virtue of the fact that historically women have had little impact on the policies and actions of male leaders of nation states, that is, those who make the wars.

In the year of *Australia Remembers* the crowds attracted to the Anzac Day events, particularly the Dawn Service, not only increased but it was noted that the crowd was the most youthful for thirty years.[26] In spite of the fact that some of these had made their 'pilgrimage' to the Melbourne Shrine straight from the local nightclubs and 'were horsing around a wee bit and there was a lot of cuddling going on, but as soon as the numbers built up they became quite serious',[27] it was apparent that the sacred nature of the occasion had been successfully conveyed. The timing of this service or 'rite of mourning for the dead' held at dawn to remind those participating that the Anzac troops were landed at Gallipoli before dawn in 1915[28] was probably influential in the trend of the young to move on from nightclub to Shrine. From my own observations of the Dawn Service over the last decade, it seems that attendance may be becoming almost trendy, followed by breakfast afterwards at any number of the nearby cafes. Furthermore, it is not only in the cities that such an increased interest and participation exists. In the Northern Territory young people were among the 2,000 who in 1995 attended 'the biggest dawn service in years', some of whom later marched with their relatives.[29]

Alistair Thomson has noted however, that such trends were already evident at the 1987 Dawn Service and march in Melbourne. A 'striking feature' was the 'diversity of the groups', with young people 'particularly prominent', many of whom marched wearing the medals of relatives unable to attend. In the same year Anzac Day became more inclusive also, with Women's Land Army veterans allowed to march for the first time.[30] Nevertheless, it may well be that few of the young have little accurate knowledge of the history of the Anzacs, judging from a 1997 survey of children between ten and eighteen years of age. All displayed only vague ideas about the geographical location of Gallipoli and what occurred there, apart from it being 'an important place to remember' as one sixteen-year-old put it.[31]

The renewed interest in the Anzac Day ceremonies on the part of the young has been interpreted by some as 'a hopeful sign that as a nation, we have progressed a bit from the angry years of the '60s and the '70s'.[32] Others have seen this to be an expression of the paradox that the further in time from war the less repellent it becomes, or that the harsh economic climate of the 1990s may have concentrated the minds of the young on 'the virtues of self-discipline and sacrifice that feature so largely in the Anzac story'.[33] Indeed, newly incumbent Prime Minister Howard expressed pleasure at the increased numbers attending Anzac ceremonies throughout the country, being particularly gratified to see more young Australians taking an active interest, believing this signified that cynicism about Anzac Day had evaporated among the younger generation.[34] For Victorian RSL president, Bruce Ruxton, the renewed popularity of Anzac Day was also welcome. In 1997, however, he manifested a contradictory desire to limit participation in the march to ex-service personnel, by seeking to exclude children and grandchildren. At the same time Ruxton recognised that by the end of the twentieth century there would need to be 'a rethink about Anzac Day altogether'.[35]

Editorial and readers' responses to Ruxton's proposed ban were consistently critical, ranging from arguing that allowing children to march 'is about recognising this wider significance of the story and preserving it',[36] to expressions of anger and disappointment by veterans who felt that the day belonged to them. Others queried what they perceived to be the secularisation of what had hitherto been effectively a holy day.[37] For veterans, memories of the war ultimately remain personal, mingled with the rather gloomy view that as the older veterans 'conk out and the Korean blokes and the Vietnam blokes, then only the kids will be left to carry on', a ritual that they hope 'goes on forever'.[38] The complexity of diggers' attitudes to war itself and memory of it was expressed by a Gallipoli veteran who wrote to his granddaughter that there were really 'three soldiers: one as imagined by a civilian, two, the one the army hopes to make and the third is the one as seen by the soldier himself'. Among his memorabilia from the First World War was a photograph of two of his mates, 'smirking in Cairo with slouch hats askew',[39] and it is these men who most strongly express the desire for peace.

Bruce Ruxton's stricture that Anzac Day would have to be 'rethought' by the end of the twentieth century was contradicted by the belief of others, inspired by the recent record attendances. Their hope was that with the passing of the last of the original diggers, the day 'will take on a new meaning—its status is growing'.[40] Such hopes do not dispel concerns, however, of a continued greed for recruits to the male, militaristic, aspect of Anzac. Such a desire was problematically suggested by a front page, one-colour photograph of a little boy wearing a scaled-down army uniform, slouch hat pushed back on his head, medals pinned on his right-hand side, as he sat on the ground with an Australian flag beside him, saluting the march as it passed by. This image was described as 'the symbol of the new spirit of Anzac—Australia's children honouring with salute and flag those who fought wars the nation won't forget'. Further links between the generations—and the legend—were ensured by the announcement that thousands of veterans would be involved in a lecture program within NSW high schools, to give first-hand accounts of 'Australia's wartime achievements', the scheme being described by Premier Carr as 'the most potent form of teaching Australian military history' and of 'keep[ing] alive the Anzac spirit'.[41]

Indeed the death of Ted Matthews in 1997, 'the last original Anzac...who waded ashore on the narrow beach at Gallipoli before dawn on 25 April 1915'[42] had the effect of strengthening the tradition. His state funeral with full military honours at St Stephens Uniting Church in Sydney[43] provided an occasion for reflection on the meanings of Anzac. Much touted in the media as 'an ordinary man pitched into an extraordinary time, combining a larrikin's sense of adventure with a decent bloke's sense of duty', Ted Matthews was quoted as regarding Gallipoli as a fiasco caused by the 'bloody fools of the British Empire'.[44] A not uncommon attitude among World War I veterans, but the anti-British sentiment resonated with much of *Australia Remembers'* resolutely 'Australian' focus. The media's highlighting of the 'ordinary man' remained within the 'egalitarian ideology' that inspired the Anzac tradition.[45] Being 'vital symbolic embodiments of the Australian nationalist imagination because they established an identity', the Anzacs have enabled Australian nationalism to be founded not in the state but in the nation, which being conceived as separate from the state, expresses the nationalists' dislike of hierarchy because of its association in their world view with English social distinctions.[46] War and death in war have become the common themes in modern nationalism and Anzac 'supports the thesis that nationalism has become a dominant religion', which was expressed for the first time during the First World War itself and in the first Anzac march in London in 1916 after the devastating loss of the Dardanelles. This march was used by both British and Australian authorities, through a public recognition of the Anzacs' heroism, to boost morale.[47] In the same year the Toowoomba City Council established an Anzac Day Commemoration Committee to organise appropriate public recognition, out of which the ritual of Anzac Day has developed and been defined over time, self-consciously initiating the younger generation 'into the roles and duties of being "patriotic Australians"'.[48] By the mid-1920s Anzac Day had become a national holiday and by the end of the decade it 'was institutionalised as a popular patriotic pageant' organised by the Returned Sailors and Soldiers Imperial League of Australia (RSSILA).[49]

For some observers the Anzac traditions of 'drinking, fighting, gambling and insubordination' were 'metaphors of both an Australian and an Anzac culture of individual autonomy'.[50] This is suggestive of the ways in which the construct 'Australian' has privileged the male as the dominant factor and subsumed women's participation in the nation under the catch-all imagery of egalitarianism. The participation of politicians of all ideological persuasions in Anzac Day ceremonies, and prime ministerial appropriations of its meanings to their respective political and personal agendas, has been interpreted as 'illustrative of their concern to be identified with the people'.[51] Anzac Day has been regarded as 'too sacred to risk it being tarnished' by becoming simply an excuse for another long weekend. Such views have suggested that this day emphasises 'what it is to be Australian' and also creates feelings of 'community'. In these ways Australians have been said to have found clues about how to answer questions about themselves, that the occasion has 'given them a starting point in finding a national identity'.[52] Such a process however has remained firmly controlled by males in spite of the inclusion of women in Anzac Day ceremonies. The 1980s protests by women against rape in warfare and feminist critiques of male glorification of militarism and the ritual of mourning dead soldiers, whilst contesting these masculinist values, have been unable to fundamentally change the ways in which the nation has engaged in public commemoration of the legend each year.

The particular sacredness of Australia's 'holy day'[53] was translated by Australia's official historian of World War I, C.W. Bean, into the building of 'the finest monument ever raised to any army', variously named by him as a temple or a shrine to the 'sacred memories of the AIF', whose commemoration he regarded as a 'sacred task'.[54] When the national memorial to the glorious dead, the Australian War Memorial, was finally opened on Remembrance Day 1941 after years of delay and controversy, Prime Minister Curtin declared it would 'give continuity to the Anzac tradition'.[55] By this time thousands of Australian troops, including Ray Walsh of the *Australia Remembers* logo, had been captured by the Germans, and the Japanese attack on Pearl Harbor was less than a month away. The need for such a formal representation of the tradition at the time, given that a new generation of Anzacs was actually perpetuating the tradition, was indicative of the perceived importance of symbolic representation of the Anzac legend. The gendered representation of warfare was also ensured within the Hall of Memory, the design and building of which was beset by controversy.[56] Within the Hall of Memory are three windows in which fifteen figures from the First World War are depicted, only one of which is female. Each figure depicts a quality supposedly associated with Australian conduct in war, such as 'social qualities' (comradeship and patriotism), 'fighting qualities' (coolness, bravery and endurance), and 'personal qualities' that include the virtues of 'resource, candour, devotion (a nurse), curiosity and independence'. There is also at each corner of the Hall of Memory a glass mosaic-constructed, uniformed figure 'representing the three services and nurses from 1939–1945'. It has been remarked that these 'disparate elements' within the Hall of Memory actually fail to 'engender that mood of reverence, that sense of entering a sacred place' so longed for by Bean, merely causing confusion in visitors as to how to define its intended nature.[57] There could be little uncertainty however, about the gendered representation in this Hall of Memory, where women's roles in both wars is represented in a one-dimensional manner, solely as nurses.

As has been noted, war memorials have played a particularly important part in the creation of national myths, with the Anzac Day rituals being 'the closest thing…to a ceremony of nationalism'.[58] They have been particularly important, perhaps, to the strand of nationalism that has developed within non-Indigenous Australia in which memorials to the war dead have been exclusively for white males,[59] which has also perpetuated the myth that there was no warfare on the various 'frontiers' between white settlers and Aborigines.

Aotearoa/New Zealand on the other hand, where the tradition of erecting such memorials began earlier, by 1900 had ten memorials to those who had 'fallen' in the New Zealand wars, the first of which memorialised 'friendly Maori' who had died defending the township of Wanganui from Hau-hau attacks.[60] Whilst in both countries there has been a strong desire to express, through memorials, their contributions to the cause of the Empire as well as mourning the dead, there have been quite marked differences in the manner in which this has been carried out, Aotearoa/New Zealand having a significantly higher percentage of soldier figures in memorials. New Zealand memorials traditionally have contained also 'iconographical images such as fern leaves or the southern cross with a distinctive national meaning'. In addition, national politics have influenced the ways in which the war dead have been memorialised. Aotearoa/New Zealand has honoured those who died far away, whereas Australia has self-consciously honoured the digger himself and recorded the names of those who served and returned, rather than simply those who died.[61] The divisiveness of the conscription issue in Australia in World War I has been a major influence in the privileging of the digger within the Anzac legend and the rituals through which this has been expressed. Aotearoa/New Zealand's national remembering on the other hand has been more inclined to include Maori, whereas Australia's remembering of warfare has been almost exclusively a European act of remembrance and the Anzac legend has been the primary focus.[62] Furthermore, the involvement of Australian Indigenous people in both world wars, as well as other wars in which Australia has fought, has been a matter of singular exclusion from the national memorialising of wars.

Pilgrimages to sites of memory

The allocation of funds by *Australia Remembers* to honour veterans through a series of pilgrimages to sites of memory overseas was in keeping with the ways in which the Anzac tradition's continuing importance was articulated, alongside the desire to make it more relevant to all Australians. Indeed, the word 'pilgrimage' with its connotations of journeys of religious devotion was redolent of the ways in which these memories were to be evoked and transmitted to Australians as a whole. The sites at which the pilgrimages took place became places where the nation's identity resides. In all there were three *Australia Remembers* pilgrimages: to England for the VE Day celebrations and two rather more sombre pilgrimages, to Papua New Guinea and Borneo,[63] in June and July respectively.

In addition, there was what turned out to be a botched pilgrimage to Anzac Cove to commemorate the eightieth anniversary of the original also botched landing on the Gallipoli Peninsula. While Australian servicemen and women, members of the peacekeeping forces in the Rwandan capital of Kigali celebrated Anzac Day with the 'traditional 5.00 am gunfire, breakfast of Bundaberg rum and coffee and a dawn service', nine descendants of the original Anzacs led by Con Sciacca and Governor-General Bill Hayden, were preparing to commemorate the original landing at Anzac Cove.[64] Possibly the only thing that went as planned on this pilgrimage was the presence of the bipartisan spirit, upheld by Con Sciacca's determination to make this aspect of *Australia Remembers* work, by including his Opposition counterpart Wilson Tuckey in each pilgrimage, briefing him 'every step of the way' and giving him the opportunity to speak.[65] In all other respects it seems the occasion was more a comedy of errors, although those directly involved perhaps failed to perceive it as such.

Whereas an introductory tour of the Gallipoli battlefields for the media and the pilgrims two days before Anzac Day had been highly successful, with 'predictable but potent' images of young Australians kneeling at the graves of Anzacs, the main event was organised to begin with the dawn service at 5.30 am. This was to be followed by an international ceremony led by the Turkish president (flown in on a special air force helicopter, with stringent security precautions) four hours later and an Australian ceremony at Lone Pine at 12.15 pm. A combination of errors by both Turkish and Australian authorities ensured instead that the commemoration was indeed reminiscent of the original event. Veterans' Affairs Minister Sciacca and the pilgrims arrived at Anzac Cove at 4.45 am, but the traditional dawn service was held up, occurring thirty-five minutes late, a second service being held at Lone Pine for the Australian and New Zealand tourists who had missed the first one which had gone ahead without Mr Sciacca and his group of tearful pilgrims who had arrived ten minutes late, being held up by over-zealous Turkish transport officials. At the same time, the busloads of mainly backpacking Australian tourists (who had paid $200 for the bus tour) were encountering trouble actually getting up from the bottom of the hill to Lone Pine. Criticisms were levelled not only at the officials from both Turkey and Australia who were held responsible in different ways for the debacle, but particularly at Governor-General Bill Hayden, who it was felt might have saved the day had he had the generosity of spirit to explain that there had been a delay and to have apologised for proceeding with the ceremony. Indeed, it seemed the only person not blamed for the debacle was Con Sciacca, who was cheered by the pilgrims upon his return from the official lunch, having waited on the balcony of their hotel for more than two hours for this purpose. As it was, the spontaneous ceremony which included the playing of the 'Last Post' on the didjeridu by a backpacker, staged by hundreds of tourists whose way to Lone Pine had been barred, was regarded as the 'best event of the day'. The pragmatic suggestion that the Governor-General should have intervened to prevent the Lone Pine ceremony from proceeding before the arrival of the pilgrims pointed to the complex semiotics of ritualised memorialising of this most sacred of days, with the symbolism of the dawn service being of central importance.[66]

From the Australian perspective it seemed the anger over the second Gallipoli disaster was confined to the series of bungles which had marred the occasion and the behaviour of the Governor-General, whereas for the British the occasion provided a clear indication that Keating's nationalist agenda was well and truly on track. A journalist for the *Spectator* newspaper later reported that he seemed to be almost the only British person present and that 'maybe it was just as well', as Britain, unlike former enemy Turkey towards whom the Australians were 'generous and forgiving', was 'unmentionable, the land whose name they neither dared nor cared to speak'. The Australian education curriculum allegedly was largely to blame for this, as well as Australian political opinion, which has built up 'a legend of betrayal by the Mother Country, the aim being not only to hasten the...republic but also to distort the history of British links with former dominions'. Claiming that the ceremony at Lone Pine had been 'thoroughly British' in its form and content but not in its participation, the journalist decried the absence of any reference to the twenty-seven British graves alongside the 153 Australian and thirty-five New Zealand 'comrades-in-arms in what is now called "the Anzac cemetery"'. To make matters worse, Governor-General Hayden's speech had repeated the 'amazing' tale of the efficient landings of the British and French eighty years earlier, which had resulted in the 'main burden of casualties to be borne by Australia and New Zealand'. Comparing figures of casualties at Gallipoli, in which Australia was overshadowed by Britain and France, he was prepared to be sympathetic to the Anzac legend only if it remained separate from a:

> campaign to drag war cemeteries and figures of men
> killed in war into politics and the debate on constitutional

reform, to portray the British not only in their traditional role as upper-class incompetents but also as cynical and treacherous mass murderers.

Readers of this outburst were doubtless left wondering at the journalist's backhanded compliment to the Anzacs. Characterising the original Anzacs as 'awesome fighters...being all volunteers and non-professional [who] sometimes irritated the British by their lack of discipline',[67] he unwittingly gave potent reinforcement of some of the legend's core elements, particularly those of fighting prowess combined with larrikinism.

If the Anzac Cove pilgrimage was something of a comedy of errors, the same cannot be said for the three official *Australia Remembers 1945–1995* pilgrimages, the first of which was for VE Day. The pilgrims on this occasion were carefully chosen from most states and the ACT, except for Tasmania and the Northern Territory. All were Anglo-Australians. Their route to the VE Day celebrations included a tour through the Australian battlefields of Greece and Crete.[68] The official Department of Veterans' Affairs video of this first pilgrimage was a fairly low-key representation, beginning with the 'Last Post' being played, with the pyramids and the *Australia Remembers* logo in the background, then cutting to scenes of the pilgrims standing in front of the pyramids, then to scenes of Greece, and the Eiffel Tower.

It was the Borneo and Papua New Guinea pilgrimages, however, which attracted close media attention, consistent with *Australia Remembers*' primary focus on the war in the Pacific. This was borne out by the Department of Veterans' Affairs video of the Papua New Guinea pilgrimage in which tribute was paid to the Royal Australian Navy and the Merchant Marine for keeping the lifeline open between the Coral Sea and Papua New Guinea. The video then focused on the fact that it was the Australian Army that drove the Japanese back, 'to eventual destruction and defeat, at great cost'. While this point was being made, archival footage of battles and the ubiquitous mud were shown and a male voice-over dramatically invoked the bombings of Darwin and Port Moresby, followed by footage of Papuans carrying supplies over very difficult terrain. The video then switched to colour, to show the pilgrims, assembled at Circular Quay in Sydney, being farewelled by schoolchildren waving Australian and *Australia Remembers 1945–1995* flags, with the commentary reminding viewers that the pilgrims were embarking on a journey to 'some of the sacred sites of our history'. In farewelling the pilgrims to Papua New Guinea, Prime Minister Keating reiterated this phrase, describing this 'heroic generation [as] very young and scarcely out of school' who had 'fought and won the battles which saved Australia', defeating an 'implacable and ruthless enemy'. The profundity of their heroism was something about which Keating's generation had learned, but would remain as indelible a hundred years from now. True to his desire for the *Australia Remembers* commemorations to be inclusive of all who had served, Keating praised the role of 'the Australian Women's Army Service, those who nursed the wounded, *all* who nursed the wounded, *all* those women who gave their energies to the war effort at home', some of whose husbands did not return and who were amongst the pilgrims. The Royal Australian and Merchant Navies were also mentioned, and the 'courage and compassion [which] forms a legendary part of our history', provided by the support given to Australians from the people of Papua New Guinea.

The pilgrims

Whilst the selection of the VE Day pilgrims had been carefully designed to achieve a balanced representation from all the forces as well as a nurse, the Papua New Guinea and Borneo pilgrims were less formally and more democratically selected, with local members of Federal parliament and *Australia Remembers* committees being directly involved in this process. This was particularly evident in rural areas, where local newspapers featured articles about the proposed pilgrimages that were often announced by the local member of parliament in association with RSL sub-branches. In what one rural newspaper called 'an exciting ballot...nationwide', one hundred and twenty positions were offered for the PNG pilgrimage and twenty-five for Borneo, it being required that nominees had seen active service in either region. In addition, the RAAF Association, the Merchant Navy

League and Naval Association were invited to provide nominations on a proportional service representation, and the War Widows' Guild was asked to nominate six representatives for the PNG Pilgrimage and two for Borneo, with the stipulation that the war widows must have lost a partner in either region.[69] The religious quest that these pilgrimages represented would be enhanced by the sacrifice and sorrow that lay behind such criteria for the war widows. Nominees were required to be medically assessed fit for overseas travel, and in anticipation of the bitter disappointment those not selected might experience, much was made of the fact that it 'must be remembered that veterans lucky enough to be drawn from the two ballots…will be representing all Australian ex-servicemen and women, as well as their country'.

The sites of remembrance taken in by the pilgrimages were to include 'visits to historic locations where some of the fiercest fighting of the entire war took place', including Port Moresby, Oro Bay (Buna, Gona and Sanananda), Lae, Kokoda, Bit Paka, Wewak and Milne Bay, and the Borneo pilgrimage would visit places such as Jakarta, Sandanan, Ranau, Labuan and Singapore, with the highlight being attendance at the RSL 'ceremony of remembrance for those who died during the infamous Sandakan "Death Marches"'.[70]

The visual images of the pilgrims presented by newspapers conveyed contradictory messages, but the most vivid was the ravaged-looking face of Owen Campbell, the only one of the three surviving Sandakan POWs still alive in 1995 who was well enough to be a pilgrim. Under a headline 'Death march survivor recalls jungle nightmare', Mr Campbell's eyes appeared heavy with the 'terrible secrets' that he carried silently for the past fifty years, because he did not 'believe in stirring up a hornet's nest—the sons and wives will start to think the worst of what happened', and his lined face was clasped in his two hands, his mouth sadly turned down at the corners.[71] In all, this photograph presented an image of suffering endlessly endured. Another photograph showed him in a happier mood in his shirtsleeves, medals pinned to his shirt, slouch hat on and camera in hand, being embraced by the son of a man who had died at Sandakan.[72] In this photograph Mr Campbell, while smiling, looked surprised and slightly stiff, perhaps preferring to be able to quietly reflect on the scenes he had brought his camera to record, or perhaps he was fearful that this show of emotion by the dead man's son might interfere with his determination to be stoical, having been described in the accompanying article as appearing 'to steel himself against any show of emotion, as he stood apparently dry-eyed before the memorial'. Yet another newspaper article, headlined 'Diggers return to bitter memories in Borneo' carried a curious photograph of 'Mr Ikeda, a former soldier of the Japanese Imperial Army, [posing] with one of the Australian veterans in the jungle near Sandakan'. Whilst the Australian veteran looked slightly nonplussed in the photograph, having one arm somewhat loosely around the shoulder of the Japanese veteran, his camera in the other hand, the latter looked thrilled that the moment was being recorded, a wide and happy smile across his face and his arm actually appearing to hug the Australian to his chest. He too was apparently intent on making his personal record of the event, sporting two cameras around his neck,[73] seemingly blissfully unaware of the Australian stereotype of the Japanese that he was fulfilling. Not all were so happy, though, at the unexpected presence of Mr Ikeda and twelve other Japanese veterans on the same track outside Sandakan. For their part, the Australians were actively unforgiving, no one having 'a good word to say about the Japanese', being unable 'to forgive nor forget because of the things I saw', one later regretting that he had not pushed the Japanese off the track. Mr Ikeda was determined to maintain his war-time innocence claiming he had never killed any Australians, who he now considered to be friends of Japan and expressing his sorrow that 'we had to come and invade Borneo and other places'.[74]

The presence of the Japanese delegation whose leader some-what blandly expressed the view that fifty years later it was 'time to forgive if not forget', adding that the veterans in his party wanted to 'rid themselves of guilt by apologising to the ex-POWs before they die', was met with determined opposition from Allied veterans. Their affronted responses ranged from the mildness of the Dutch who simply requested that the Japanese be kept away from their ceremony in Kanchanaburi, to the aggressive British response that 'If I was to meet a Japanese guard who worked on the railway I would have no compunction about belting him'. For their part, the Australian pilgrims responded by boycotting a 'peace march' across the bridge on Thailand's River Kwai because of the presence of former Japanese guards.[75] Less than two years later, following the death of the last Australian Sandakan survivor, Keith Botterill, a national appeal for Sandakan camp memorabilia was launched by the Federal Government, for a planned memorial at the campsite.[76] It seemed as if the passing of the last survivor had heightened the need to create a physical sign of the sacredness of this site of suffering which it was believed expressed a core aspect of the Australian national identity.

An aspect of the Borneo and Papua New Guinea pilgrimages, albeit a fairly minor one, was the acknowledgement of the role of the indigenous populations throughout the war. The obituaries to Keith Botterill elaborated on how he and his 'three mates' who escaped had been 'befriended by some local people, who gave them food and protection',[77] which was not only dangerous but also a considerable sacrifice given that their own dietary requirements had been severely affected by the demands of the Japanese.

Papua New Guinea and 'fuzzy wuzzy angels'

Perhaps more than any other indigenous people over the fifty years since the war, however, the Papua Guineans had become a part of the Australian consciousness about indigenous participation in the war, visualised through photographs of Papuan supply bearers and particularly through George Silk's famous *Life* photograph of Raphael Oembari assisting wounded Australian digger 'Dick' Whittington to safety. Curiously, this was not chosen for the *Australia Remembers* Papua New Guinea commemorative poster. Given that the Australian War Memorial holds the photograph and a bronze sculpture of it has been struck and placed outside a services club in a Canberra suburb, it would not have been difficult to reproduce this famous image for the Papua New Guinea commemorative poster. Instead the poster featured an Australian digger helping a wounded 'mate', his arm in a sling and head bandaged (much like 'Dick' Whittington in the George Silk photograph), the stub of a hand-rolled cigarette in his mouth. The choice of this all-Australian photograph seemed to reinforce the

Figure 6: Curiously, George Silk's famous photograph of wounded Private 'Dick' Whittington being taken to safety by Raphael Oembari was not featured on the *Australia Remembers* Papua New Guinea commemorative poster. Instead, a totally Australian image was used, which effectively mirrored this photograph. AWM Neg. No. 014028

nationalist pride taken in the often repeated fact that the first defeat of the Japanese on land was inflicted over the Owen Stanley Ranges by Australian troops. The two Australians on the poster conveyed the essence of the national identity derived from the Anzacs, with mateship as its defining characteristic.

For the past fifty years however, Australia has effectively appropriated the imagery of wartime Papua New Guinea and its people, and in the process has furthered a stereotyping of the Orokaiva people of Oro Province, as 'fuzzy wuzzy angels', taken from a poem which suggested that their presence was sufficient to make soldiers 'think that Christ was black…', and exhorting the 'Mothers of Australia' to pray for those 'impromptu angels/with their fuzzy wuzzy hair'. Raphael Oembari, who died in the year following *Australia Remembers,* became *the* 'fuzzy wuzzy angel'. Ignored in the Australian imagining of the fuzzy wuzzy angel has been that the Orokaivans 'assessed the situation and negotiated the safest strategy for the survival of themselves and their families. A few specific people with qualities of leadership took part in more dramatic action', and thus it is unwise to categorise them as a group.[78] This preferred postwar image of the fuzzy wuzzy angel endured throughout the *Australia Remembers* program, the 'angels' receiving significant media attention. A speech by a Wollumbin High School student, on the theme of the bravery of the soldiers along the Kokoda Trail and the forgotten heroes of the war, nurses, doctors and 'fuzzy wuzzy angels'[79] demonstrated the ease with which this image had been handed on through the generations. The presence of 'Angel' Raphael Oembari at the VP Day celebrations in Townsville[80] as a part of a Papua New Guinea contingent which included twelve World War II veterans and more than eighty dancers, was a source of pride for Papua New Guinea, judging from the remarks of Port Moresby Governor (and later prime minister) William Skate, who appeared to have chosen to add credence to the European construction of Oembari and the 55,000 others who had risked their lives to save wounded Australians, as 'the other'. Commenting on the heroic status of Mr Oembari within his own country, Mr Skate described his country and people as primitive, because 'we did not have educa-tion—that came after the war—so we did not have any army'. By providing a uniform identity for Papua New Guineans, he suggested they were happy to participate in the war 'because Papua New Guineans love helping their relatives and friends. It is part of our culture', at the same time adding his voice to demands that the payment withheld during the war now be made.[81] What this construction blithely overlooked, as much as the prevailing Australian version of the 'fuzzy wuzzy angel' was that they were at this time a colonised people, some of whom had not only preached independence and the eradication of Europeans from their midst, but had also participated in the massacre of some Australian missionaries. For Papuans, the sight of their white masters having to fight for survival transformed their self-perception, whereby they became 'partners in a needed role for the first time', gave them hope for the future.[82]

The 'heroic and often silent feats of the Papua New Guineans and Pacific Islanders in aid of Australia's war effort' was the central theme for the ten-day festival in Townsville, which had been designated a national *Australia Remembers 1945–1995* event, Townsville having particular relevance for many Australian soldiers, having been the final image of Australian before leaving for battle in the Pacific or New Guinea.[83] For Prime Minister Keating however, their role was particularly important also, because they were present at what he regarded as the moment of Australia's greatness. The story of the Pacific war was a collective one, he suggested, and fifty years later 'we in Australia celebrate the feats of the Pacific nations as part of our own story', including those of the legendary 'fuzzy wuzzy angel[s]'.[84] Such sentiments seemed well received in the context in which they were expressed, in spite of the complex and less than consistently satisfactory relationship between Australia and its former colony of New Guinea, as well as its at times ambiguous responses to the handling by the PNG government of the Bougainville Island secessionist movement. Arguably of more importance however, was the hint of appropriation in Paul Keating's inclusion of all within Australia's 'story', which suggested a lingering attitude of colonial ownership.

It seems Mr Oembari's visit to Townsville for VP Day celebrations was prompted more by a desire to settle what was for him fairly urgent business and to assert some personal autonomy, expressing his unhappiness that his photograph was 'all over Australia but he had not benefited for the brave things he had done during the war'. The necessity to discuss the question of compensation for his vital assistance more than fifty years ago, for which he had an appointment with Prime Minister Keating, was exacerbated by the fact that during his previous trips to Sydney and Canberra, 'he was not given pocket money and said the government had forgotten he lived in the bush and had very little money to spend'.[85] Indeed, Mr Oembari appeared less interested in gaining compensation in the European sense in which the word was used by the media, on the whole sympathetic to his case. Rather, something more like a traditional reciprocal exchange with very specific personal needs was being articulated. He expressed the view that:

> If the Australian Government feels my help was so important, then they could give me a house in my village, a vehicle to get back and forth to the hospital, a generator to give light in the night, and a little bit of money to live off until I die.[86]

Perhaps the fact that he had been persuaded to reverse his initial refusal to participate in the Townsville commemorative events was in his eyes further reason for the government to reciprocate in the tangible ways he had outlined. In spite of Mr Oembari petitioning the prime minister in 1992, seeking compensation on behalf of those carriers from the southern Kokoda Trail near Port Moresby who had not benefited from compensation payments of the mid-1980s,[87] the prime minister claimed only to have 'received a note' from Mr Oembari, to which he would reply as quickly as possible, adding that 'we appreciate very much what these people did for us'. In true politician's style, but also with an unfortunate touch of paternalism, Mr Keating sought to place responsibility for Mr Oembari's case upon the PNG Government, by adding 'but we would like to be able to do something for him'. The poignancy of Mr Oembari's plight was made visual with the inclusion of photographs of him being helped on to the stage by an Australian soldier for the VP50 ceremony in Townsville. Beneath this photograph was the flashback to the other, famous photograph of him leading the Australian soldier to safety. The images of both photographs were juxtaposed further by another of Mr Oembari in 1995, leaning on a walking stick held in his left hand, much in the manner that Private Whittington had leant on a similar stick in his right hand all those years ago.[88] Almost a year later, upon his death, Raphael Oembari was eulogised by the RSL's Major–General Digger James and Australia's Minister for Defence, Ian McLachlan, and at a memorial service in his south-eastern Oro Province he was honoured by a memorial guard of four Australian and one Papua New Guinean soldiers.[89]

In his gesture that simultaneously honoured Raphael Oembari, as well as continuing to construct him as 'other', Paul Keating had also ventured that the wartime deeds of 'soldiers from our own indigenous communities' would probably never adequately be recorded,[90] because discriminatory practices during the war years had indeed made this difficult to record accurately. Furthermore, the vexed question of compensation extended beyond consideration of the 50,000 'fuzzy wuzzy angels' who had been drafted to assist the Australian war effort, the majority of whom received compensation in the mid-1980s, with follow-up offers to the outstanding cases in 1992, although clearly Raphael Oembari believed not all had been included in this.

Australian Indigenous peoples and service recognition

As Ken Inglis has observed, 'World War II imposed on Australians another difficulty not experienced by most other peoples in constructing a rhetoric of commemoration. You can't be born, or come of age, twice'.[91] *Australia Remembers*' commemoration of the Pacific theatres of war provided a solution to this dilemma. It represented the war as a time in which the national identity, traceable to the Anzacs at Gallipoli, was consolidated in the mud of Borneo and Papua New Guinea. It was here in the Pacific theatre that Australians, in the spirit of the Anzacs, fought and saved Australia.

Like the circumstances surrounding their wartime enlistment and service, the honouring of the Aboriginal and Torres Strait Islander contribution by *Australia Remembers* remained problematic, with a tension between the spoken praise of the prime minister and Veterans' Affairs Minister, and the unresolved dissatisfactions of some of those being praised. For the Prime Minister, reflection on Indigenous Australians' war efforts was included merely as part of a speech paying tribute to Pacific Island veterans at the Townsville VP50 celebrations. This seemed to suggest a belief in Indigenous homogeneity, with a paragraph or so being allocated to each nation's veterans. Such an absence of differentiation had the effect of detracting from his praise for the figure of perhaps 'as high as one in five' of the Aboriginal population who had served either in the armed forces or as labourers, along with the reassuring statement that:

> even if the Australia of the 1940s was blind to their bravery and loyalty, we see it clearly now. And we acknowledge it now. It must not be forgotten…These are stirring tales.[92]

The difficulty in stating the figure for Aboriginal and Torres Strait Islander involvement in the war arose because neither Commonwealth nor state governments had kept adequate records of the racial background of those enlisting, but it has been estimated that as many as 3,000 formally enlisted in the armed forces, with another 150–200 involved as *de facto* service personnel, in surveillance activities for which they received no formal recognition or pay. In addition, an estimated 3000 Indigenous men and women also worked as civilian labourers or in the war industries, making the overall contribution of Indigenous Australians 'higher than that for Australians as a whole'. Whilst their involvement in the war did not bring many of their desired political changes, it did provide albeit briefly, the experience of being treated as valued equals. It also gave many non-Indigenous Australians an appreciation of Indigenous living and working conditions, as well as knowledge about the denial of civil rights which they continued to experience once they removed their military uniforms.[93]

For his part the Minister for Veterans' Affairs had been anxious to encourage the Aboriginal and Torres Strait Islander Commission (ATSIC) to 'come up with events to recognise the involvement of about 3,000 of their people in wartime defence of Australia', and in a widely ranging speech on Indigenous Australia's contribution, had referred to the Anzac Day 1991 announcement that about 100 'Black Diggers' were finally to receive payment for their services as well as becoming eligible for repatriation benefits, with a total payout of about $1.4 million anticipated. Perhaps in response to this rather limited gesture, the people of Bathurst Island were more concerned to press for $90,000 compensation for war work for which they had yet to be paid.[94] Attending a memorial service at Nguiu airstrip in honour of Matthias Ulungura, a twenty-one-year-old Tiwi Islander who captured the first Japanese on Australian soil, Con Sciacca wished to acknowledge 'what [the Tiwi people] did fifty years ago', adding that *Australia Remembers* provided the opportunity to remedy the previous lack of official and public recognition. On the other hand, the Bathurst Islanders were more intent on gaining full recognition and monetary compensation, Bathurst Community Government Council President, Barry Puruntatmeri, pointing out that the war had been an important period in Tiwi culture, which the Australian Government had failed to fully appreciate.[95]

The Papua New Guinea and Tiwi people were not the only ones to use the occasion of non-Indigenous Australia's desire to remember the glorious past of the Second World War as a means to press their own specific demands, as Prime Minister Keating was to find when he visited Thursday Island with his three daughters for a ceremony at Anzac Park in order to lay a wreath in remembrance of locals who died in the war. Pictured in a clearly relaxed mood, with a floral wreath around his neck, both hands being shaken by locals, he was keen to praise the results of the High Court's Mabo decision and to reiterate his vision of an Australia that 'doesn't simply come from the traditions and customs of the people of European descent'. Perhaps to dispel any impression on the prime minister's part that this necessarily spelt an easy relationship between European Australians and Torres Strait Islanders, the Mayor of Thursday Island used the occasion to remind him of his 'vision that Australia will be a republic by the year 2001', and that the Torres Strait Islander people had their own 'vision of attaining self-government by the year 2000'. Keating's response, advocating a process for reaching a regional agreement through the Native Title Tribunal to resolve island land issues, and the establishment of a committee to examine the possibility of either increasing the powers of the TSI Regional Authority or perhaps creating a new commission separate from ATSIC, seemed to be received as adequate, at least for the time being.[96]

Consideration of the question of compensation for Indigenous ex-service personnel had not begun in earnest until the 1980s, when over seven million dollars were paid to more than 800 Aborigines and Torres Strait Islanders who had been underpaid during the war. This process continued until 1994, with the payment of more than one million dollars and the presentation of service medals to Aborigines who had patrolled the remote north Australian coast armed only with traditional weapons. Such payment also provided recognition of their exceptional bush skills but also as a means of preventing any Japanese invading forces from realising that they were in fact an organised military unit.[97] Three of these Aboriginal guerrilla fighters, from Geliwinku (Elcho Island), Maningrida and the outstation of Rurru, were reunited in an Arnhem Land Anzac Day service in 1995 with ex-Sergeant Ritchie who had helped form their special northern reconnaissance unit, and 'shared memories of the months they spent together walking vast distances across the Top End, preparing for a feared Japanese invasion'.[98] On the advice of anthropologist Donald Thomson, who had lived among the Yolngu people of East Arnhem Land for lengthy periods since the mid 1930s and who served in the air force during the war, forty-nine of these Aborigines had been formed into a guerrilla unit and informed that the government would be happy for them to kill any Japanese they encountered. Apart from being instructed in the European art of the use of Molotov cocktails, to be used against any Japanese aircraft attempting to land, these guerrilla fighters were to employ their traditional military weapons and skills, and were issued with three 'shovel-nosed' fighting spears and one wire fish spear for hunting. Fifty years later, former Sergeant Ritchie remained sure that 'the Japs [sic] would not have had much of a chance' had they landed in the north of Australia because of the superior military and survival skills of the Aboriginal unit. Payment however had consisted of a weekly issue of three sticks of tobacco.[99]

The minister's speech suggested a strong desire to redress past 'basically racist' practices and attitudes, and to dispel non-Indigenous Australia's ignorance of the extent of Aboriginal and Torres Strait Islander—unpaid or underpaid—involvement in the defence of Australia. He noted the enthusiasm with which this was done, and that Aboriginal and Islander people had begun to join the services as soon as war was declared, for which formal recognition had not been forthcoming for fifty years. Absent from both the prime minister and the Veterans' Affairs Minister's speeches however, were references to the second-class citizen status which Aborigines and Torres Strait Islanders resumed upon returning to civilian life, such as the right to drink in public bars only being extended to those who were exempted from the provisions of the Aboriginal 'Protection' laws of the various states. Torres Strait Islander and military medal winner Charles Mene, recalled the ways in which the war broke down racism, only to be experienced again in peacetime, having been refused entry to Brisbane hotels to have a drink with his 'mates' from the war, which made him 'very upset'.[100]

The precedent for Indigenous involvement in World War II had been set by over 300 Aboriginal and Torres Strait Islander servicemen in the First World War. A number of these had been awarded for bravery, for example Private Reginald Rawlings from Victoria who received the Military Medal. While the army was trying to develop a policy on Indigenous enlistment when the Second World War started, many simply went ahead and enlisted, reflecting the view that the war provided an impetus to their demands for citizens' rights, and that war service should be directly linked to this political struggle. Indeed, men from the Torres Strait regarded their participation as being sanctioned by God, as well as an opportunity to pursue the goal of full citizenship, one leader advising younger men that 'If you want freedom, now is your time'.[101] Some white people in authority, however, questioned the loyalty of Indigenous people. This not only manifested a peculiar paranoia, but also suggests an awareness—

perhaps unconsciously—of the legacies of violent dispossession and the immorality of the continuing denial of citizenship rights.

Having decided that the enlistment of Aborigines and Torres Strait Islanders was 'undesirable in principle', the basis upon which they were in fact 'allowed' into the forces rested upon a variety of racially motivated formulae to do with 'colour'. This had drawn protests from Aboriginal political organisations and state governments that were in support of the principle of Aboriginal enlistment. The ease with which Aborigines and Torres Strait Islanders enlisted varied, the RAAF being the easiest force to enter because of its need for large numbers of personnel.[102] Like many of their white 'mates', many also joined up because the war provided the opportunity to travel overseas, as well as gaining skills that might assist in obtaining employment after the war. Significantly, it also provided the opportunity for Aborigines and Torres Strait Islanders, as non-commissioned officers, to command white Australians thereby enjoying an authority that had been and would again be an alien experience in peacetime Australia. Reg Saunders' leadership qualities led to promotion to Lance Corporal six weeks after enlisting in the army, and to Sergeant three months later, eventually being recommended for officer training, and completing his wartime service as a platoon commander in the 2/7th Infantry Battalion. He had joined up because of what he defined as 'a sense of duty to the country' and because he saw himself as merely following:

> in the footsteps of hundreds of other Aboriginals in World War I. The men that I grew up with—you know, my schoolmates' fathers and that—they were nearly all soldiers or involved in the military. So I thought it was just a normal thing.

Saunders, who was a nephew of World War I hero Reginald Rawlings, was adamant that he was fighting for Australia and that he did not owe any loyalty to Britain, which 'tried to bloody destroy me, and my family, my tribe, my people'.[103]

Notably absent in the commemorations were references to the fact that Australian Indigenous servicemen had also had been

Figure 7: The *Australia Remembers* Aboriginal people
and Torres Strait Islanders commemorative poster
featured a photograph of Sgt. Leonard Waters, the only
Aboriginal fighter pilot of the Second World War. This
inset photograph of Lt. Reg Saunders shaking hands
with fellow officer graduate resonated the 1990s theme
of 'Reconciliation'. AWM Neg. No. 083166

prisoners of the Japanese, including at Sandakan[104] and at Changi
where the brothers of the poet and Australian Women's Army
member, Oodgeroo Noonuccal had been captive.[105] Like their white
counterparts, they too starved and suffered and returned with physical and mental wounds. Similarly, their families, mothers, sisters and
lovers would also have had to cope with the worry while they were
imprisoned, and with the ongoing effects of their experiences after
their return.

Aboriginal and Torres Strait Islander women served as nurses
and support personnel during World War II, as well as bearing the

brunt of economic and personal hardships. These women were ignored throughout the *Australia Remembers* commemorations of Indigenous Australians. This silenced important gendered memories such as those of Torres Strait Islander women. Thanks to an oral history project, some of these women had the opportunity to speak of their 'real fear' of 'white men, men in uniforms, men with guns, and fear of the machines of modern warfare', with bombs dropped on Nurupai being heard 'and vibrations felt on neighbouring islands'. As well, these women shared the universal impact of warfare—the care of the children and constant worry about their safety. With the Torres Strait declared a war zone, they struggled to maintain their families, with restrictions on their movement exacerbating their difficulties in obtaining adequate food from their gardens. Positive aspects of the war's impact on these women were similarly ignored, such as the manner in which they filled the gap left by evacuated white teachers, thereby contributing to the realisation of the goal of an improved standard of education as a part of their struggle for citizenship rights. Similarly, the departure of whites had enabled Torres Strait Islander women to become the dispensers of medical advice and treatment. A particularly significant aspect of this was that they reclaimed their cultural knowledge by resorting to the previously outlawed bush medicines as supplies of western medicines ran out.[106]

Not only was the war a time when Indigenous men and women were able to enjoy a degree of freedom from the constraints of the various state and territory restrictive legislation, and also to gain acceptance and educational, employment, and training opportunities from the Anglo-Australian system, but Aboriginal men were to find that starvation and the diseases of beri-beri and malaria did not know racial barriers. In such cases the phenomenon of mateship, born among white Australian men in the bush they had often brutally taken from Aborigines, was an important added dimension to their wartime experiences. This made it easier for men such as Charlie Livermore of Tamworth to cope, recalling that 'there was a lot of my mates there with me. We were together all the time'. As James Duffield observed in a film about Aboriginal and Torres Strait Islander service men and women who had fought in Australia's twentieth-century wars and peacekeeping missions, 'the colour of your skin don't stop bullets'.[107] For men like Mr Livermore *Australia Remembers 1945–1995* provided the first occasion on which they felt able to overcome their shyness—and perhaps feelings of having been marginalised again upon returning from the war—by joining in the VP Day events.[108]

Attempts by *Australia Remembers* to commemorate the assistance and service of Indigenous veterans was limited in its success however, in spite of what was clearly a genuine attempt to address issues of racial discrimination which had prevailed at the time and to include their participation in the 'story' of World War II. Those Aborigines and Torres Strait Islanders who did participate in events such as VP Day appear to have done so in modest numbers, as members of their wartime units, rather than under their own flag as had occurred in Brisbane on Anzac Day in 1994.[109] Indeed, it would seem that generally speaking they did not take much interest in remembering the war,[110] or in the program. There was a continuity in this, it having been noted that in the 1980s members of the National Aboriginal and Islander Ex-Service Association had conducted their own separate commemorations on Anzac Day,[111] and it was not until 2001 that they included themselves in this event, as is discussed in the next chapter. Except in pressing their demands for recognition or compensation, Aboriginal and Torres Strait Islander voices were mostly absent from the national remembering of their involvement. This was indicative, perhaps, of their continuing marginal status within the state in spite of some significant formal gains since the war. In terms of 'national identity', Aborigines and Torres Strait Islanders remained outside of this. At key moments they were 'allowed in' but this was carefully contained, indicative of what Ghassan Hage has defined as a European practice of managing the national space, through gestures of tolerance and inclusion.[112] The Eurocentric celebrations of the nation may have simply appeared irrelevant in the context of the continuing struggles for justice and rights.

CHAPTER 6

The Legacy of
Australia Remembers 1945–1995

'If we forget, who will remember?'[1]

'Some people had to wait fifty years to be recognised—particularly the women who didn't go [overseas]...'[2]

'I am surprised that there has been no official mention of the sacrifices made by the Timorese people during World War II...'[3]

THE official activities of the *Australia Remembers* program ended on Remembrance Day, 11 November 1995, although a number of local groups continued to meet beyond that date. One of the four main themes articulated by *Australia Remembers* had been 'legacy', the desire to leave 'a permanent memory in our history'.[4] To this end, a 'Freedom Wall' was erected in Brisbane, so chosen because it had been Australia's main supply and service centre for the Allies throughout the Pacific war. The location of this national site of memory, explicitly linked to the Pacific war that had been privileged in the year-long national remembrance, resonated with the desire to remake Australia's wartime narrative. The 'Freedom Wall' also provided a permanent monument to *Australia Remembers* itself, the entrance proclaiming it the 'National *Australia Remembers* Freedom Wall'. Consisting of brass plaques purchased and inscribed by members of the public, the wall was dedicated on Remembrance Day 1996.

War widows and fields of remembrance

Other less permanent, but highly symbolic acts of public remembrance of an individual nature had been witnessed in 1995 through an initiative of the War Widows' Guild, involving the creation of fields of crosses in the various states. These enabled members of the public, who enthusiastically took advantage of the opportunity, to 'plant a cross' bearing a name or other inscription, in a very personal and direct act of commemoration. In Melbourne, a 'Field of Remembrance' had been set apart and dedicated at an ecumenical service at the Shrine of Remembrance at eleven o'clock in the morning of 2 July 1995, on a fine, sunny Sunday morning, before an estimated crowd of about 3000 people,[5] most of whom wore the medals of their deceased loved ones. Most of those present came in groups or family groups. Some included young children or grandchildren and a number of spontaneous reunions appeared to occur, and there was quiet, cheerful chatting before the ceremony began. As a media event, this seemed fairly low-key, with Channel Nine being the only TV channel present. It was not until around VP Day that the field—by now with some 7,000 crosses planted[6]—began to receive media attention and promotion of this quite visually dramatic means of commemoration.

In dedicating the Field of Remembrance, the Anglican Archdeacon of Melbourne prayed for God to bless the Field, and to keep it holy, 'that it may be a fitting place for memorials of honour and love to be placed within it'. The first cross was planted by Mrs Eileen Watt, President of the War Widows' Guild. As the last strains of the 'Last Post' were sounding, a jogger ran through the ceremony, and turned to cast a surprised look at what he had interfered with. After some stirring words about those being remembered being 'young, strong of limb [and] staunch', people then proceeded to a booth where they obtained crosses and marking pens to inscribe their messages or remembrances. They then dutifully formed themselves into a queue, where they were shortly urged to 'move around the front' by women bearing crosses and plastic buckets for donations. Brown and Dureau, a subsidiary of the Amcor Australia paper group, donated the crosses, which had been made by prisoners at the Coburg Prison Complex under arrangements made by the Victorian Department of Corrective Services. A number had been adapted to make them suitable for members of the Jewish community and carried inscriptions such as the stark 'Kiev 1941–42', and the poignant 'To all Jewish people who died in the Holocaust. And my great grandparents. 1995'. Single, more secular, stakes marked with the Star of David offered remembrance of 'righteous Gentiles' Oskar Schindler and Raoul Wallenberg with the inscriptions 'Brave beyond belief', while a German exchange student confronted her country's past with an apology and wondered whether forgiveness was possible. The desire for peace was evident in the inscription of a Japanese visitor, translated into English as, simply, 'Peace, please'.[7]

There were several crosses dedicated to the 'Unknown Soldier', and many messages to 'mates', while one cross particularly evoked the multicultural nature of postwar Australian society, with the message 'To all the brave soldiers who fought in the war, thank you for making our country the great place it is today', and on the vertical part, simply, 'Peace', with the names Kristy Martin, Nicky Doherty, and Phuong Huynh. AWPS '95'. The POW experience was not far from people's minds in planting these crosses, with one, for example, planted for 'Noel Taylor. Died POW Camp...the Uncle I never new [sic] with love', while the very brevity of others evoked the horrors of imprisonment. One such said, simply, 'Sgt Frank Reid—20.6.45. Last march—Sandakan'. Others spoke of the traumatic legacy of the war, a cross being dedicated 'For Dad—he never spoke about the war!!' The double marks of exclamation expressed, perhaps, the ways in which this silence had been a burden on other members of the family.

Four months later, the ashes from these crosses were scattered as a part of the Remembrance Day ceremony at Melbourne's Shrine.

Groups of women of the war generation arrived together, many wearing medals. A number also wore a sprig of rosemary, and *Australia Remembers* badges were a common sight. A schoolboy wearing his Cadet uniform attended with his parents and grandparents. As the World War II planes flew overhead just before eleven o'clock to coincide with the sounding of the 'Still', many in the crowd—young and old and male and female—wept, and continued to do so while the ashes from the crosses were scattered by members of the War Widows' Guild. Some of these women looked slightly discomforted by their role as actors in this ultimately personal drama, watched by the assembled crowd. One war widow in particular seemed determined to assert the personal significance of her actions, crossing herself as she began to scatter ashes over the ground where the field of crosses previously had been planted. After a while this part of the ceremony became too lengthy for some, and people began to drift away before it finished.

The Freedom Wall

In Brisbane, the ashes of Brisbane's Field of Crosses in King George Square during 1995 were incorporated in the 'Freedom Wall'. The Brisbane Field of Crosses had also been an initiative of the state branch of the War Widows' Guild, which, consistent with its record of quietly achieving rights for war widows since its inception in October 1945, had tended to maintain a fairly low profile throughout *Australia Remembers* events. A result of this was that in the national remembering of the war, the very particular sacrifices of war widows tended to be acknowledged within wider contexts of sacrifice, such as the VP Day Gala Concert in Melbourne or the Flame of Freedom performance at the conclusion of Brisbane's VP Day functions. In this way, the grief and suffering of war widows, consistently presented as widowed mothers, was managed and mediated through a range of other experiences, including that of male suffering and sacrifice. Representing war widows as mothers conveyed two main impressions, both of which were suitable to the overall process of national imagining and memorialising throughout 1995. Firstly, these women thereby attained a status of continuing respectability because they were settled and responsible people who now had to cope with rearing the children alone. This effectively rendered them as sexless objects of sympathy. Lastly, the representation of war widows as mothers added poignancy and pathos to their sacrifice.

The original vision for the 'Freedom Wall' had been based on the expectation that it would attract more than 35,000 commemorative plaques, but the change in federal government and a new Minister for Veterans' Affairs had resulted in a less than enthusiastic commitment to the concept. One result of this was that the absence of promotion of the concept resulted in only 15,000 plaques being sold, leading to the suggestion that the scheme be abandoned and plaques already received be returned. When this possibility became known, however, significant negative publicity in the Queensland newspapers and other media resulted in the future of the event, albeit scaled down, being assured. This meant that revised plans had to be prepared by the architect, and the original date of the opening of the Freedom Wall, 15 August 1996 (VP Day), was rescheduled for Remembrance Day.[8]

Located in the Brisbane Botanic Gardens at Mt Coot-tha, the memorial was designed by Brisbane architect, Robin Gibson, to be approached across a bridge, symbolising the fact that most of Australia's forces travelled overseas 'to defend our island continent'. The memorial is in the form of two straight walls intersecting a circular wall where the brass plaques are located, which represent the 'heart of the memorial...commemorating those men and women who contributed so much to Australia's freedom'. The walls radiate out to represent all parts of Australia. The plaques, which sold for $9.95 each, were arranged in groups of ninety-six, and engraved and arranged in five sections: alphabetical, schools, ex-service organisations, local authorities and community groups. They were specially treated to withstand the effects of the Brisbane climate and graffiti,[9] in spite of which their condition quickly deteriorated. The sour and almost farcical element that this introduced into this final act of the *Australia Remembers* program, seemed in a way to encapsulate the difference in style and degree of commitment to the project on the part of the incoming minister. The State Coordinator of *Australia Remembers* regarded the wall as insurance that the legacy of remembrance would endure beyond the program of commemoration, and that the plaques would provide an opportunity for 'women and their various roles' to be honoured. Indeed, the participation in the Order of Service of Mrs Jean Walters, President of the Queensland War Widows' Guild, provided a rare high-profile moment for the Guild. She spoke of the significance of the fiftieth anniversary for the Guild itself, and of how *Australia Remembers* had inspired 'very emotional, powerful memories, and also...wider understanding, particularly among the young', numbers of whom had particularly impressed her through their involvement in the planting of crosses in the Fields of Crosses in all the states during 1995.

Inscriptions on the plaques mirrored many of the messages which had been placed on the crosses in the various Fields of Crosses throughout Australia in the previous year, addressed to absent or un-met fathers, and giving thanks for 'freedom'. More recently deceased veterans were also included, such as 'Peter Jones, RAAF No. 59279 1924–1990. Remembered with love by wife Josephine and son Stephen'.

Themes of the Freedom Wall dedication ceremony

Perhaps mindful that this was the final act of *Australia Remembers*, Brisbane's Lord Mayor, whose strong commitment to social justice was to provide his themes, began by placing his friend and colleague Con Sciacca firmly at the centre of the ceremony, reminding those present that they would not be 'here today without the vision and drive of...Con Sciacca', and then thanking 'the new minister...for finishing this memorial'. The event, Lord Mayor Soorley continued, aimed 'to do a sacred deed', which linked those present to those 'men and women from every tribe and nation [who] have gathered to build and dedicate memorials...' throughout history.

The contemporary relevance of the 'Freedom Wall', he suggested, was to remind us 'that young Australians laughed and cried—yes, Aborigines too—were wounded and cared for', in many theatres of warfare. Touching upon other contemporary political agendas, the occasion provided Mr Soorley with the opportunity to

A.G. (BILL) JONES
VX46238
4TH ANTI TK REGT POW CHANGI
DIED AGE 40 YEARS 1959
ALWAYS REMEMBERED
KATHRYN, PAUL & DAUGHTERS

ALBERT EVAN JONES VX10744
29/46 AUSTRALIAN INFANTRY BATTALION
WITH LOVE FROM YOUR FAMILY
HOW, PROUD WE ARE

ALFRED THOMAS JONES
VX22435
MIDDLE EAST, MOROTAI & BORNEO
2ND 9TH DIV
25.3.1920 - 6.10.1995
SERVED HIS COUNTRY

NX69224. SPR. ARTHUR R. JONES
2/3 FLD. COY RAE 7TH DIV 2ND AIF
WITH LOVE & THANKS TO MY HUSBAND,
OUR FATHER & GRANDFATHER
FROM YOUR WIFE, CHILDREN &
GRANDCHILDREN

FOR MY UNCLES
BERT, STAN, KEVIN & KEITH JONES
(DALBY)
THANK YOU FOR THE FREEDOM
YOU HAVE GIVEN ME
LOVE HELEN

GRATEFUL THANKS TO
OUR HUSBAND, DAD AND POP.
"BUCK"
JONES

CLIFF JONES
HMS VICTORIOUS
JOAN JONES (NEE VENUS)
W.A.A.F.
CHARLES VENUS
MERCHANT NAVY

GUNNER GLEN HAROLD JONES QX35633
2/11 AUST FD. REGT
THANKS FOR YOUR EFFORT
DURING WORLD WAR 2
LOVE FROM YOUR WIFE BETTY &
DAUGHTERS JANICE, DIANE, BEVERLEY & ANN

SON LDR HARRY JONES BEN RAAF 1943 - 1976
OUR ETERNAL THANKS FOR YOUR DEDICATED
SERVICE TO RAAF AND AUSTRALIA
FROM SONS PETER AND TONY
GRANDCHILDREN DANNY, SARAH, DAMIEN
AND BRENDAN

TO MY LATE BROTHER
HENRY MAXWELL JONES
A.I.F. 1939 - 45
FROM RUTH

H.E.R. JONES (MACK)
78737
30 SQUADRON RAAF
THANKS FOR THE FREEDOM AND
PEACE WE SHARE TODAY
THE JONES FAMILY

PTE NORMAN FREDERICK JONES
VX53991
2/6TH INF BATT 17TH BRIGADE
FROM YOUR LOVING WIFE MAISIE
& PROUD CHILDREN PAMELA,
BRENDA & WAYNE

IN LOVING MEMORY OF
NORMAN SPENCER JONES
1909 - 1953
FROM FAMILY AND DESCENDANTS

THANKS FOR FREEDOM - MAINLY BELGIUM
TO PERCY DAVID JONES MC DCM ED
AND BERTHIE BILLAINE (BRACKE) JONES
(0893 - 1978)
(0936 - 1970)
JONES/MCCOMB/BURTON/FAMILY

R.A.A.F.
W/O P.G. (GEORGE) JONES
A 1413
LOVINGLY REMEMBERED BY HIS FAMILY

TO MY BROTHER
PERCY GUY JONES
A.I.F. 1939 - 45
FROM RUTH

TO MY LATE FATHER
PERCY MORRIS JONES
10TH LIGHT HORSE 1914 - 18
FROM RUTH

FROM MILDURA (VICTORIA)
PETER JONES
RAAF NO. 59279
1924 - 1990
REMEMBERED WITH LOVE BY
WIFE JOSEPHINE & SON STEPHEN

425663 F/SGT JONES T.S.
LOVINGLY REMEMBERED
BY
FAMILY AND FRIENDS

NO 21612 SPR T.W. JONES
A DUTY NOBLY DONE
FROM HIS FAMILY
VALERIE, PATRICIA & GAIL

CPL VIVIAN T. JONES
036876
42ND AUST INF BTN
ALWAYS CHERISHED

V.R.A. JONES QX 17479 2/26TH
JOY FOR THOSE WHO RETURNED
WE BEGIN TO UNDERSTAND
THE SILENCE

JONES, WILLIAM ARTHUR 43422
F/O D.P.R. RAAF
MAY FREEDOM PREVAIL
FROM YOUR LOVING FAMILY

TREASURED MEMORIES OF
SGT. WILLIAM C.M. JONES
2/3 ANTI TANK REGIMENT
9TH AUST DIVISION
HAZEL, GARRY, SUE & BRETT JONES
LISA & SCOTT BRADY

TO GUNNER WILLIAM F.A. JONES
WITH PRIDE
FROM
WIFE DOROTHY, LORRAINE LAW,
LAWRENCE MILLS, STANLEY & ELIZABETH
JONES, JEAN CONNELLAN

remember that many of those young Australians had died 'in Asian and Pacific lands with Asian and Pacific friends and Asian and Pacific comrades in arms'. With this memory refreshed, he hoped the wall would 'compel us to build up the institutions of our country, to challenge our politicians, parliaments, and civic leaders to enlarge our vision to build a country of greatness'.

As a media event, the opening of the 'Freedom Wall' was not particularly significant, it seems, except in its home state of Queensland. It received only passing mention in the *Australian*'s account of Remembrance Day around the country, whereas the *Age* appeared more interested that the racial discourse of Queensland Independent MP (later One Nation Party leader), Pauline Hanson, who was also at this event, had been countered by Jim Soorley in his speech. Neither newspaper bothered to include of the 'Freedom Wall' among their photographs of Remembrance Day in various parts of the country.

Australia Remembers 1945–1995—evaluation of its success

Before passing judgement on the program overall it is worth considering firstly, the ways in which the various state and territory committees assessed their work, and secondly, the reflections of Veterans' Affairs Minister Sciacca at the end of 1996. A submission to the Public Relations Institute of Australia prepared by the Community Communications program for *Australia Remembers* by consultant Peter Thomas of Turnbull Fox Phillips evaluated the ten key objectives of the '*Australia Remembers* Community Communications program'. These were to ensure nationwide publicity; to promote

Figure 8: The 'Freedom Wall' in Brisbane which was unveiled as the final event of *Australia Remembers 1945–1995*. The individual plaques provided a lasting monument through the expressions of personal memories as shown in these varied inscriptions.

selected major events to 15 August 1995; to promote state and local community events; to encourage all ex-service organisations to associate their activities with the commemorations; to encourage all communities to participate in commemorations and celebrations; to involve all Australians including various ethnic groups; to raise the awareness of young Australians and to promote the education kit throughout the country; to attract sponsorship for national, state and local events; to obtain oral histories and memorabilia from the war and the immediate postwar period; and to ensure *Australia Remembers* was recognised beyond 1995 as 'a meaningful program [which] captured and documented in our national history'.

All objectives were evaluated as having been achieved, with the exception of sponsorship about which it was noted there had been 'very limited success'. It was too early to evaluate the last objective, regarding the legacy of *Australia Remembers*. According to this evaluation, media attention to the program exceeded all other programs seen in Australia, with press clippings filling thirty-four lever-arch files by October 1995 and television news and current affairs segments monitored in Canberra alone producing more than fifty-seven hours of *Australia Remembers* segments. Over ninety per cent of ex-service organisations and of communities throughout the country were deemed to have participated, and an 'excellent success rate' of approximately seventy per cent of all Australians were estimated to have been involved in activities of various sorts, while the collection of oral histories and memorabilia was continuing.[10] Overall, the assessment of the various committees was positive, with nearly all noting the failure to attract corporate sponsorship or other financial support anticipated, as a 'disappointment'. Con Sciacca's view on this was that 'corporate sponsors were just shocking', the major corporations all refusing requests to become involved. He regarded their rejection as indicating that 'they didn't see anything in it for them', whereas he had 'thought they would be certainties', pointing out that BHP had 'made millions out of the war', as had Telstra (or PMG at the time). Australia Post, however, was 'fantastic' in its support, and there were some small companies who had good contacts with some of the chairpersons, but generally corporate sponsorship was 'a dud'. It was only when it was clear that *Australia*

Remembers had indeed struck a significant chord within the community that some of the corporations initially approached offered support, late in the program, at which time the minister told them, in no uncertain terms, that they were too late. Upon reflection, Sciacca felt that the absence of corporate support had actually been a good thing because it meant that the Australian public owned the events, because each time (twice) he went to Cabinet, he got what he wanted in terms of support, saying 'colleagues, if this doesn't tug at your heart strings, you haven't got one'.[11]

Not that private enterprise did not make money from *Australia Remembers*, with official licensed merchandise bearing the logo, being marketed by Bladon Australia Pty Ltd and seventeen other licensees, ranging from spoons, badges, flags, key ring holders and pens to port wine crocks, pilsener glasses, coasters, mugs, as well as shirts, jackets, jumpers, caps and sports bags. A compact disc or cassette featuring 'twenty-two unforgettable songs from the most popular artists of the war years, proudly supplied by CBS Records' no doubt was a popular purchase at $24.95.[12]

The Northern Territory Committee noted a further disappointment in relation to Aboriginal involvement, with responses from only three communities and/or Land Councils out of the eighty-three canvassed for their views on how the role of Aboriginal people could best be commemorated. Nevertheless, this Committee felt able to point to several positive events that had recognised Aborigines' roles during the war. These included the wreath-laying at Bathurst Island by Con Sciacca at the memorial to Matthias Ulunguru, who took the first Japanese prisoner of war in Australia after his plane crashed near the Island; presentation of Civilian Service Medals in Darwin to Mrs Phyl Hatch, an Aboriginal woman who had served in the Australian Women's Land Army in Queensland; and an oral history extract from Nellie Cam Foo in the Territory's education kit. Other positive outcomes included an Aboriginal Nursing Scholarship funded by the *Australia Remembers* Committee in conjunction with the Red Cross, the Australian Kidney Foundation and the Northern Territory University, as well as events that recognised the cultural significance of oral history. Also cited as key successes were the 'Back to the Track' military convoy re-enactment, and the 'Adopt-a-Vet' scheme whereby schools 'adopted' veterans, this being so successful that it would continue beyond 1995.[13]

For the Northern Territory *Australia Remembers* Committee, however, it was women's involvement in the war which was not only listed as one of its successes, but became the focus of a national reunion of ex-servicewomen in Darwin in June. This reunion had been planned since June 1993 when four women, two of whom were members of the NT Council of ex-servicewomen, were sitting in a spa and discussing ways to celebrate the fiftieth anniversary of the war's end. The idea of holding a reunion having been adopted by the Council, the initiators were 'staggered' by the response to their initial mail-out for what was to become the largest gathering of women from all ex-service organisations in Australia. While hardly 'corporate funding', it was in relation to more modest and specific events such as this, perhaps, that local businesses at least were generous in their support.

Similarly, the Canberra business community, while unwilling to provide 'significant sums of money', had assisted with smaller donations of up to $5000, and assistance by way of goods, services and venues. Overall the ACT's program was judged by its organisers to have been a success, the most outstanding event nominated being the 'Time Tunnel', an interactive display of Australian life in the 1940s. Some 60,000 people had visited this, free of charge, during its ten days of operation in May. The original plan for this display to run for only four days clearly did not anticipate the appeal of such opportunities to visit the past.[14]

It seems that Victoria was the sole exception with regard to relative success with corporate sponsorship. This had included $50,000 from Cadbury Schweppes, which doubtless also profited from sales of its 'quarter-pounder' blocks of chocolate in wrappings reminiscent of those used in 1945, $20,000 from Kodak (Australasia) Pty Ltd, and $22,000 from Tooheys Brewing Co Pty Ltd. A 'Tooheys Blue Commemorative Can' featured three designs commemorating the efforts of Australia's Army, Navy and Air Force. There were also smaller amounts from Fosters Brewing Group Ltd, the Phillip Morris Group (Kraft), Tattersalls and Transfield Defence Systems. Corporate support was also acknowledged in kind by the Victorian organisers, for example, the extensive and free promotion by Radio Station

Magic 693 of the 'Back to the Track', Ticker Tape Parade and Victory Ball, and the promotion and provision of 'significant resources' to assist with the organisation and conduct of events within the City's boundaries by the City of Melbourne, including some 120 large *Australia Remembers* banners commissioned by the City and displayed throughout August and for a week during November.[15]

Tasmanian organisers regarded the more memorable events in their state as being the Youth Forums of a hundred students and ten veterans who gathered into groups of ten to hear the veterans' wartime experiences. The main outcome of this was the students' realisation that the veterans had gone to war when they were the same age as the students. The state's first interfaith church service to coincide with VE Day, at which a representative from the Christian, Jewish and Islamic faiths each presented a reading in a Catholic church, each attendee being presented with an olive branch after the service, was also ranked among the more significant achievements in that state. Other noteworthy events included an International Peace Ball, as well as numerous reunions of former Divisions of the three forces. These shared the desire to focus on peace by avoiding any glorification of war, remembering instead 'sad, frightening and at times even funny situations'. While requests that ATSIC send a representative to the *Australia Remembers* meetings proved unsuccessful, members of Tasmania's Aboriginal communities organised an afternoon tea held by the Sports Aboriginal Corporation of Tasmania, a combined wreath-laying by the Flinders Island Community, a tree planting by the Mersey Leven Aboriginal Corporation and a photographic display of Aboriginal veterans from Furneaux Island Group which would form part of a book.[16]

When I interviewed Veterans' Affairs Minister Sciacca towards the end of the year of *Australia Remembers*, he suggested that response to the program within Western Australia had been fairly negative to start with. He felt this had been because a Labor government had proposed it, but that once the commemorations got under way the state had been impelled to join in. Perhaps this was even more reason for the satisfaction on the part of the WA *Australia Remembers* Committee chairman, Keith Mattingley, who felt that the 20,000 who had turned out for the VP parade in Perth, even though short of the hoped-for 50,000, had 'responded magnificently'. Particularly pleasing had been the 'tremendous' attendance of young people, many of whom paraded. This confirmed the trend, evident in recent Anzac Day events elsewhere in the country, 'that the community is becoming increasingly appreciative of what our veterans did'. Nevertheless, state–federal political tensions were not done away with even on this day, with State Liberal Premier, Richard Court, using the occasion to attack what he claimed was an unacceptably low level of defence personnel in WA, which he deemed 'a disgrace' in the light of the state being Australia's biggest export earner. The *West Australian*, however, did carry a remarkable story and photograph of reconciliation between British ex-POW Eric Lomax and ex-guard Takashi Nagase, who had been contacted by letter by Mr Lomax's wife in an attempt to help 'confront the demons which were still destroying his life' (and hers also, one assumes, although this was rarely mentioned in such accounts). A series of letters followed between the two, until Eric Lomax was convinced that his former tormentor was genuine in his desire to expiate the crimes committed during the war, and agreed to meet at the Kwai bridge. The reconciliation, believed by the Medical Foundation for Victims of Torture to be the only such case, enabled both men finally 'to put their own personal ghosts to rest'.[17]

Such a spirit of reconciliation was not always present in the streets of Brisbane on VP Day 1995, some Japanese tourists taking photographs of a giant kangaroo sculpture as well as enthusiastically waving Australian flags during the parade, prompting bitter reactions from some ex-diggers. Others warmly applauded RSL President Digger James' wreath-laying speech that dealt with the POW experience and the need for openness within Japan today about the 'hideous chronicle' of Japanese actions. No doubt some also gained satisfaction from the visible discomfort experienced by the Japanese Ambassador, seated among the official diplomatic party. His presence reflected his personal wish to express a sincere apology on behalf of his country,[18] an action that (by that time former) Veterans' Affairs Minister Sciacca highlighted when interviewed in the year following *Australia Remembers*.

During that interview in Brisbane on Remembrance Day 1996, Sciacca listed a number of particular achievements of *Australia*

Remembers. The first of these was what he termed 'proof in the pudding [that it] reignited a sense of gratitude and of the importance in history of that generation of Australians', noting that Anzac Day 1996 had been the biggest ever, which he regarded as a result of 1995. *Australia Remembers* had also provided 'a new lease of life and sense of belonging and appreciation to that generation'. He regarded the ways in which not just the soldiers were remembered, but also 'the ladies, the women, and all people on the home front', as a possible counter to his concern that Australian society was becoming a 'throwaway society'.

Sciacca also assessed the achievements of *Australia Remembers* in terms of having managed to avoid controversy, noting that with his 'excellent consultant, Greg Rudd', everything had been carefully calculated to anticipate any potential negatives. He paid tribute again to the bipartisan support he had gained immediately from his counterpart, Wilson Tuckey, who was 'there every step of the way' throughout the year. He appeared unconcerned, therefore, with the thought that some of the big issues of the war had been sidelined by the official program, and had received fairly limited media examination in Australia, most notably the anniversary of the use of atomic weapons against the people of Hiroshima and Nagasaki. Reminded by Gareth Evans of these anniversaries when initially discussing the concept of *Australia Remembers* with his Cabinet colleagues, Sciacca's response had been to avoid them, concentrating instead on the fiftieth anniversary of the lasting peace since then. Thus, he was able to feel convinced that by the time the anniversary of these bombings came about, the *Australia Remembers* program was 'so steeped and accepted in the psyche of the Australian people and the mainstream media' that any attempts to highlight what he termed 'the bad parts of what happened' would not get very far. The history he seemed concerned to 'remember' remained resolutely focused on what he perceived to be Australian concerns, and in this sense Australia seemed divorced from the task of engaging with the moral concerns arising from the war.

For Sciacca, the year of *Australia Remembers* more than achieved his goals and will doubtless remain a high point in his life, both personally and politically. As the photographs and other memorabilia on the walls of his Brisbane legal office attest, there was a lot of emotional investment by him in the program. This arose partly from the ways in which, because of his recent loss of his own young son, he was able to empathise on a fundamentally personal level with those of the wartime generation affected by the loss of their young men. In addition were the unique awards conferred upon Sciacca during 1995, as well as expressions of continuing respect and affection by organisations with which he had a formal relationship as minister, and the spontaneous appreciation of this 'man of the people' that I witnessed in Brisbane on the occasion of the 'Freedom Wall' opening.

Indeed, for a program which was so extensive and which touched virtually all communities throughout the nation, there were surprisingly few complaints in the media about *Australia Remembers,* and these may be divided essentially into two categories: from those who for whatever reason felt left out or insulted in some way, and those expressing a political critique. Of the latter, the failure of *Australia Remembers* to pay adequate tribute to the East Timorese people's assistance and suffering arising from this during the war and the shameful complicity of the Whitlam Labor government in the Indonesian invasion and occupation of that country were frequent themes. Such reminders remained fairly low-key, however, usually being expressed through letters to the editors of various newspapers, along the lines of 'I am surprised that there has been no official mention of the sacrifices made by the Timorese people during World War II. They stood by our soldiers suffering atrocious casualties at the hands of the Japanese and they are still suffering'.[19] It was surprising that more did not seek to explore the links between this silence over East Timor's role in the war, and the Keating Labor government's relationship with Indonesia. One letter-writer from Avoca did make this link explicit, providing detailed information and sources on the significance of East Timorese wartime assistance to Australian troops during 1942, when 'Australia was then wide open to invasion'. Similarly, an Adelaide correspondent reminded readers that while *Australia Remembers* celebrated a fiftieth anniversary, 1995 marked the twentieth anniversary of the invasion of East Timor by Indonesia. This letter linked the two anniversaries 'against an imperialist aggressor', suggesting that the Australian government in 1975, however, had been content to bury its head in the sand when 'another imperialistic power' invaded East Timor.[20] Indeed, it is difficult to avoid being sceptical about the absence of reference to the East Timorese role in the war by either the Veterans' Affairs Minister in his relevant media releases, or by Prime Minister Keating in his 14 August speech paying tribute to Pacific Island Veterans. Ranging from the peoples of Papua New Guinea, the Solomon Islands, Tonga, Vanuatu, New Caledonia, New Zealand, to Aborigines and Torres Strait Islanders, East Timor was tellingly absent. Such silence on Con Sciacca's part no doubt reflected his desire to avoid controversy, whereas one imagines a more insidious motive behind Prime Minister Keating's.

Fears of political opportunism were also raised by the RSL, seeking reassurance from the government of 'the fidelity of [its] intent'.[21] Paul Keating's response, accepted as satisfactory by Major-General James, focused entirely upon the war against Japan, and his perception that Australians need to be taught more about this conflict. The fact that his response did not mention Europe was reported in a favourable light, as indicative that he was 'not afraid of raising the aggressive past of Australia's most important trading partner'.[22] On the other hand, what those RSL members who had seen battle against the Germans felt about this response, especially in the light of the almost complete neglect of prisoners of war in Europe was not aired publicly.

The formal *Australia Remembers* events were judged to have been an 'extraordinary' success, which 'refreshed some old memories, provided some modern Australian history to those too young to have known it [gave] some additional recognition to those diggers who never came home'. It also remained 'largely immune from partisan criticism and speculation about the program's spin-offs in the electorate', although it was anticipated that the 'profound reach into the Australian community' would not have harmed the government's standing with voters over sixty-five years of age.[23]

This did not prevent criticisms or—perhaps more accurately—carping about the program, much of which seemed simply ill-informed and misdirected. For example, a letter to the editor in the

West Australian after VP Day complained about 'A poorly organised march in Perth last Sunday with not enough onlookers to line the streets and a few other small events'. The correspondent pointed out that WA did make a significant contribution to the war effort, and boasted a deputy prime minister and other senior ministers, but that the state had not been recognised, that 'Australia remembers but WA is forgotten'.[24] If indeed WA's commemoration had been as poor as portrayed, this may have reflected a lack of commitment by or support for the state taskforce, in line with Con Sciacca's view that any Labor initiative was automatically rejected in that state. The state committee's lack of response to my own letter inviting it to evaluate its program of events perhaps suggested a deeper malaise within that body. 'Canberra', often a code word for Paul Keating, was similarly accused of neglect, and of regarding 'Far North Queensland [as] the "arse end" of Australia' by a writer from Cardwell in the north of Queensland, which had witnessed the Battle of the Coral Sea 'some miles out to sea', and was said to have been angered by the absence of a military presence at its annual memorial service in May.[25]

A more fundamental criticism came from a letter-writer, terming VJ Day's processing in Sydney as a:

> travesty of the spirit and purpose of VJ Day—an utterly inappropriate "folk procession" to "celebrate" a "national festival"; brainchild of our new culture merchants—with the veterans envisaged as the tail in this circus, in jeeps. Nothing to tell us who did not live through that magnificent joint effort of the Australians, Americans, British and indigenous peoples about their triumphs and terrors.[26]

This complaint, the only of its kind to be printed, touched on the distinction decided upon by the *Australia Remembers* organisers as the most appropriate way to encompass the two major events of the war. VP Day had been designed to celebrate, whereas the events held earlier in the year had been designed to commemorate specific aspects of the war, the program's organisers believing it was appropriate to celebrate only the anniversary of the war ending. The aim of the VP Day celebrations, therefore, was to recreate the ecstatic atmosphere and outpouring of relief and thanksgiving that the war had ended. In so doing, it was hoped that those who had served at home and abroad, many of whom had not yet arrived back in Australia by 15 August in 1945, would be honoured and thanked.

Lingering suspicions over the motivations of the federal government with regard to its choice of the term VP Day remained throughout the year of *Australia Remembers,* but even these appeared to be confined to a relatively small number of individuals and the *Australian* newspaper. By August 15 the latter had almost fetishised the term 'VJ Day'. The result of this was that writers of letters to its editor apparently also universally used this term, leaving readers to wonder whether mail containing the words 'VP Day' was automatically excluded from publication. Indeed, a letter to that newspaper following VP Day had congratulated it for 'spurning the euphemism "VP Day" and consistently using the historically accurate VJ title'. Another, from University of New England historian Carl Bridge, had somewhat sarcastically accepted Con Sciacca's assurance that his choice of VP had not been in response to pressure from the Japanese. Bridge went on to suggest that 'for whatever reasons, Australia apparently had anticipated Japanese desires',[27] ignoring the fact that the Japanese themselves had used the term VJ Day, as was reported in the *Sydney Morning Herald* on 16 August.[28] Whilst this issue had been addressed by the Minister for Veterans' Affairs at the outset, his arguments that 'VP Day' had been a term employed during 1945 clearly failed to satisfy a minority of hardcore critics. Perhaps this had been exacerbated by President Clinton's changes of preference from 'VJ' to 'VP' and then back to 'VJ' again under pressure from US veterans' groups, as well as Britain's unwavering use of 'VJ Day', possibly expressive of a lingering anti-Japanese racism.

Another source of success for *Australia Remembers* was the support it received from the workers' movement, which appeared content to engage in symbolic tribute, such as the CFMEU's banner that graced the building site of the Princes Theatre in Melbourne, in the process of restoration at the time of the VP Day parade. Con Sciacca's links as a 'numbers man' in Queensland Labor politics doubtless contributed to the state branch of the Australian Workers' Union and the ACTU jointly producing a glossy, thirty-two page booklet titled *Fighting the War at Home: Queensland workers remember,* with a foreword written by him.[29] Mostly consisting of wartime photographs and reproductions of newspaper headlines such as Prime Minister Curtin's appeal to Australia in the *Courier Mail* after the bombing of Darwin in February 1942, the booklet portrayed men and women workers raising funds for the victims of German bombing of Britain during the Blitz of 1940–41. The booklet proudly restated Australian unionists' record of opposition to fascism dating back to the early 1930s, especially during the Spanish Civil War. The contributions of Aboriginal workers during this period were noted in a photograph, with the caption referring simply to the men pictured as 'pastoral workers [who] were often the unrecorded heroes of the Australian war effort', but neglecting to explicitly state that Aborigines had generally received unequal wages (if paid at all) during this period. There was no elaboration of Aboriginal workers' roles during the war, nor of the various trade unions' attitudes towards them.

Two particularly successful aspects of the *Australia Remembers* program can be suggested. Firstly, the program did achieve what the minister primarily set out for do, in that members of the Second World War generation were thanked, remembered and celebrated, and a significant impact—at least at the time—was made on the minds of those generations since the war. Many of these continue to manifest an interest and participation in rituals of remembrance such as Anzac Day. Indeed, the increasing numbers of young Australians travelling to Gallipoli for Anzac Day has led to the ceremonies being expanded to two days from 2003. The dawn service will continue to be held at Lone Pine on 25 April, but the Turkish international, the French and Commonwealth services will be held the day before. This had been initiated by the Turkish Government in order to 'alleviate problems with traffic and overcrowding'. There will also be a 'large video screen and superior sound system' provided.[30]

It remains unclear, however, to what extent this renewed interest in commemoration of Anzac Day might indicate a renewed nationalism and interest in war itself, or whether it expresses a desire for peace and perhaps a curiosity as to the meanings of such rituals. It is likely that more complex and intimate aspects of memory as well as a search for individual and possibly national meaning are being expressed. Bruce Scates in his recent ethnographic and collaborative survey of 'pilgrims' to Gallipoli has suggested varied motivations and composition of those surveyed, ranging from 'family pilgrimages' to young backpackers, few of whom travelled directly from Australia but rather include the visit as a part of 'a rambling world tour'.[31] For many of these young pilgrims, however, Gallipoli was more than just a place to go, describing it as 'spiritual' and Anzac Day the '[closest] to a sacred day as Australians ever get'.[32]

Secondly, *Australia Remembers* made important advances in the ways in which women in Australian society were represented, even if the manner of representation was at times problematic. The explicit intention, spelled out by Prime Minister Keating on the occasion of the national commemoration of women in the defence forces, that women should be honoured as never before, was realised to a significant extent, as were the contributions of women on the home front, unfortunate as this gendered division of labour in warfare remained. The visible representation of women, with the two *Australia Remembers* posters dedicated to them, as well as the ways in which women veterans of both the fronts responded to the year-long commemorations, suggest that women were no longer being included as tokens. Rather, a genuine desire was being expressed, not only to right previous wrongs in national commemorations, but also to promote women to an equal place in the public memory. It may be that future commemorations of the nation have the potential to build upon the very real advances that *Australia Remembers* made in this regard. In addition, as the initiatives of the four women who organised the national reunion in Darwin demonstrated, the *Australia Remembers* program encouraged women to seize the opportunity to create their own events in ways that gave meaning to their own experiences.

Australia Remembers was at pains to make women heroes too, which on one level was a worthy aim, but also reinforced the tendency to legitimise the idea of warfare. Nevertheless, the representation of wartime women as heroes clearly struck a chord with many of that generation, suggestive of the fifty years they had waited for recognition. Given the physical and emotional hardships endured by women during the war years, including for many the sole responsibility for the care of their children, it was not surprising that the term 'heroic' was avidly grasped. This was clearly the case for the children of women such as Varlie Walsh of the *Australia Remembers* logo, remembered by her children as a true hero of the war. The inclusion of Varlie Walsh in the logo may also have provided additional satisfaction for those who welcomed the heroic status conferred upon wartime women.

On the other hand, women's experiences as prisoners of war of the Japanese were almost entirely absent. The privileging of male POWs of the Japanese also marginalised and effectively belittled the experiences of prisoners of war of the Germans, using the rather too bland generalisation that these men suffered little more than the problems inherent in losing their freedom. Photographic and other evidence suggests that for those incarcerated in German camps to the east, such as Ray Walsh, life was far from easy. For these men perhaps the most important factor in survival was that, unlike the Japanese, the Germans were signatories of the Geneva Convention, and prisoners therefore received their Red Cross parcels (if somewhat erratically), which made the difference between starvation and survival.

Women's exclusion from the prisoner-of-war experience was most evident in the POW poster representation. This was not out of any deliberate attempt to sideline their experiences, but more likely because of gender blindness. This was slightly balanced by the award of the $20,000 *Australia Remembers* National Play Competition prize to John Misto for his play, *The Shoe-Horn Sonata*. The play depicted a reunion between two women who had been prisoners of the Japanese, probing questions of loyalty, friendship, sacrifice, betrayal and reconciliation, and was performed to positive reviews both within Australia and Britain throughout 1995. Sciacca's desire that the winning play should 'produce more female role models',[33] was answered by Misto's sensitive and sympathetic play, based on considerable research of the diaries of women prisoners as well as interviews with a number of them.[34]

Some questions were simply not asked, for example, about conscientious objection to the Second World War, which had not occurred at significant levels, but which one could be forgiven for assuming had not occurred at all. Nor were the experiences of alien internees included in the national remembering. Such omissions probably did not result from a conscious decision to exclude—and it is necessary to be mindful of how much was actually included—but it is in the gaps in the national remembering that fascination may reside in another fifty years' time.

The commemorations of Aborigines and Torres Strait Islanders reflected the fact that fifty years after the war, fundamental questions relating to recognition of Indigenous sovereignty and rights to land remained unresolved. In spite of a specially designed poster and inclusion of fighter pilot Len Waters in the Australia Post VP commemorative stamps, as well as speeches by the prime minister that paid tribute to their wartime roles, Indigenous 'memories' remained largely absent throughout the national events. At the state or territory level, judging from the assessments already noted, particularly by the Northern Territory Committee, Indigenous people seem to have fared somewhat better in terms of inclusion, although this does not seem to have been uniformly so. The apparent non-response of the peak body ATSIC to approaches by state and federal *Australia Remembers* organisers suggested a perception that this process of national remembering had little relevance to more pressing present-day struggles for advancement. Six years later some Aboriginal organisations chose to include themselves in the nation's remembrance, approaching the WA branch of the RSL with the idea of marching together. The result was the decision that Indigenous returned servicemen and women would lead the Anzac Parade in Western Australia. When the Indigenous contingent of sixty people marched past the 25,000 spectators lining Perth's streets, all showed 'enormous' support, and one marcher expressed the view that 'Anzac Day means a great deal…[and] hopefully in the future…will also have a unifying effect by bringing more of our veterans and their families forward to take their rightful place' in the nation's remembrance of their war service.[35] This event arguably reflected the influence of the Reconciliation process more than *Australia Remembers*. More recently the story of Aboriginal peoples' involvement in warfare has been recorded in Glen Stasiuk's forty-minute documentary, *The Forgotten: Indigenous servicemen in European and American wars*, which combines a personal and historical homage to these men, many of whom were Stasiuk's kin.[36] Furthermore, a letter from Cecil Fisher, Indigenous veteran of the Korean War, correcting the *Koori Mail*'s designation of the Perth march as the first led by Aboriginal veterans, similarly suggested that Indigenous peoples' initiatives in this regard were independent of government-sponsored events. Fisher stated that an approach had been made by the Kombumerri Aboriginal group at the Gold Coast in 1993, and that about fifty personnel, including eleven children, carrying a full-length, Aboriginal-designed street banner, had led the 1993 Gold Coast march. Among the marchers had been Oodgeroo Noonuccal and the wife of Captain Reg Saunders.[37]

Another letter from Cecil Cook in the same issue of the national Indigenous newspaper included his poem 'Black Anzac' which speaks of Indigenous fighters who, being no longer needed by the nation, were 'forgotten' in spite of having served in all wars since World War I. This poem, which celebrated only male fighting exploits, was matched by a letter from Don Elphick, invoking 'the spirit of Kalkadoon' which provided a continuity between the Kalkadoon warriors' defence of their lands in the 1880s and Aboriginal men 'in the best Anzac tradition'. Other writers wondered whether on:

> the next Anzac Day we could begin to memorialise warriors like Namarluk, the 1928 Coniston massacre and a hundred more "incidents" buried and forgotten and ill-served by continued blinkered shame.[38]

Indigenous peoples' engagement with Anzac Day and more broadly with issues of national remembrance arguably have little direct connection with the legacy of *Australia Remembers*. Instead, involvement in commemorative events such as at Cape Barren Island and Perth in the years after 1995 and the Gold Coast in 1993, is suggestive of a selective Indigenous agency, as these occurred because of the initial approach being made by Indigenous communities themselves, on their own terms. As well, the momentum of the Reconciliation process may have been an influential factor. It is noteworthy that the male warrior remained privileged in Indigenous articulations of their prowess in warfare both prior to and since colonisation. Rather than being interpreted as indicative of an internalisation of the gendered nature of non-Indigenous remembrance, the focus on the Indigenous male can be seen as a manifestation of the continuing contestation over the occurrence and extent of warfare on the colonial frontiers and the necessity to ensure that this is recognised.

Ultimately, the extent of success of *Australia Remembers 1945–1995* must lie in the ways in which commemoration touched all parts of the country. The numerous local events may have appeared quaint to those in the cities with their official galas and parades, but these enabled local communities to unite in ways they may not have done for years. These expressions of local interests enabled a sense of place and identity to be encouraged and validated. In the context of rural decline, these 'imagined communities' became at least momentarily tangible.

Comparisons with other commemorations of Australia

Australia Remembers managed to avoid the cringe-making tendencies of many of the Australian Bicentenary events during 1988, suggesting that some lessons had been gained from that expensive series of extravaganzas. Other factors which might have contributed to this include the short notice with which the *Australia Remembers* program was devised, in comparison to the decade or so, wracked by internal problems, which led up to the Bicentenary celebrations. Another factor was the modest budget of *Australia Remembers* and the uncomplicated manner in which funds were allocated equally to each electorate. The fact that many taskforce staff throughout the country worked overtime with no payment, there being no provision for this in the budget, indicated their commitment to the program and, for some of them, to the minister himself.

Furthermore, *Australia Remembers* did not seek to be the final arbiter of the ways in which the war might be 'remembered' or indeed imagined. A number of local *Australia Remembers* groups continued to meet after 1995, and the possibility remains for a renewal of the narrative of the war and its meanings. Ongoing contestation within

Australia over the meanings and uses of history, as well as accusations that former Prime Minister Keating was seeking to 'rewrite' Australia's history, ensure that debate over our past and national identity will continue. While it is doubtful that the year of remembrance of times past made a significant impact in arresting the decline in the teaching of history in schools, the ways in which *Australia Remembers* employed terms such as 'memory', 'remembering' and 'history' itself, however, may have added to students' confusion about the meanings of such terms. Similarly, popular understandings of the role of memory in history may have been further confused or encouraged in the notion that memory and history are one and the same.

Former Veterans' Affairs Minister, Con Sciacca, when interviewed twelve months after *Australia Remembers,* felt that the year of commemorations and celebrations had been successful because 'we did it better because Labor Party people, I think, have a better heart'. We can only speculate about what kind of program a Coalition government might have initiated. It is clear that it would not have been *Australia Remembers 1945–1995,* for all the bipartisan support this received. An incident just before Anzac Day two years after *Australia Remembers* perhaps provided some hints. A park in Canberra, a joint effort with its Japanese sister city, Nara, to symbolise their links, became the focus of angry objections from Prime Minister John Howard to the proposal, previously presumed to be uncontroversial, to name this small garden the Canberra–Nara Peace Park. In the midst of rather more pressing regional concerns, such as the threat of civil war erupting in Papua New Guinea and Mr Howard's imminent first trip to China as prime minister, this park, however, dominated the prime ministerial attention, with Mr Howard threatening to withdraw the required approval for the park if the word 'peace' remained.[39]

The irony of Prime Minister Howard's apparent obsession with the word 'peace' cannot be lost when one reflects on his similar obsession with another five-letter word, 'sorry', which he has consistently refused to utter.

NOTES

Chapter 1: Introduction—Memory and World War II

1   *Age*, 4 April, 1995, p. 10.

2   ibid., 17 April, 1995, p. 6.

3   W. Melion & S. Küchler (eds), *Images of Memory: On remembering and representation*, Smithsonian Institution Press, Washington, 1991, p. 7.

4   ibid., p. 3.

5   Quoted in H. Nelson, 'Gallipoli, Kokoda and the Making of National Identity', *Journal of Australian Studies*, No. 53, 1997, p. 160.

6   ibid.

7   L. Spillman, *Nation and Commemoration: Creating national identities in the United States and Australia*, Cambridge University Press, Cambridge, 1997, p. 30, emphasis added.

8   ibid., p. 54.

9   D. O'Brien, *The Bicentennial Affair: The inside story of Australia's 'Birthday Bash'*, ABC, Sydney, 1991, p. 4.

10   'White Australia has a Black History' was a multi-layered slogan of 1988.

11   Spillman, *Nation*, p. 97.

12   G. Turner, *Making it National: Nationalism and Australian popular culture*, Allen & Unwin, St Leonards, 1994, p. 66.

13   See for example, J. Hutchinson, 'State festivals, foundation myths and cultural politics in immigrant nations' in T. Bennett (ed.), *Celebrating the Nation: A critical study of Australia's Bicentenary*, Allen & Unwin, St Leonards, 1992, p. 17.

14   P. Cochrane & D. Goodman, 'The Great Australian Journey: Cultural logic and nationalism in the postmodern era', in Bennett (ed.), *Celebrating the Nation*, pp. 177–90.

15   Sciacca has since regained his seat.

16   J. Damousi, *The Labour of Loss: Memory and wartime bereavement in Australia*, Cambridge University Press, Cambridge, p. 2.

17   Quoted in A. Shoemaker, 'Selling Yothu Yindi', in G. Papaellinas (ed.) *Republica: All same as family in big 'ouse*, Angus & Robertson, Sydney 1994, pp. 26–7.

18   T. O'Connor, 'Hatred and bitter memories fade out', *Sunshine Coast Daily*, 23 May 1995, p. 11.

19   L. Carlyon, 'A sorry substitute for an apology', *Age*, 17 August 1995, p. 13.

20   F. Devine, 'The war with Japan is long over, boys', *Australian*, 3 July 1995, p. 13.

21   *Guardian Weekly*, 20 August 1995, p. 1.

22   S. Hewitt, 'Japan's apology too little: Ruxton', *Sunday Age*, 13 August 1995, p. 2.

23   'Partners: Time for a full Japanese role', *Courier-Mail*, 29 April 1995, p. 8. (Editorial)

Chapter 2: Small nations remember—Canada, Australia and New Zealand remember

1   J. Chrétien, Prime Minister of Canada, *Canada Remembers*, St Clair Group Inc., Toronto 1995, p. 9.

2   The Hon. Con Sciacca MP, Interview, Melbourne, 15 November 1995.

3   The Rt. Rev. Manu Bennett, quoted in *New Zealand Remembers The Second World War*, Department of Internal Affairs/Te Tari Taiwhenua, 1995, p. 43.

4   The Hon. Paul Keating MP, House of Representatives, *Hansard,* 30 May 1994, pp. 927–9.

5   J. Robertson, *1939–1945, Australia Goes to War*, Doubleday, Sydney, 1984, p. 219.

6   The Hon. Con Sciacca MP, Interview, Brisbane, 11 November 1996.

7   The Hon. Con Sciacca MP, Maiden Speech, The House of Representatives, *Historic House Hansard,* 24 September 1987, pp. 699–700.

8   M. Frith, 'The Minister for Nostalgia', *Age*, 14 August 1995, p. 11.

9   Sciacca, Interview, Brisbane, 11 November 1996.

10   Frith, 'The Minister for Nostalgia'.

11   The secretary of his department, Dr Allan Hawke, agreed that the Veterans' Affairs Department prior to Sciacca had been a sleepy department, historically driven by a welfare mentality, which soon changed, as reflected also in payments to veterans no longer being called 'benefits' but 'compensation'; ibid.

12   Correspondence from the Hon. Con Sciacca, 14 January 1997. There is only one person in Australia who holds the award higher than Commendatore: Mr Belgiorno-Nettis, the Founder and Managing Director of the Transfield Corporation, who is a 'Grand Officiale'.

13   Sciacca, Interview, Melbourne, 15 Melbourne 1995. At this time he felt that despite his obviously genuine intention to keep the program bipartisan, 'it was not doing any harm electorally', a perception that was to prove considerably off-key, including in his electorate.

14   Sciacca, Interview, Brisbane, 11 November 1996. As well, though, he was aware that the Opposition could not afford to be negative about such a proposal, adding 'how could you rubbish this?'

15   Media Release, 'The Nation Remembers World War II', 24 November 1994.

16   Executive Summary, *Australia Remembers 1945–1995* Community Communication Program, 28 August 1995.

17   Sciacca, Interview, Melbourne, 15 November 1995.

18   ibid.

19   *Executive Summary*, pp. 7–8. Actor Jack Thompson was chosen to intro-
        duce the recollections of 'hundreds of ordinary Australians' about their
        wartime experiences on more than sixty radio stations from March to
        August, Media Release, The Hon. Con Sciacca MP, *'Australia Remembers*
        on the air', 17 March 1995, C11/95.

20   House of Representatives, *Hansard*, 9 February 1995, pp. 914–20.

21   That is, not the *Age* and the *Sydney Morning Herald*, although he did go
        to the *Australian.*

22   Sciacca, Interview, Melbourne, 15 November 1995.

23   *Australia Remembers 1945–1995*, 'Background information', Department
        of Veterans' Affairs, Canberra, 1994, p. 8.

24   Recollection of Mrs Shirley Walsh (wife of Arthur), Nowra, 14 December
        1996.

25   Sciacca, Interview, Melbourne, 15 November 1995.

26   Private conversation, Canberra, Easter 1996.

27   Which has been described as the 'Scum and the Cream of Australia', Ian
        Sabey, *Stalag Scrapbook,* F. W. Cheshire Pty Ltd, Melbourne and London,
        1947, p. 24.

28   Arthur Walsh, Interview, Nowra, 14 December 1996.

29   D. Rolf, *Prisoners of the Reich: Germany's Captives 1939–1945*, Leo
        Cooper, London, 1988, p. 175.

30   Sabey, *Stalag Scrapbook*, pp. 133–4.

31   *Australia Remembers,* 'Background information', pp. 8–9.

32   Telephone interview with Mr Peter Thomas, media head of the national
        taskforce, 23 October 1995.

33   E. Stacey, 'Behind the embrace that touched a nation', *The Mercury*,
        5 May 1995, p. 1.

34   Walsh family, Interview, Nowra, 14 December 1996.

35   ibid.

36   *Australia Remembers 1945–1995*, 'Background information', p. 8.

37   Sabey, *Stalag,* pp. 61, 70, 102.

38   ibid., p. 69.

39   ibid.

40   ibid., p. 102.

41   Walsh family, Interview, 14 December 1996. In Stalag VIIIb, fifty ciga-
        rettes bought a bar of chocolate, and two cigarettes equalled one mark,
        which was the equivalent of a little more than one day's work, Sabey,
        Stalag, p. 81.

42   Sabey, *Stalag,* p. 85.

43   Recollection of Robyn Robinson (nee Walsh), and of her mother being
        cross about this, Walsh family, Interview.

44   Walsh family, Interview.

45 Arthur Walsh was particularly concerned about the initial misinformation surrounding the photograph, Walsh family, Interview.
46 ibid.
47 Speech by the Prime Minister, the Hon. Paul Keating MP, Launch of *Australia Remembers 1945–1995*, Australian War Memorial, Canberra, 14 August 1994.
48 ibid.
49 Sciacca, Interview, Brisbane, 11 November 1996.
50 K. S. Inglis & J. Phillips, 'War Memorials in Australia and New Zealand: A Comparative Survey', in J. Rickard and P. Spearritt (eds), *Packaging the Past? Public histories*, Melbourne University Press and Australian Historical Studies, Melbourne, 1991, p. 190.
51 L. Watt, *Mates and Mayhem: World War II frontline Kiwis remember*, Harper Collins NZ Ltd, Auckland, 1996, p. 211.
52 Extracts from the speech of the Minister for Veterans' Affairs at the launch of *Australia Remembers 1945–1995* at the Australian War Memorial, 14 August 1994, 'Background information', p. 12.
53 D.B. Scott (ed.), *About Canada: The home front in the Second World War*, Canadian Studies Program, *Canada Remembers*, 1995, p. 8.
54 ibid., p. 9.
55 *Canada Remembers*, p. 9.
56 ibid.
57 D. B. Scott, 'The March to Victory', *Canada Remembers*, p. 22.
58 Patrice A. Dutil, 'A Summer Chill', *Canada Remembers*, pp. 15–19.
59 The subtitle of section in ibid., p. 53.
60 This was apparently the basis upon which unemployment rates were calculated, *Canada Remembers*, p. 53; presumably, therefore, the actual unemployment rate was higher, if one took into account the non-unionised.
61 C. Oberdorf, 'Pulling out the Stops', *Canada Remembers*, p. 54.
62 Scott, 'The March to Victory', p. 28.
63 ibid.
64 H. Halliday, 'On the Frontline'; ibid., pp. 31, 39.
65 ibid., p. 31.
66 ibid., pp. 34, 36.
67 R. Collins, 'Capturing the Moments'; ibid., p. 49.
68 Oberdorf, 'Pulling out the stops', p. 63.
69 *Canada Remembers*, p. 4.
70 R. Collins, 'An Arsenal for Democracy', *Canada Remembers*, pp. 44, 46.
71 ibid., p. 44.
72 *Canada Remembers*, pp. 65–73.
73 ibid., p. 75.
74 J. L. Granatstein & D. Morton, 'The war changed everything', *Canada Remembers*, p. 79.

75   *Canada Remembers*, p. 5.

76   Mike Mountain Horse, First World War Veteran.

77   The exact number of Native recruits is not known, as some Indians and most Métis and Inuit were excluded from the Indian Affairs Department's tally, p. 20. The booklet, p. 2, contains a note on terminology, in which it is explained that of the various terms, 'Native' includes all of Canada's first peoples. Thus, for purposes of this discussion, 'Native' will be used unless in direct quotations.

78   J. Summerby, *Native Soldiers, Foreign Battlefields*, Communications Division, Veterans' Affairs Canada, Ottowa, Ontario, 1995, p. 31.

79   ibid., p. 6.

80   ibid., pp. 8, 20.

81   ibid., p. 21.

82   Correspondence from D. M. Stevens, Manager Ceremonial, Visits and Ceremonial Office, The Department of Internal Affairs, Te Tari Taiwhenua, 26 March, 1996.

83   ibid., p. 3.

84   ibid.

85   *New Zealand Remembers*, p. 6.

86   ibid., p. 61.

87   ibid.

88   'Commemorating the 50th Anniversary of the End of World War II', monthly newsletter from the Office of the Coordinator of *New Zealand Remembers*, No. 1, April 1995, p. 2.

89   'New Zealand at War—A New Documentary Series', ibid., p. 4.

90   ibid., p. 4.

91   ibid., p. 54.

92   She remembered that there were essentially three options for women: the army or land army, nursing (for which she was too young), or 'essential work which was ammunitions', which presumably had little attraction for her.

93   Similarly, Reg Rolfe remembered the difficulty of settling back into life after the war, when 'your wife doesn't understand. It's a different life'.

94   She also remembered the Maori Women's Welfare League being formed then, and providing 'a platform for Maori women to come into their own'.

95   ibid., p. 39.

96   *New Zealand Remembers*, p. 5.

97   This bell is the largest of four new brass bells housed in the National War Memorial tower, and when finished the Carillon will rank as the third largest in the world, ibid., p. 45.

98   Watt, *Mates and Mayhem*, pp. 211, 215.

99   *New Zealand Remembers*, p. 23.

100   ibid., p. 25.

101   ibid., p. 25.

102   ibid., pp. 40–1.
103   G. Preston and J. Fyfe, *War Stories Our Mothers Never Told Us*, Penguin
       Books NZ, Auckland, 1995, p. 7.
104   ibid., pp. 9–12.
105   Correspondence from D. M. Stevens, Manager Ceremonial, Visits and
       Ceremonial Office, Department of Internal Affairs, Te Tari Taiwhenua,
       26 March 1996.
106   Reminiscent of William Cooper of the Australian Aborigines League,
       who strenuously sought to argue that Aboriginal enlistment should be
       conditional upon the recognition of their political demands of the period,
       for equal citizenship rights.
107   *New Zealand Remembers*, pp. 42–3.

Chapter 3: History and memory: Australia Remembers 1945–1995 and uses of the past

1   Speech by Paul Keating at *Australia Remembers* Women in Defence
       Forces Ceremony, Canberra, 25 July 1995.
2   Japanese woman, quoted in Kenzaburo Oe, 'A Voice of Conscience',
       Weekend Australian, 12–13 August 1995, p. 24. (Focus)
3   Centenary of Federation: National Program List at <www.centenary.gov.
       au/cgi-bin/eve>, 7 April 2002.
4   Quotations taken verbatim from ABC TV's screening of this event on
       9 September 2001. Pederson's emphasis on the word 'federation' was
       accompanied by enthusiastic cheers and whistling by the crowd.
5   Centenary web page.
6   D. Lowenthal, *The Past is a Foreign Country*, Cambridge University Press,
       Cambridge, 1993, p. xix.
7   J. Hutchinson, 'State festivals, foundation myths and cultural politics
       in immigrant nations', in Tony Bennett (ed.), *Celebrating the Nation:
       a critical study of Australia's Bicentenary*, Allen & Unwin, St Leonards
       1992, p. 14.
8   M. McKenna, 'Tracking the republic', in D. Headen et al (eds) *Crown or
       Country. The Traditions of Australian Republicanism*, Allen & Unwin, St
       Leonards, 1994, pp. 3–5.
9   P. Spearritt, 'Making the Bicentenary', *Australian Historical Studies*,
       Vol. 23, No. 91, 1988, p. 4.
10   ibid., p. 10.
11   ibid., pp. 7–8.
12   ibid., p. 11.
13   ibid., p. 8.
14   ibid., p. 13.
15   G. Turner, *Making it National: Nationalism and Australian popular cul-
       ture*, Allen & Unwin, St Leonards, 1994, p. 69.

16   This spelling is only one of many and use here because it was the most common at the time of the event described.

17   B. Attwood & A. Markus, *The Struggle for Aboriginal Rights*, Allen & Unwin, Sydney, 1999, p. 317.

18   Turner, *Making it National*, p. 71.

19   Hutchinson, 'State festivals', pp. 17–18.

20   Turner, *Making it National*, pp. 84–5.

21   ibid., p. 87.

22   Attwood & Markus, pp. 316–17.

23   J. J. Matthews, 'Making the Bicentenary', *Australian Historical Studies*, Vol. 23, No. 91, 1988, p. 94.

24   ibid., p. 95.

25   'Memories of war on parade', *Cairns Post*, 15 August 1995, p. 2.

26   '6,000 remember end of the war', *NT News*, 14 August 1995, p. 2.

27   H. Pitt, 'A time to pause and reflect, but not all remembered', *Sydney Morning Herald*, 16 August 1995, p. 5.

28   *Mercury* (Tasmania), 15 August 1995, p. 19.

29   'An "unshakeable partnership" built on goodwill', *Canberra Times*, 15 August 1995, p. 2.

30   'War of words rages on', *Sydney Morning Herald*, 15 August 1995, p. 4.

31   C. Bridge, 'Make no mistake: we mean VJ Day', *Australian*, 11 August 1995, p. 13.

32   'Peace, pretty as a picture', *Courier-Mail*, 15 August 1995, p. 1.

33   R. Samuel, *Theatres of Memory*, Vol. 1, Verso, London, 1994, p. x.

34   N. Wood, 'Memory's Remains: Les lieux de mémoire', *History and Memory. Studies in representation of the past*, Vol. 6, No. 1, Spring/Summer 1994, pp. 129, 131.

35   P. Nora, 'Between Memory and History: Les lieux de mémoire', *Representations*, No. 26, Spring 1989, p. 23.

36   Wood, 'Memory's Remains', p. 124.

37   ibid.

38   Australian War Memorial, '1945: War and Peace' Inform audioguide script, 1995.

39   S. Küchler & W. Melion (eds), *Images of Memory: On remembering and representation*, Smithsonian Institution Press, Washington and London, 1991, p. 76.

40   Wood, 'Memory's Remains', p. 130.

41   J. Winter & E. Sivan (eds), *War and Remembrance in the Twentieth Century*, Cambridge University Press, Cambridge, 1999, p. 1.

42   ibid., p. 126.

43   Marie-Noelle Bourguet et al (eds), *Between Memory and History*, Harwood Academic Publishers, 1990, p. 5.

44   Wood, 'Memory's Remains', p. 145.

45   Bourguet et al, *Between Memory and History*, pp. 60–4.

46   Wood, 'Memory's Remains', p. 147.

47   J. E. Toews, 'Intellectual History after the Linguistic Turn: The autonomy of meaning and the irreducibility of experience', *The American Historical Review*, Vol. 92, No. 4, Oct. 1987, pp. 884–5.

48   Media Release, The Hon. Con Sciacca MP, 'Australia remembers the important role of women to the war effort', C8.85, 8 March 1995.

49   Part of a prayer at the *Australia Remembers* Women in the Defence Forces Ceremony, Canberra, 25 July 1995.

50   B. Melman, 'Gender, History and Memory: The invention of women's past in the nineteenth and early twentieth centuries', *History and Memory: Studies in representation of the past*, Vol. 5, No. 1, Spring/Summer, 1993, pp. 5–6.

51   ibid., pp. 10–11.

52   K. Inglis, 'Men, women, and war memorials: Anzac Australia' in R. White & P. Russell (eds), *Memories and Dreams: Reflections on 20th Century Australia*, Allen & Unwin, St Leonards, 1997; K. Inglis, *Sacred Places*, Melbourne University Press, Carlton 1998, esp. p. 367.

53   Inglis in White & Russell (eds), *Memories and Dreams*, p. 55.

54   Speech by the Prime Minister, The Hon. Paul Keating MP, 'Australia remembers women in defence forces ceremony', Canberra, 25 July 1995.

55   M. Cook & A. Woolacott (eds), *Gendering War Talk*, Princeton University Press, Princeton, NJ 1993, p. ix.

56   J. Hartley (ed.), *Hearts Undefeated: Women's writing of the Second World War*, Virago Press, London, 1994, p. 26.

57   ibid., pp. 69–70.

58   ibid,, pp. 112, 199.

59   ibid., pp. 210, 209.

60   Cook & Wallacott, *Gendering War Talk*, p. ix.

61   Kenzaburo Oe, 'A Voice of Conscience', p. 24

62   'Big gathering of WWII female veterans to be held in Canberra', Media Release, C24/95 23 May 1995.

63   'Wartime friendships endured', *Gympie Times*, 4 March 1995, pp. 4–5.

64   S. Oxford, 'Enduring mateship', *South West News* (Brisbane Suburban), 2 August 1995, p. 7.

65   The Hon. Paul Keating MP, 'Australia remembers women in defence forces ceremony'.

66   M. Frith, 'Keating salutes women veterans' gallantry', *Age*, 26 July 1995, p. 3.

67   *Australian*, 26 July 1995, p. 3.

68   Nora, 'Between Memory and History', pp. 12–13, 15.

69   ibid., p. 17.

70   ibid., p. 19.

71   G. McCormack & H. Nelson (eds), *The Burma–Thailand Railway: Memory and history*, Allen & Unwin, St Leonards, 1993, p. 162.

72 J. Robertson, *1939–1945 Australia Goes To War,* Doubleday, Sydney, 1984, p. 206. The passing mention of women typifies ways in which their wartime experiences have been marginalised, often when discussing the war itself, and Robertson neglects to mention that women were also taken prisoner by the Japanese.

73 ibid., p. 153.

74 H. Nelson, *POW: Prisoners of War, Australians under Nippon,* ABC, Sydney, 1985, p. 215.

75 McCormack & Nelson, *The Burma–Thailand Railway,* pp. 162–4. Page 164 contains a somewhat contradictory table (Table B.1) of prisoner deaths in the war against Japan, sourced to R. J. Pritchard & S. Zaide (eds), *The Tokyo War Crimes Trial,* Garland Publishing, New York and London, 1981, Vol. 16, pp. 40, 537, which lists Australian POW deaths as 7,416 (34%), followed by the US (33%), New Zealand (26%), UK (25%), 'Dutch (white)' (23%) and Canada (16%).

76 J. Beaumont (ed.), *Australia's War 1939–45,* Allen & Unwin, St Leonards, 1996, p. 49.

77 ibid.

78 M. Barter, *Far Above Battle: The experience and memory of Australian soldiers in war 1939–1945,* Allen & Unwin, Sydney, 1994, p. 251.

79 *The Australian,* 30 May 2001, p. 12.

80 Beaumont, *Australia's War,* p. 48

81 Warner & Sandilands, *Women Beyond the Wire,* pp. 210–11.

82 ibid., p. 5.

83 ibid., p. 11.

84 ibid., p. 14.

85 ibid., p. 102.

86 Warner & Sandilands, *Women Beyond the Wire,* p. 264.

87 Once the Japanese realised that music enabled the women to transcend the camp's horrors, they often cancelled performances; ibid., p. 207.

88 Nelson, *POW,* pp. 26–7.

89 Warner & Sandilands, p. 221.

90 ibid., p. 120.

91 ibid., pp. 92, 95.

92 ibid., pp. 206, 227.

93 ibid., p. 230.

94 ibid., pp. 251, 257.

95 ibid., p. 260.

96 ibid., pp. 263, 267–9; Nelson, *POW,* p. 212.

97 Nelson, *POW,* pp. 26–27.

98 Walsh family, Interview, Nowra, 14 December 1996.

99 Nelson, *POW,* p. 214.

100 ibid., p. 267.

101   J. Misto, *The Shoe-Horn Sonata,* Currency Press, Sydney, 1996, Introduction.

102   Nora, 'Between Memory and History', p. 17.

103   Samuel, *Theatres of Memory,* p. 13.

104   ibid., p. 22.

105   I. Willox, 'PM links republic to N-tests', *Age,* 4 November 1995, p. A9.

106   S. Lipski, 'Keating's voice fails to strike the right note', *Age,* 29 May 1995, p. 13.

107   ibid.

108   ibid.

109   ibid.

110   'Paul's tailored view of history', *Geelong Advertiser,* 18 February 1995, p. 6.

111   Ryan, *Advancing Australia,* p. 64.

112   ibid., pp. 65–8.

113   ibid., p. 69.

114   ibid., p. 70.

115   ibid., p. 187.

116   E.g. Asia–Australia Institute address, Sydney, 7 April 1992; ibid. pp.189, 196; 'The story of Australia', National Library twenty-fifth anniversary, Canberra, 13 August 1993, p. 55.

117   J. Lahey, 'Family recalls snapshots of political saint', *Age,* 24 June 1995, pp. 4 and 1–3, 'Saturday Extra'.

118   J. Lahey, 'PM finds room in history for Curtin', *Age,* 6 July 1995, p. 2.

119   L. Slattery, 'Heroic stature eludes Labor's wartime leader', *Australian,* 5 July 1995, p. 2.

120   'A time to remember John Curtin', *Australian,* 5 July 1995, p. 12. (Editorial)

121   'Flaunting the flag', *Age,* 26 April 1996, p. A12. (Editorial)

Chapter 4: Nostalgia unbounded—VP Day as spectacle

1   'Passing on the torch', *Herald Sun,* First edition, 16 August 1995, p. 12. (Editorial)

2   Male veteran in ABC documentary series 'True Stories: Faces of war, battle for empire'.

3   D. Lowenthal, *The Past is a Foreign Country,* Cambridge University Press, Cambridge, 1985, pp. 36, 40.

4   ibid., p. xix.

5   ibid., p. 8.

6   *Australia Remembers 1945–1995: Commemorating the 50th Anniversary of the end of World War II,* Background Information, Department of Veterans' Affairs, Canberra, 1994, pp. 15–17.

7   P. Spearritt, 'Celebration of a nation: The triumph of spectacle', *Australian Historical Studies,* Vol. 23, No. 91, 1988, p. 20.

8   Lowenthal, *The Past*, pp. 206, 348–9.

9   ibid., pp. 350, 356.

10   J. Lack, 'Media accounts of VE Day don't reflect confusion of time', *Age*, 11 May 1995, p. 15.

11   ibid.

12   *Australian*, 8 May 1995, pp. 1, 6.

13   *Weekend Australian*, 6–7 May 1995, p. 13.

14   Lowenthal, *The Past*, p. 4.

15   The Hon. Con Sciacca, 'Australia gears up for VE Day commemoration', Press Release, May 2 1995, C21/95.

16   Speech by the Prime Minister, the Hon. Paul Keating, MP, *VE Day—Australia Remembers commemorative ceremony*, Australian War Memorial, Canberra, 8 May 1995.

17   *Age*, 9 May 1995, pp. 6–8.

18   Gideon Haigh, 'Captive eyewitnesses to Europe's dark days', *Australian*, 8 May 1995, p. 10

19   'World War II: the just war', *Sydney Morning Herald*, 8 May 1994, p. 14. (Editorial)

20   'Ceremonies focus on major wartime events', *Daily Mercury*, 8 May 1995, p. 2.

21   'Memories flood back for VE Day revellers', *Gladstone Observer*, 9 May 1995, p. 7.

22   'Girl serenaded soldiers on train', *Morning Bulletin* (Rockhampton), 8 May 1995, p. 6.

23   *Courier-Mail*, 15 August 1995, Editorial.

24   'Passing on the torch', *Herald Sun*, First edition, 16 August 1995, p. 12 (Editorial)

25   G. Easdown, 'Mystery sweater girl speaks across time', *Herald Sun*, 14 August 1995, p. 5. The jumper is now an exhibit in the Australian War Memorial.

26   'Passing the torch', *Herald Sun* First Edition, 16 August 1995, p. 12. (Editorial)

27   V. Gurvich, 'VP mess...just part of the job', *Age*, 17 August 1995, p. 7.

28   R. Myer, 'The cookie's crumbling', *Sunday Age*, Business Section, 14 January 1996, p. 17.

29   P. Charlton, 'United States occupation of Queensland', *Courier-Mail*, 15 August 1995, p. 4.

30   'The Flame of Freedom' program notes.

31   Kate Darian-Smith, 'War Stories: Remembering the Australian home front during the Second World War', in K. Darien-Smith & P. Hamilton (eds), *Memory and History in Twentieth-Century Australia*, Oxford University Press, Melbourne, 1994, p. 137.

32   M. Gibson, 'What's in a name anyway?' *Daily Telegraph Mirror*, 11 August 1995, p. 10.

33   'Memory of peace sparks off a new war dance', *Mercury* (Tasmania), 4 August 1995, p. 3; 'Battle erupts over icon of peace', *Advertiser*, 5 August 1995, p. 3.
34   'Dancer in the streets', *Daily Telegraph-Mirror*, 9 August 1995, p. 12.
35   T. Stephens, 'Famous pirouette of peace stepping up to a war dance', *Sydney Morning Herald*, 10 August 1995, p. 7.
36   'Hot shoe revival for Drew', *Daily Telegraph-Mirror*, 15 August 1995, p. 4.

Chapter 5: *Australia Remembers* and national identity

1   Con Sciacca, quoted in P. Ellingson, 'Gallipoli's tears for our roll of honour', *Age*, 25 April 1995, p. 1.
2   Speech by Paul Keating at 'Tribute to Pacific Island Veterans', Townsville 14 August 1945.
3   Speech by Paul Keating, 'Farewell to the *Australia Remembers* Pilgrimage to Papua New Guinea, Sydney, 29 June 1995.
4   J. Beaumont, 'Long Shadow of Gallipoli's gravestones', *Australian*, 14 August 1995, p. 13.
5   ibid.
6   ibid.
7   'Flaunting the flag', *Age*, 26 April 1996, p. A12.
8   G. Turner quoted in M. Simons, '30 things that still say Australia', *Weekend Australian*, 27–28 January 1996, p. 2.
9   P. Fuery, 'Introduction', in P. Fuery (ed.) *Representation, Discourse and Desire*, Longman Cheshire, Melbourne, 1994, p. 5.
10   M. Ryan, *Advancing Australia*, Big Picture Publications, Sydney, 1995, p. 279.
11   ibid., pp. 280–1.
12   P. Ellingsen, 'Gallipoli's tears for our roll of honour', *Age*, 25 April 1995, p. 1.
13   H. Trinca, 'New guard "pilgrims" keep Anzac spirit alive', *Australian*, 24 April 1995, p. 5.
14   A. Thomson, *Anzac Memories. Living with the Legend*, Oxford University Press, Melbourne, 1994, p. 198.
15   ibid.
16   Ellingsen, 'Gallipoli's tears', p. 2.
17   I. Willox and F. Farouque, 'No flag change without vote', *Age*, 25 April 1996, p. 1.
18   'Howard sets his position on the flag', *Australian*, 26 April 1996, p. 12. (Editorial)
19   'Time to remember sacrifices', *Courier* (Ballarat), 25 April 1995, p. 8. (Editorial)
20   J. Giles, 'Anzac Day revives memories of mates', *Bayside Bulletin* (Brisbane Suburban), 25 April 1995, p. 7.

21   N. McKean, 'Surviving on mateship', *Westside News* (Brisbane Suburban), 26 April 1995, p. 4.

22   'Growing up and leaving the folks', *Sunday Age*, 12 November 1995, p. 14. (Editorial)

23   M. Lake, 'Anzac and the women who bear the children', *Age*, 24 April 1995, p. 15.

24   B. Anderson, *Imagined Communities: Reflections on the origin and spread of nationalism*, Verso, London, 1991, revised edn, p. 7.

25   ibid. p. 9.

26   R. Buchanan, 'Day of tribute and play', *Age*, 26 April 1995, p. 1.

27   'Hushed crowds honour the dead in dawn services', *Australian*, 26 April 1995, p. 4.

28   P. Kitley, 'Anzac Day ritual', *Journal of Australian Studies*, No. 4, June 1979, p. 60.

29   N. Bane, 'Anzac flame burns bright', *Northern Territory News*, 26 April 1995, pp. 4–5.

30   Thomson, *Anzac Memories*, pp. 197–8.

31   B. Parsons, 'Bringing Australia's students up to date on the Gallipoli story', *Age*, 1 April 1997, p. A4.

32   P. Gray, 'Healing postwar wounds', *Herald Sun*, 16 August 1995, p. 12.

33   'The Anzac resurgence', *Age*, 27 April 1995, p. 13. (Editorial); Record crowds were also reported in Britain for the Remembrance Day parade, swelled by the earlier commemorations of VE and VJ Days, *Guardian Weekly*, 19 November 1995, p. 8.

34   D. Greenlees, 'PM hails youthful supporters', *Australian*, 26 April 1996, p. 4.

35   C. Milburn, 'Marching orders for Anzacs' children', *Age*, 18 March 1997, p. A2.

36   'Passing the torch', *Age*, 19 March 1997, p. A14. (Editorial)

37   B. Parsons, 'Veterans denounce march ban fearing death of their legacy', *Age*, 19 March 1997, p. A3; 'Time to remember', *Access Age*, 19 March 1997, p. A14.

38   S. Rintoul, 'A nation pays homage to its heroes', *Age*, 26 April 1996, p. 1.

39   C. Le Grand, '"Third Soldier" will march alone', *Australian*, 25 April 1996, p. 2.

40   N. Bane, 'Our day to remember', *Northern Territory News*, 26 April 1996, p. 14.

41   *Daily Telegraph*, 26 April 1996, pp. 1, 4, 5.

42   D. Conway, 'A spirited life ends for the last original Anzac', *Age*, 11 December 1997, p. A1.

43   G. Henderson, 'Lasting legacy of the First', *Age*, 23 December 1997, p. A11.

44   Conway, 'A spirited life'.

45   B. Kapferer, *Legends of People Myths of State: Violence, intolerance, and political culture in Sri Lanka and Australia*, Smithsonian Institute Press, Washington and London, 1988, p, xi.

46   ibid., pp. 127, 7, 13.

47   ibid., pp. 144–5.

48   Kitley, 'Anzac Day ritual', p. 58.

49   Thomson, *Anzac Memories*, pp. 129, 131.

50   Kapferer, *Legends of People*, p. 178.

51   ibid., p. 179.

52   'When we all remember', *Mercury* (Tasmania), 8 December 1994, p. 19.

53   K. S. Inglis, 'A Sacred Place: The making of the Australian War Memorial', *War and Society*, Vol. 3, September 1985, p. 99.

54   ibid., pp. 99–103.

55   ibid., p. 111.

56   ibid., pp. 114–22.

57   ibid., pp. 122–3.

58   K. S. Inglis & J. Phillips, 'War memorials in Australia and New Zealand', in J. Rickard & P. Spearritt (eds), *Packaging the Past? Public histories*, Melbourne University Press and *Australian Historical Studies*, 1991, p. 179.

59   See R. Frances & B. Scates, 'Honouring the Aboriginal Dead', *Arena* 86, 1989, pp. 72–80 for an account of memorialising Aboriginal fighters prior to 1995.

60   Inglis & Phillips, 'War Memorials', p. 181.

61   ibid., pp. 181–4.

62   ibid., p. 190.

63   Con Sciacca, Interview, Melbourne, 15 November 1995.

64   'Descendants' pilgrimage', *Townsville Bulletin*, 25 April 1995, p. 5.

65   Con Sciacca, Interview, Brisbane, 11 November 1996.

66   H. Trinca, 'Debacle at dawn'; Sue Quinn, 'Gallipoli Shambles', *Herald Sun*, 26 April 1995, pp. 1, 4.

67   N. Bethel, 'The great Anzac lie', *Sunday Age*, 21 May 1995, p. 16; Elsewhere Lord Bethel was quoted as elevating this nationalist version of history beyond simply 'the great Anzac lie' to 'the great Australian lie'.

68   J. Lahey, 'Veterans begin official pilgrimage', *Age*, 29 April 1995, p. 7.

69   'Veterans invited to join PNG pilgrimage', *Tumut and Adelong Times*, 21 April 1995, p. 4.

70   'Veterans sought for PNG and Borneo pilgrimages', *Blue Mountains Gazette*, 26 April 1995, p. 20.

71   L. Murdoch, 'Sandakan pilgrimage', *Age*, 12 July 1995, p. 11.

72   G. Feeney, 'Stoic survivor salutes the dead of Sandakan savagery', *Australian*, 12 July 1995, p. 3.

73   L. Murdoch, 'Diggers return to bitter memories in Borneo', *Age*, 11 July 1995, p. 9.

74   ibid.

75   N. Cater, 'Aussies boycott camp guards', *Advertiser*, 15 August 1995, p. 2.

76   'POW march appeal', *Age*, 27 January 1997, p. A6.

77   'Survivor of the death marches', *Age*, 28 February 1997, p. C2.

78   J. Newton, 'Angels, Heroes and Traitors: Images of some Papuans in the Second World War', *Research in Melanesia*, No. 20, 1996, p. 155.

79   'Courage, bravery, sacrifice', *Daily News* (Warwick), 2 May 1995, p. 4.

80   Having been to Australia for five official commemorative visits leading up to the *Australia Remembers* events, ibid., p. 142. Mr Oembari's name was spelt 'Oimbari' in the caption of George Silk's photograph.

81   D. Kingston, 'Angel to fly in for peace festival', *Townsville Bulletin*, 5 August 1995, p. 5.

82   Newton, 'Angels, Heroes and Traitors', p. 155.

83   'Townsville to thank 'fuzzy wuzzy angels' and Pacific Islanders for war effort', Media Release, the Hon. Con Sciacca MP, 25 November 1994, C32/94.

84   Transcript of the Prime Minister, *Australia Remembers* Pacific Tribute Official Luncheon, Townsville, 14 August 1995, p.2; Speech by the Prime Minister, Tribute to Pacific Island Veterans, Townsville, 14 August 1995, p. 2.

85   'Fuzzy wuzzy angel seeks reward for war effort', *Townsville Bulletin*, 11 August 1995, p. 1.

86   ibid.; 'Angel of mercy', *Daily Telegraph-Mirror* (First Edition), 15 August 1995, p. 4.

87   M. Brown, 'PNG angel feted as hero', *Herald Sun* (Second Edition), 15 August 1995, p. 4.

88   J. Camplin and R. Callinan, 'At last, some favours returned to an angel', *Courier-Mail*, 15 August 1995, p. 1.

89   'Symbol of wartime compassion', *Age* (Obituary), 17 July 1996, p. B2.

90   Camplin and Callinan, 'At last, some favours'.

91   K. Inglis, *Sacred Places*, Melbourne University Press, Carlton, 1998, p. 349.

92   Speech by the Prime Minister, the Hon. Paul Keating, MP, Tribute to Pacific Island Veterans, Townsville, 14 August 1995, p. 3.

93   R. A. Hall, *Fighters from the Fringe: Aborigines and Torres Strait Islanders recall the Second World War*, Aboriginal Studies Press, Canberra, 1995, pp. 195–7.

94   G. Alcorn, 'Government moves to salute the wartime service of blacks', *Age*, 20 February 1995, p. 4; Media Release, *Australia Remembers* the Aboriginal and Islander contribution to victory in WWII', the Hon. Con Sciacca MP, p. 5.

95   A. Toulson, '53 years on, war heroes honoured', *Northern Territory News*, 20 February 1995, p. 1; 'Salute to Kooris', *Telegraph Mirror*, 20 February 1995, p. 2.

96   K. Middleton, 'Keating suggests increased independence for Islanders', the *Age*, 13 September 1995, p. 4.

97   ibid., p. 3; Hall, *Fighters from the Fringe*, p. vi.

98   'Dawn service, parades draw record crowds', *Age*, 26 April 1995, p. 4.

99   D. Nason, 'Elite black force guarded against invasion', *Australian*, 24 April 1995, p. 5.

100   'War broke racist barriers, says vet', *Northern Territory News*, 15 August 1995, p. 20.

101   E. Osborne, 'Torres Strait Islander Women. An interpretation of some recollections on their experiences during the Pacific War 1942–1945', *Northern Perspective*, Vol. 18, No. 2, 1995, Wet Season, p. 33.

102   Hall, *Fighters from the Fringe*, pp. 5–13, 45; D. Huggonson, 'Lest we forget our Indigenous diggers', *Koori Mail*, 28 June 1995, p. 29.

103   Hall, *Fighters from the Fringe*, pp. 64, 68, 77–8.

104   ibid., p. 25.

105   ibid., pp. 14, 194.

106   Osborne, 'Torres Strait Islander Women', pp. 33–5.

107   G. Stasiuk, *The Forgotten: Indigenous servicemen in European and American wars*, A Black Russian Production, Perth, 2002.

108   K. Pretty, 'Comrades in arms: Aboriginal vets urged to join *Australia Remembers* parade', *Northern Daily Leader* (NSW), 24 May 1995, p. 1; 'Aboriginal vets: Who to contact', ibid., 26 May 1995, p. 6.

109   Hall, *Fighters*, p. vi.

110   Pers. comm., the late Alick Jackomos OAM, Melbourne, 7 May 1997, and evaluation of the various state and territory *Australia Remembers* committees; See chapter 6.

111   Thomson, *Anzac Memories*, p. 199.

112   G. Hage, *White Nation: Fantasies of White supremacy in a multicultural society*, Pluto Press, Sydney, 1998, p. 90.

Chapter 6: The Legacy of *Australia Remembers 1945–1995*

1   One of two quotes believed to best encapsulate the philosophy of *Australia Remembers* by Bob Alford, Chairman *Australia Remembers* NT, in Remembrance Day Auction booklet, 11 November 1995.

2   Con Sciacca, Interview, Brisbane, 11 November 1996.

3   'Missing in action', *Age*, 17 August 1995, p. 12.

4   *Australia Remembers 1945–1995* 'Background information', Department of Veterans' Affairs, Canberra 1994, p. 6.

5   R. Buchanan, 'Emotions flow as a nation remembers', *Age*, 14 August 1995, p. 1.

6   S. Coomber et al, 'Time for solemnity amid VJ euphoria', *Australian*, 14 August 1995, p. 1.

7   M. Flanagan, 'Making a mark in a forest of feeling', *Age*, 14 August 1995, p. 1.

8   Information supplied by Mr Errol Davis, *Australia Remembers* State Coordinator, Queensland, 22 January 1996 and 3 July 1996.

9   Background information from The Hon. Bruce Scott MP, Minister for Veterans' Affairs and the Right Honourable The Lord Mayor of Brisbane, Jim Soorley, Media Release 145/96, November 11 1996.

10   *Australia Remembers 1945–1995* Community Communication Program Executive Summary, 28 August 1995, pp. 5, 10, provided by Peter Thomas, 23 October 1995.

11   Con Sciacca, Interview, Melbourne, 15 November 1995; Peter Thomas, media head of the national taskforce suggested the failure was largely due to fears that *Australia Remembers* would glorify war, and that there was a failure to grasp what was intended by the program.

12   Bladon Australia Pty Ltd, *Australia Remembers* Wholesale Price List, Effective March 15th 1995.

13   Correspondence from Robyn Smith, Executive Officer, NT Committee, 22 January 1996.

14   Correspondence from Stephen Lalor, Branch Head Parliamentary and Corporate Affairs, Commonwealth Department of Veterans' Affairs, Canberra, 13 February 1996.

15   Correspondence from Tony Carr, State Coordinator, Victoria, 24 January 1996.

16   Correspondence from Karina Ceron, Veterans' Affairs Network, Tasmanian Branch Office, 27 February 1996.

17   *West Australian*, 14 August 1995, pp. 10–11; John McCarthy, 'Broken on the Burma Railway', *International Express* (Australian Edition, by satellite), 9–15 August 1995, p. 37.

18   C. Johnstone, 'Anger lingers in era of peace', *Courier-Mail*, 16 August 1995, p. 1.

19   'Missing in action', Access Age, *Age*, 17 August 1995, p. 12.

20   R. Mumford, 'Australia Remembers—East Timor?', *Southern Highland News* (Bowral), 17 February 1995, p. 8; Martin Smee, 'Remember our true allies in East Timor', *Advertiser*, 30 January 1995, p. 10.

21   'Keating: war anniversary non-political', *Courier-Mail*, 13 February 1995, p. 6.

22   ibid.; 'No politics behind war events: PM', *Advertiser*, 13 February 1995, p. 8.

23   N. Richardson, 'Victory in the electorate', *Bulletin*, 22 August 1995, p. 27.

24   'WA the forgotten state', Letters to the Editor, *West Australian,* 17 August 1995, p. 13.

25   'Cardwell Remembers "Canberra Forgets" ', *Tully Times,* 4 May 1995, p. 4;
      Keating's remark that Australia was 'the arse end of the world' returned
      to haunt him in a variety of contexts.
26   'Folksy pageant', Letters to the Editor, *Australian,* 23 August 1995,
      p. 12.
27   *Weekend Australian,* 19–20 August 1995, p. 12.
28   *Sydney Morning Herald,* 16 August 1995, p. 12.
29   Forewords by Bill Ludwig, Queensland Branch Secretary and National
      President of the AWU, and John Thompson, Acting General Secretary
      of the ACTU (Queensland) respectively touched on workers fighting
      against fascism and oppression, and the success of the massive domestic
      campaign being a direct result of the cooperation and support of the
      trade union movement.
30   M. Forbes, 'Anzac Day to last 48 hours', *Age,* 17 December 2002, p. 3.
31   B. Scates, 'In Gallipoli's Shadow: Pilgrimage, mourning and the
      Great War', *Australian Historical Studies,* Vol. 33, No. 119, April 2002,
      pp. 3–7.
32   ibid., p. 8.
33   Media Release, 16 February 1995, C6/95.
34   *Paradise Road,* directed by Bruce Beresford, released in mid-1997 was
      based upon extensive research from sources such as Australian nurse
      Betty Jeffrey's 1954 book (reprinted in 1993 by Angus & Robertson,
      Pymble) *White Coolies,* and interviews with women who had been
      POWs.
35   J. Hoffman, 'Aboriginal pride to the fore in Anzac Day march', *Koori Mail,*
      2 May 2001, p. 11.
36   G. Stasiuk, *The Forgotten: Indigenous servicemen in European and
      American wars,* Black Russian Production 2002.
37   C. Fisher, 'Anzac Day marching on the Gold Coast in 1993', *Koori Mail,*
      2 May 2001, p. 9.
38   A. R. Coward, 'Lest we forget the "forgotten" heroes', *Koori Mail,* 2 May
      2001, p. 8.
39   G. Green, 'War and peace: how a word upset the PM', *Age,* 19 April 1997,
      p. A27.

BIBLIOGRAPHY

Books

Adam-Smith, P., *The Anzacs*, Thomas Nelson, Melbourne, 1978.

Anderson, B., *Imagined Communities: Reflections on the origin and spread of nationalism*, Verso, London, 1991.

Barker, A.J. & Jackson, L., *Fleeting Attraction: A social history of American servicemen in Western Australia during the Second World War*, University of Western Australia Press, Nedlands, 1996.

Barter, M., *Far Above Battle: The experience and memory of Australian soldiers in war 1939–1945*, Allen & Unwin, St Leonards, 1994.

Beaumont, J. (ed.), *Australia's War 1939–45*, Allen & Unwin, St Leonards, 1996.

Bourguet, M. N. et al. (eds), *Between Memory and History*, Harwood Academic Publishers, 1990.

Buruma, I., *The Wages of Guilt*, Meridian, New York, 1995.

Cooke, M. & Woollacott, A. (eds), *Gendering War Talk*, Princeton University Press, Princeton New Jersey, 1993.

Damousi, J. & Lake, M. (eds), *Gender and War: Australians at war in the twentieth century*, CUP, Melbourne, 1995.

Darian-Smith, K. & Hamilton, P. (eds), *Memory and History in Twentieth-Century Australia*, Oxford University Press, Melbourne, 1994.

Hall, R. A., *Fighters From the Fringe: Aborigines and Torres Strait Islanders recall the Second World War*, Aboriginal Studies Press, Canberra, 1995.

Hartley, J. (ed.), *Hearts Undefeated: Women's writing of the Second World War*, Virago Press, London, 1994.

Inglis, K. S. & Phillips, J., 'War Memorials in Australia and New Zealand' in J. Richard and P. Spearritt (eds), *Packaging the Past? Public histories*, Melbourne University Press and *Australian Historical Studies*, 1991.

Kapferer, B., *Legends of People, Myths of State: Violence, intolerance and political culture in Sri Lanka and Australia*, Smithsonian Institute Press, Washington and London, 1988.

Küchler, S. & Melion, W. (eds), *Images of Memory: On remembering and representation*, Smithsonian Institution Press, Washington and London, 1991.

Lowenthal, D., *The Past is a Foreign Country*, Cambridge University Press, Cambridge, 1993.

McCormack, G. & Nelson, H. (eds), *The Burma–Thailand Railway: memory and history*, Allen & Unwin, St Leonards, 1993.

Misto, J., *The Shoe-Horn Sonata*, Currency Press, Sydney, 1996.

Nelson, H., *POW: Prisoners of war, Australians under Nippon*, ABC, Sydney, 1985.

Robertson, J., *1939–1945 Australia Goes To War*, Doubleday, Sydney, 1984.

Rolf, D., *Prisoners of the Reich: Germany's captives 1939–1945*, Leo Cooper, London, 1988.

Ryan, M., *Advancing Australia*, Big Picture Publications, Sydney, 1995.

Samuel, R., *Theatres of Memory*, Vol. 1, Verso, London, 1994.

Thomson, A., *Anzac Memories: Living with the legend*, Oxford University Press, Melbourne, 1994.

Thorpe Clark, M., *No Mean Destiny: The story of the War Widows' Guild of Australia 1945–85*, Hyland House, South Yarra, 1986.

Warner, L. & Sandilands, J., *Women Beyond the Wire: A story of prisoners of the Japanese 1942–1945*, Michael Joseph, London, 1982.

White, R. and Russell, P. (eds), *Memories and Dreams: Reflections on 20th Century Australia*, Allen & Unwin, St Leonards, 1997.

Journals

Frances, R. & Scates, B., 'Honouring the Aboriginal Dead', *Arena* 86, 1989, 72–80.

Inglis, K., 'A Sacred Place: The making of the Australian War Memorial', *War and Society*, Vol. 3, No. 2, September, 1985.

Kitley, P., 'Anzac Day Ritual', *Journal of Australian Studies*, No. 4, June, 1979.

McCormack, G., 'Remembering and forgetting: the war, 1945–1995', *Journal of the Australian War Memorial*, No. 27, October, 7, 1995.

Matthews, J. J., '"A female of all things": Women and the Bicentenary', *Australian Historical Studies*, Vol. 23, No. 91, 1988, 90–102.

Melman, B., 'Gender, History and Memory: The invention of women's past in the nineteenth and early twentieth centuries', *History and Memory: Studies in representation of the past,* Vol. 5, No. 1, Spring/Summer, 1993, 5–42.

Newton, J., 'Angels, Heroes and Traitors: Images of some Papuans in the Second World War', *Research in Melanesia* 20, 1996, 141–56.

Nora, P., 'Between Memory and History: Les lieux de mémoire', *Representations*, No. 26, Spring, 1989, 7–25.

Osborne, E., 'Torres Strait Islander Women: An interpretation of some recollections on their experiences during the Pacific War 1942–1945', *Northern Perspective*, Vol. 18, No. 2 (Wet Season), 1995.

Scates, B., 'In Gallipoli's Shadow: Pilgrimage, mourning and the Great War', *Australian Historical Studies*, 1–21.

Spearritt, P., 'Celebration of a Nation: The triumph of spectacle', *Australian Historical Studies*, Vol. 23, No. 91, 1988.

Wood, N., 'Memory's Remains: Les lieux de mémoire', *History and Memory: Studies in representation of the past*, Vol. 6, No. 1, Spring/Summer, 129, 1994, 123–49.

Interviews

The Hon. Con Sciacca MP, Minister for Veterans' Affairs, Melbourne, 15 November 1995.
The Hon. Con Sciacca, Brisbane, 11 November 1996.
Walsh family, Nowra, 14 December 1996.

Films

The forgotten, A Black Russian Production, Perth, 2002.
Paradise road, Fox Searchlight Pictures, 1997.

Other sources

1945: War and Peace, Inform audio guide script, Australian War Memorial, 1995.
Australia Remembers 1945–1995: Commemorating the 50th Anniversary of the end of World War II, Background Information booklet, Department of Veterans' Affairs, Canberra, 1995.
Background information from the Hon. Bruce Scott MP, Minister for Veterans' Affairs, 1996.
Personal communication from Errol Davis, *Australia Remembers* State Coordinator, Queensland, 1996.
Personal communication from Karina Ceron, Veterans' Affairs Network, Tasmanian Branch Office, 1996.
Personal communication from Robyn Smith, Executive Officer, *Australia Remembers* NT Committee, 1996.
Personal communication from Stephen Lalor, Branch Head, Parliamentary and Corporate Affairs, Commonwealth Department of Veterans' Affairs, Canberra, 1996.
Personal communication from the late Alick Jackomos, OAM, Melbourne, 7 May 1997.
Prayer at the *Australia Remembers* Women in the Defence Forces Ceremony, Canberra 25 July, 1995.

Speeches

The Hon. Paul Keating PM, 'Australia Remembers Women in Defence Forces Ceremony', 25 July 1995.
The Hon. Paul Keating PM, VE Day address, 1995.

Media releases

The Office of the Hon. Con Sciacca MP, Minister for Veterans' Affairs, 1995.
The Office of the Hon. Paul Keating PM, 1995.
The Office of the Right Honourable The Lord Mayor of Brisbane, Jim Soorley, 1996.

Newspapers (1995)

Advertiser
Age
Australian

Bayside Bulletin (Brisbane Suburban)
Blue Mountains Gazette
Border Mail (Albury–Wodonga)

Cairns Post
Canberra Times
Courier-Mail

Daily News (Warwick)
Daily Telegraph Mirror

Gladstone Observer
Gold Coast Mail
Great Southern Star
Guardian Weekly
Gympie Times

Herald-Sun

International Express

Kalgoorlie Miner
Koori Mail

Mercury (Tasmania)
Malvern/Prahran Leader
Morning Bulletin (Rockhampton)

Northern Daily Leader (NSW)
Northern Territory News

Richmond River Express Examiner

South West News (Brisbane Suburban)
Southern Highland News (Bowral)

Sunday Age
Sunday Mail
Sunraysia Daily
Sunshine Coast Daily
Sydney Morning Herald

The Times
Townsville Bulletin
Tumut and Adelong Times

Weekend Australian
West Australian
Westside News (Brisbane Suburban)

INDEX

Aborigines (see also Indigenous
    Australians and Torres Strait
    Islanders), 4, 9, 36, 50, 94, 130,
    144, 146, 147, 161, 163, 167, 170,
    174
and Anzac Day, 130, 151, 173–4
Aboriginal and Torres Strait
    Islander Commission (ATSIC),
    17, 53, 146, 163, 173
and treaty, 53
and Indigenous war
    commemoration, 145
Aboriginal women and World
    War II, 149–50
Arnhem Land guerrilla unit
    reunion, 146
Australia Remembers 1945–1995
    commemoration of, 143–51,
    173
Bicentenary, 4, 59, 60, 61, 62
'Freedom Wall' dedication
    ceremony, 157, 161, 163, 167,
    169, 170
sovereignty, 55, 61
training as guerrilla fighters during
    World War II, 146–7
World War I precedent and
    political aims, 147–8
Anzac
Anzac Cove, 5, 25, 131, 134
Anzac Day, 38, 69, 74, 98, 121, 122,
    123, 124, 125, 126, 127, 128,
    130, 131, 132, 145, 151, 165,
    170, 173, 174, 176
protests by women, 129
Anzac Legend, 5, 25, 84, 96, 105,
    119, 120, 121, 122, 124, 128,
    133, 135, 143, 144, 174
Indigenous Australian participation
    in, 170–1, 173

comparison with 'Kalkadoon spirit',
    174
Aotearoa/New Zealand, 2, 4, 11, 25,
    49
Aotearoa/New Zealand Remembers,
    26, 35, 37–40, 42, 44, 94, 130
and Maori, 41, 44, 49, 50, 130–1
commemoration of women, 47–8
logo, 40–1
theme of peace, 44–6
use of spectacle, 46
Atomic bombs, 32, 67, 101, 107, 111,
    165
Australia Remembers 1945–1995, 3–9
commemoration of Aborigines
    and Torres Strait Islanders, 3,
    143–51, 173
commemoration of women, 71–83
compared with other
    commemorations, 101, 175
corporate sponsorship, 160–1
criticized for ignoring East
    Timorese, 166, 167
evaluation of its success, 159–76
'Flame of Freedom', Brisbane, 15,
    114–16
Gala Concert, Melbourne, 90–3
launch of, 24–5
logo, 18, 20, 35, 77
privileging of VP Day over VE Day,
    103, 153
relationship with *Aotearoa/New
    Zealand* and *Canada
    Remembers,* 25-51
structure of, 14–16
target audiences, 16–17
use of spectacle, 100–1, 110–16
Australian War Memorial, 14, 129
Aborigines' 'Invasion Day' protest
    at, 60

launch of *Australia Remembers 1945–1995*, 24
'1945: War and Peace exhibition', 69–70

Barunga Festival and Statement, 61
Beaumont, Joan, 119, 120
Bicentenary (1988 Australia), 3, 4, 6, 7, 25, 52, 55, 56, 57, 59, 60, 62, 93, 101
and Australian Bicentennial Authority (ABA), 6
and Barunga Statement, 61
compared with *Australia Remembers 1945–1995*, 175–6
logo, 58
and women, 61
Blamey, Sir Thomas, 63, 66
Bosnia (VP Day 1995 cartoon), 65

Canada, 2, 4, 11, 12
prime minister Chrétien, 27
Canada Remembers, 25, 26, 28, 31, 45
commemoration of indigenous soldiers, 35, 36, 50
logo, 34–5
'Captives' Hymn, 81
Centenary (1888, Australia), 6, 25, 54, 55, 121
Changi (see also POWs—Japanese), 23, 84, 86, 87
and Burma–Thailand Railway, 85, 95
and Muntok and Banka Island, 86
and Sandakan, 95
Chifley, Ben (Prime Minister), 67, 91, 110, 112
Clinton, Bill (President), 1, 169
Cook, Cecil, 174
'Black Anzac' poem, 174
Curtin, John (Prime Minister), 97–8, 107, 122, 129, 170

Damousi, Joy, 8
'Dancing Man', 116–18
Delegate (township of), 68
Dunlop, Sir Edward 'Weary', 94, 95, 96
memorial to, Melbourne, 106

East Timor, 166, 167

Federation (Australia 1901), 6, 52–3, 56
and Centenary of, 4, 53, 55
and White Australia policy, 121
and Yeperenye festival, 55
Fields of Remembrance, 153–5, 157
'Flame of Freedom' (VP Day 1995, Brisbane), 15, 114–16
Freedom Wall (Brisbane), 152–3, 155–6, 159
dedication ceremony, 157–9
plaques, 156, 158
French Nuclear Tests in Pacific, 94

Gala Concert (VP Day 1995, Melbourne), 90–3
Gallipoli, 99, 110, 121, 127, 133, 170–1
and Anzac legend, 143
Glenn Miller and Vera Lynn, 91–2, 110, 111, 112

Hage, Ghassan, 151
Hayden, Bill, 7, 131–3
Holocaust, 67, 105
Howard, John, 123, 126
and 'sorry', 176

Indigenous Australians (*see also* Aborigines and Torres Strait Islanders), xi–xii, 3, 6, 54, 61, 119, 131, 173
and Anzac Day, 173–4
exclusion from 1901 Constitution, 121
'Invasion Day' 1988, 6

inclusion in 1995 commemorative programs, 49
recognition of World War II service, 143–151
women's roles in World War II, 150
Inglis, Ken, 74, 143

Japan, 8, 9, 10, 63, 66, 67, 69, 108, 129, 137, 138, 164, 167, 169, 176
and apology, 9, 76, 110
attempted individual apologies to POWs, 1995, 137, 164
and VP Day 1995, 65, 66

Keating, Paul (Prime Minister), 5, 25, 58, 63, 70, 74, 79, 80, 82, 93, 94, 95, 96, 97, 105, 116, 120, 121, 122, 123, 135, 167, 168, 171, 176
and 'Fuzzy Wuzzy Angels', 141–3
commemorative speech regarding Aborigines and Torres Strait Islanders, 147
Redfern Park speech, 94
Tribute to Unknown Australian Soldier, 94
visions of Republic, 146
visit to Thursday Island, 145

Langton, Marcia, 9
Livermore, Charlie, 150–1
Lowenthal, David, 56, 99

MacArthur, General, 63, 110
Mateship (see also Anzac Legend/ Day), 7, 70, 74, 92, 95, 123, 124
Mene, Charles, 147
Misto, John (and 'Shoehorn Sonata'), 90, 172

National Museum of Australia, 55
Ngata, Sir Apirana, 49
Noonuccal, Oodgeroo, 149, 174
Nora, Pierre, 69, 83, 90
Nostalgia, 3, 4, 99–102, 109

Oembari, Raphael, 138, 139, 140, 141–3
and George Silk photograph, 138–9
Olympic Games (Sydney 2000), 53, 54, 55

Papua New Guinea, 63, 69, 107, 121, 122, 134, 140, 141, 144, 167, 176
and commemorative poster, 138
and 'Fuzzy Wuzzy Angels', 138, 140, 141, 143
Pederson, Aaron, 54
Pilgrimages/pilgrims, 5, 15, 119, 131, 134–8
and acknowledgement of local indigenous populations, 138
Prisoners of War (POWs)
of Germany, 8, 12, 84, 106
Ray Walsh, 22, 172
Canadian Natives and Métis, 36
of Japan, 8, 22, 67, 102, 112, 124, 136, 164, 172
commemorative poster, 83–6
gendered remembrance of, 83–7
Indigenous Australian prisoners, 149
Women, 80, 86–90, 124, 172

Rawlings, Reg
World War I Military Medal, 147, 148
'Reconciliation', 53, 173
Remembrance Day, 5, 69, 154, 164
Returned Servicemen's League (RSL), 13, 143, 167
and Aborigines and Anzac Day, 173
and ballot for pilgrimages, 135
and Bruce Ruxton, 10, 112, 126, 127
Delegate sub-branch, 68
Rubuntja, Wenten, 61

Samuel, Raphael, 68, 91
Saunders, Reg, 9, 93, 148–9, 174
Scates, Bruce, 171
Sciacca, Con (Minister for Veterans'
    Affairs), xii, 7, 12–14, 17, 18, 23,
    25, 26, 58, 63, 77, 78, 90, 109, 122,
    145, 147, 159, 160, 161, 163, 165,
    166–9, 172, 176
  Anzac Cove pilgrimage, 131–2
  commemoration of Aborigines and
    Torres Strait Islanders, 144–5
  compensation for Indigenous ex-
    service personnel, 146–7
  Freedom Wall ceremony, 157
  Italian knighthood, 14
  'Sites of Memory', 68–71, 101
Spillman, Lyn, 6
Stasiuk, Glen, 173–4

Torres Strait Islanders (see also
    Aborigines and Torres Strait
    Islanders/Indigenous Australians),
    9, 145, 146, 147, 148, 150, 167, 173
Trade unions, 112–13, 169–70
Tuckey, Wilson, 14, 165
  Anzac Cove pilgrimage, 132

Ulungara, Matthias, 145, 161

VE Day, 1, 14, 63, 102–7
  and World War II bombing of
    Dresden, xi, 9, 107
VP Day, 4, 9, 10, 14, 63–7, 68, 71, 91,
    99, 100, 102, 103, 108–10, 114,
    116, 119, 140, 155, 164, 168, 169
  and Aotearoa/New Zealand and
    Canada Remembers, 38, 45–6
  controversy over use of term 'VP'
    or 'VJ', 17, 66–7, 101, 109, 116,
    168–9

Indigenous Australian participation
    in, 151
  observation of two minutes silence,
    65
  Paul Keating's speech, 63
  spectacle, 100, 108–16

Walsh, Ray and Varlie
  and Australia Remembers logo, 7,
    16, 18, 20, 21, 22, 23, 129, 172
Walsh family, xii, 20–4, 89
War Widows, 153–5, 156, 157
Waters, Leonard, 9, 149, 172, 173
Watson, Don, 94, 95
Women, 5, 7, 8, 25–6, 28, 61–2, 70,
    79–82, 107, 135, 162, 171–2
  Aboriginal and Torres Strait
    Islander, 150–1
  Anzac Day protests, 129
  and Aotearoa/New Zealand
    Remembers, 40, 47–8
  Australia Remembers
    commemorative poster, 72–3
  Australia Remembers
    commemorative ceremony,
    76–82
  and Canada Remembers, 29, 31–2
  and 1988 Bicentenary, 59
  'Flame of Freedom' performance,
    115
  International Women's Day, 1995,
    71
  Prisoners of War, 84, 86–90, 124,
    172

Yeperenye Festival, 54–5
Yolngu people's 'Bark Petition', 61
Yothu Yindi, 54, 93
Yunupingu, Galarrwuy, 61
Yunupingu, Mandawuy, 93